ETHICAL ISSUES IN COMMUNITY-BASED RESEARCH WITH CHILDREN AND YOUTH

Edited by Bonnie Leadbeater, Elizabeth Banister, Cecilia Benoit, Mikael Jansson, Anne Marshall, and Ted Riecken

Efforts to apply ethical guidelines and regulations to research with vulnerable populations such as children and youth are often problematic. Consequently, health and social scientists sometimes shy away from research with these groups, particularly when it means addressing value-laden social problems such as sexuality, drugs, and racism.

This collection of original essays discusses the unique challenges of community-based research, outlining many of the ethical concerns that it engenders. The contributors examine such issues as the complexity and scope of informed consent in situations involving multiple stakeholders, the protection of privacy and maintaining consent, weighing benefits and preventing harm, and research with groups. The volume suggests that a more collaborative and sustained approach is needed by researchers and by ethical review boards to ensure that research on sensitive social problems with high-risk populations receives adequate support, and that it is conducted with a clear understanding of the potential problems and with the highest ethical standards possible.

BONNIE LEADBEATER is a professor in the Department of Psychology at the University of Victoria.

ELIZABETH BANISTER is a professor in the School of Nursing at the University of Victoria.

CECILIA BENOIT is a professor in the Department of Sociology at the University of Victoria.

MIKAEL JANSSON is a professor in the Department of Sociology at the University of Victoria.

ANNE MARSHALL is a professor in the Department of Educational Psychology and Leadership Studies at the University of Victoria.

TED RIECKEN is a professor in the Department of Curriculum and Instruction at the University of Victoria.

D1005429

Ethical Issues in Community-Based Research with Children and Youth

Edited by
Bonnie Leadbeater, Elizabeth Banister,
Cecilia Benoit, Mikael Jansson,
Anne Marshall, and Ted Riecken

Anne Marshall

UNIVERSITY OF TORONTO PRESS
Toronto Buffalo London

© University of Toronto Press Incorporated 2006
Toronto Buffalo London
Printed in Canada

ISBN 13: 978-0-8020-3839-5 (cloth)
ISBN 10: 0-8020-3839-5 (cloth)

ISBN 13: 978-0-8020-4882-0 (paper)
ISBN 10: 0-8020-4882-X (paper)

Printed on acid-free paper

Library and Archives Canada Cataloguing in Publication

Ethical issues in community-based research with children
and youth / edited by Bonnie Leadbeater ... [et al.].

ISBN 0-8020-3839-5 (bound)
ISBN 0-8020-4882-X (pbk.)

1. Children – Research – Moral and ethical aspects.
I. Leadbeater, Bonnie J. Ross, 1950–

HV715.E85 2006   174.2'8   C2005-905623-1

University of Toronto Press acknowledges the financial assistance to
its publishing program of the Canada Council for the Arts and the
Ontario Arts Council.

University of Toronto Press acknowledges the financial support for
its publishing activities of the Government of Canada through the
Book Publishing Industry Development Program (BPIDP).

Contents

Part VI: Summary and Recommendations for Ethical Guidelines, Research, and Training

Preface

This book grew out of a need for more guidance in ethics in community-based research with vulnerable populations. In January 2001 the editors of this volume, along with Drs Gordon Barnes and Nancy Galambos, were the recipients of five years of funding from the Community Alliance for Health Research (CAHR) grant program of the Canadian Institutes for Health Research (CIHR). The grant was titled 'Healthy Youth in a Healthy Society: A Community Alliance for Preventing Injury in Children and Youth.' Ours was one of nineteen CAHR projects (as they have come to be known) awarded across Canada. In each of these innovative research projects, university researchers and members of the wider community collaborated to investigate a serious health concern.

What is unique about the Healthy Youth in a Healthy Society team grant? Our research team has been drawn from five university disciplines (nursing, psychology, child and youth care, education, and sociology), and from many different professional groups (educators, police, social workers, health care providers, and administrators) and service agencies (not-for-profit groups, health clinics, and schools). Collectively, the researchers have considerable expertise in a variety of methodologies, including program evaluations, large-scale surveys, qualitative and quantitative studies, and participatory action research. Such variability is rare in a single research project, and findings drawn from these diverse methods are not often recognized across disciplines and almost never published in the same journals and books. Most of the researchers had previously established ad hoc collaborations with community partners (in schools, service agencies, health care units, and police groups), and most had direct experience working with young people as educators, nurses, or psychologists, or in agencies serving youth. We also share a common frustration with the inability of our previous research to improve the well-being of young people, families, and communities.

The ongoing research of the Health Youth in a Health Society CAHR has two aims: to increase understanding of the risks and protective factors (both common and unique) associated with injuries among youth from a variety of social circumstances; and to work to reduce these injuries through targeted prevention programs. We consider a variety of problems facing high-risk and vulnerable youth – which we had previously investigated independently – including dating violence, sexual exploitation, sexually transmitted infections, peer aggression, and alcohol abuse. Some of the young participants in this study are living on the street. Some attend alternative schools for high-risk youth. Others live in rural communities that are undergoing dramatic economic restructuring because of declines in marine, mineral, and forest resources and in related employment opportunities. Others are living in relatively secure circumstances but are at risk for injuries because of their race, sexual orientation, or other identifying factors.

While preparing the grant, our university and community-based research team members spent many hours building relationships with one another and mapping out common research questions. However, none of us anticipated the challenges for research ethics that this work would pose. Few ethics guidelines exist that are specific to research with high-risk youth, and we found that routine procedures such as obtaining parental consent for adolescents' participation could not apply to youth who were living independently or who were privately seeking health care for sexually transmitted infections. While ethics guidelines are widely written and available, we encountered a profound gap in the research literature when it came to applying these to the unique circumstances of community-based research. This book is the result of our efforts to come to terms with this gap, and of our discovery of colleagues who are struggling with these concerns and who are even beginning to conduct research to resolve their questions.

Six of the fifteen chapters in this book describe ethical concerns encountered and solutions found in ongoing CAHR target projects. These projects include a city-wide, population-based survey of injuries and related risk and protective factors among youth (Jansson, Mitic, Hulten, and Dhami); a participatory-action health educators' program led by Aboriginal youth (Reicken and Wilson); a mentoring program for pro-

moting healthy relationships and preventing dating violence and
sexual transmitted infections among high-risk girls (Banister and Daly);
a longitudinal study of the health and well-being of street youth (Jansson and Benoit); and a qualitative focus-group study investigating the
health and community engagement of young people (Marshall and
Shepard). Also, our graduate students relate their own experiences in
the overall CAHR project (Slatkoff, Corrin, Phillips, Rozeck-Allen,
Hulten, and Wilson).

The authors of the other chapters joined us as invited consultants,
because of their interests and expertise in working with vulnerable
populations. Their research experiences, and the ethical concerns they
had considered, ranged widely as they conducted their own research
with ethnic minorities and adolescents (Fisher & Masty); collected controversial sociometric data with peers of young people (Underwood,
Mayeux, Riser, and Harper) bullying and victimization in children
(Yuile, Peplar, Craig, and Connolly), involved themselves in school-
based research collaborations with educators (Sippola); and investigated
suicidal ideation and behaviours in youth (Vaillancourt and Igneski),
maltreatment in children and adolescents (Walsh and Macmillan), and
the teaching of research ethics to graduate students (Moretti). Two
ethicists – Conrad Brunk and Kathleen Glass – also joined this book
project and challenged us all to think beyond our own research to
consider more deeply the interests of all our participants.

Greater understanding of the health risks facing vulnerable populations (including those marginalized by poverty, aboriginal status, youth,
sexual orientation, and so on) is badly needed to inform effective prevention strategies, social policies, and treatment protocols for addressing long-standing health and social problems (see Leadbeater and Glass,
this volume). However, many roadblocks to research with vulnerable
populations exist, and these have impeded our efforts to understand
these populations and to measure the effectiveness of interventions
designed to improve their lives. For example, surveys of adolescents
that ask sensitive questions about sexuality, reproductive health, religious backgrounds and so on have been stopped by individual parents,
by school authorities, or by politicians who object to the content or
who anticipate objections from others. A dramatic example, from 1992,
was the cancellation, by the Secretary of Health and Human Services,
based on political considerations, of the American Teenage Study investigating youth sexuality. This decision overturned the peer review process of the Public Health Service, which had endorsed the study. Faced

with such barriers, university-based researchers can choose a smoother path and turn to other research. Our goal is to increase knowledge of, and foster dialogue about, research ethics in order to decrease these barriers to research with vulnerable populations. We hope this book will be viewed as a foundation for the extensive dialogue and empirical research that is required to ensure that ethical research practices are responsive to the unique needs and circumstances of these populations.

Much of the research described in this book reflects the authors' expertise in research with children and youth, which is where the need for improvements in ethics guidelines and practice is most conspicuous. However, we believe that our experiences and the ethics principles we derive from them also have implications for research with vulnerable populations more generally. The social problems experienced by youth are not exclusive to them, and neither are the ethical concerns relating to investigations of these problems. Problems such as substance use and abuse, homelessness, poverty, lack of education or employment, sexually transmitted infections, and interpersonal violence affect many vulnerable populations. These problems also involve the complex interplay among biological, physical, socio-economic, and cultural characteristics – an interplay that is ideally investigated by interdisciplinary teams of university-based researchers and community partners. To ensure ethical research practice with vulnerable populations, we must consider such issues as competence to give informed consent, confidentiality and protection of privacy, and maximization of benefits and minimization of harms – the same issues that are key to research with young people. The process-oriented approach described in this book, to establishing and maintaining ethical research practices and to training graduate students and clinical researchers, can be extended to investigations involving other vulnerable groups.

An introductory chapter explains some of the unique characteristics and benefits of community-based research and outlines some of the ethical challenges that are often encountered in working with vulnerable populations (including those relating to obtaining informed consent, assessing the competence of vulnerable populations, engaging in dual roles as research-practitioners, reporting suspected child maltreatment or harm to self or others, the ownership of data, and the dissemination of research findings on sensitive social issues). Parts 1 to 5 are organized around ethics 'themes' that intersect with the sometimes unique methodologies used in our research. These methodologies include ecological analyses, longitudinal studies, sociometric and observational data collecting that can reveal risks for victimization or aggression among children or youth, and the use of focus groups for data collection. Each chapter takes a case-study approach and presents ethical dilemmas encountered in the course of actual research projects, as well as the solutions that were designed to address these dilemmas. The first two chapters in Part 6 make recommendations for improving ethics training for students and clinical researchers as it relates to community-based research with vulnerable populations. The final chapter summarizes the ethical dilemmas described in this book and appeals for continued discussion and research. We argue for a more dynamic, problem-solving approach, one that is fuelled by ongoing dialogue across a broad spectrum of interested parties to identify varying and sometimes conflicting values as they relate to the risks and benefits of research, not only for individuals but also for families and communities.

Acknowledgments

This book was made possible with the support and participation of many bright and talented researchers, students, community partners, administrators, and institutions. Financial support for the writing of this book came from several sources. A development grant from the University of Victoria's Health Research Initiative (funded by the Canadian Institutes of Health Research [CIHR]) provided a first opportunity for faculty, graduate students and experts in ethics research, from the University of Victoria and the Greater Victoria community to examine ethics in community-based research. The workshop exposed the need for further research and debate.

The Institute of Human Development, Child and Youth Health of the CIHR provided funding for the authors of this book to meet at a two-day workshop in Victoria, British Columbia, on 3 and 4 October 2003. There, they discussed their own community-based research efforts, shared and debated the ethical issues they encountered, and developed the recommendations for researchers working in community-based research that are made in this volume. We thank Cindy Bachop for organizing the workshop.

Funding was also provided through a grant from CIHR titled: 'A Community Alliance for Reducing Risks for Injury in Children and Adolescents.' This innovative five-year grant program fosters multidisciplinary community-based research.

Thanks also go to Shelley Booth, who worked tirelessly and with good humour to organize, review, and format (and reformat) the manuscripts. Finally, we thank all of our community partners for their support, for their willingness to collaborate in the research, for sharing their unique perspectives, and for providing us with the feedback we need to continue to develop ethics practices that increase our ability to work with vulnerable populations.

Contributors

Elizabeth Banister, PhD — School of Nursing, University of Victoria

Cecilia Benoit, PhD — Department of Sociology, University of Victoria

Conrad Brunk, PhD — Director, Centre for Studies in Religion and Society, University of Victoria

Jennifer Connolly, PhD — Department of Psychology, York University

Sarah Corrin, MA — Department of Education, University of Victoria

Wendy Craig, PhD — Department of Psychology, Queen's University

Kim Daly, RN, MA — Victoria Youth Clinic, Victoria, BC

Mandeep Dhami, PhD — Institute of Criminology, University of Cambridge

Celia Fisher, PhD — Director, Center for Ethics Education, Fordham University

Kathleen Glass, DCL — Director, Biomedical Ethics Unit, Departments of Human Genetics and Pediatrics, McGill University

Bridgette Harper, MA — Behavioral and Brain Sciences, University of Texas at Dallas

Tracey Hulten, MA — Department of Psychology, University of Victoria

Violetta Igneski, PhD — Department of Philosophy & Communication Studies, McMaster University

Mikael Jansson, PhD — Department of Sociology, University of Victoria

Bonnie Leadbeater, PhD — Department of Psychology, University of Victoria

Harriet MacMillan, MD, MSc, FRCP(C) — Offord Centre for Child Studies; Department of Psychiatry and Behavioural Neurosciences and Pediatrics; McMaster University

Anne Marshall, PhD — Department of Educational Psychology and Leadership Studies, University of Victoria

Jessica Masty — Department of Psychology, Fordham University

Lara Mayeux, PhD — University of Oklahoma

Wayne Mitic, EdD — School of Child and Youth Care, University of Victoria

Marlene Moretti, PhD — Department of Psychology, Simon Fraser University

Debra Pepler, PhD — LaMarsh Centre for Research on Violence and Conflict Resolution, York University

Rachel Phillips, MA — Department of Sociology, University of Victoria

Ted Riecken, EdD — Department of Curriculum and Instruction, University of Victoria, Faculty of Education

Scott Risser — Behavioral and Brain Sciences, University of Texas at Dallas

Tamara Rozeck-Allen, MA — Department of Educational Psychology and Leadership Studies, University of Victoria

Blythe Shepard, PhD — Department of Educational Psychology and Leadership Studies, University of Victoria

Lorrie Sippola, PhD — Department of Psychology, University of Saskatchewan

Josh Slatkoff, MA — Department of Psychology, University of Victoria

Teresa Strong-Wilson, PhD — McGill University Department of Integrated Studies in Education

Marion Underwood, PhD	Behavioral and Brain Sciences, University of Texas at Dallas
Tracy Vaillancourt, PhD	Department of Psychology, McMaster University
Christine Walsh, PhD	Faculty of Social Work, University of Calgary
Amy Yuile, MA	Department of Psychology, York University

PART ONE

The Ecology of Informed Consent in Vulnerable Child and Youth Populations and First Nations

1 Community-Based Research with Vulnerable Populations: Challenges for Ethics and Research Guidelines

BONNIE LEADBEATER, TED RIECKEN, CECILIA BENOIT,
ELIZABETH BANISTER, CONRAD BRUNK, AND
KATHLEEN GLASS

University–community research alliances have ushered in new methods for investigating social problems, as well as innovative or best practices for preventing or treating them. Typically, these alliances or partnerships bring together teams of university-based researchers from various disciplines with targeted members of the non-university community (for example, policy makers, police, grassroots operations, not-for-profit groups, health service providers, teachers, parents, and children or youth themselves) to address issues of mutual concern in ways which ensure that relevant questions are posed and that valid research findings can be rapidly disseminated to users as well as written up for publication in academic books and journals (Benoit, Jansson, Millar & Phillips, in press). In response to researchers' past neglect of many groups, federal funding agencies in Canada and the United States are now highlighting – and in some jurisdictions even mandating – the inclusion of women, children, and minorities in research that can benefit them. Such policies have the potential to increase fairness in the distribution of the benefits and burdens of research; however, the practical and ethical difficulties of accessing, engaging, and working with these traditionally neglected and sometimes vulnerable populations has received less attention.

Community–university research partnerships have ushered in a host of new strategies. They have expanded the reach of research to include populations marginalized by age, Aboriginal status, stigmas, poverty, low formal education, poor mental health, or non-heterosexual orientation – that is, individuals and groups who have often been neglected by or actively excluded from research in the past. However, because they extend the research lens beyond individuals or families and consider more broadly the characteristics of schools, communities, agencies, or governments, these alliances generate new roles and responsibilities for both investigators and research participants, as well as new ethics questions.

In Canada and the United States, research with both humans and animals is subjected to careful scrutiny by ethics review boards,[1] which have been established by the educational institutions or hospitals where the research is conducted. In Canada in the 1990s, recognizing the common themes in these guidelines, the major federal research funding councils – the Medical Research Council (now called the Canadian Institutes for Health Research or CIHR), the Natural Sciences and Engineering Research Council (NSERC), and the Social Sciences and Humanities Research Council (SSHRC) – founded an Interagency Working Group to discuss and advise on ethics issues as they related to research on human subjects. The working group's final report, the *Tri-council Policy Statement: Ethical Conduct for Research Involving Humans*, was adopted by the three councils in August 1998. This statement is today considered the overseer of research practice in Canada. The Interagency Advisory Panel on Research Ethics and the Secretariat on Research Ethics are responsible for promoting high ethical standards of conduct in research involving humans; they do so by developing, interpreting, and implementing the *Tri-council Policy Statement*. Other disciplines, professions, and countries have similar sets of guidelines.

Ethics guidelines for research seek to minimize risks, burdens, and harms; to increase the benefits of research for individual participants; to ensure that the consent given by participants or their guardians is freely offered and informed by knowledge of what the participants are being asked to do; and to maintain participants' privacy and confidentiality. The same ethics concerns are central to community-based research alliances. However, in part because these research partnerships are so new, precedents for applying established ethics guidelines, organizational policies, and even child protection laws are not widely available to guide research practices or the decisions of university and community ethics review boards.

The characteristics of community-based research are unfamiliar to many in the current research ethics review system. University- and hospital-based research ethics boards and centralized research councils are more accustomed to considering the dynamics of control over research practices by researchers and the need to protect participants' interests. These boards often have limited understanding of the multiple perspectives represented by research partnerships. There is a clear need to enhance researchers' access to guidelines and to provide examples of ethical practices in community-based research. This book attempts to address this need.

By its very nature, community-based research creates a certain amount of unpredictability in the research process (Janesick 2000; Weijer, Goldstand & Emanual, 1999). In this chapter we describe the benefits of community-based research and outline some of the ethics questions that arise from this research. The chapters which follow present case studies to illustrate ethics concerns that can and do arise in community-based research as well as the practices that have been followed to address these concerns. Collectively, these papers suggest that research-ers and ethics review boards need to take a more collaborative, ongo-ing, and discursive approach in order to ensure that research on sensitive social problems with high-risk populations is conducted with a clear understanding of the highest standards possible.

What Is Unique about Community-Based Research?

Each of the chapters in this book is linked in some way to a community-based research project. A single, unified conception of community-based research cannot be applied uniformly to all of the projects described in this book; that said, the different projects share certain characteristics that are specific to a community-based approach model of interconnected stakeholders and long-term research partnerships. Always an important goal is to engage non-academics in the research process for the purpose of enhancing the production of relevant, scien-tifically sound knowledge that can be rapidly disseminated.

Projects that adopt a community-based approach involve a network of interconnected stakeholders, in partnership with university-based researchers. These partners may be government departments, health or social service practitioners, not-for profit organizations, school boards, or parents and their children. These stakeholders may have an interest in the research itself and may have some claim on the data because of their role as participants or as members of a partner community. They may also have a claim on the time of the researchers, or an interest in obtaining a share of project resources allocated to the research project. Because these groups are among the most likely to be affected by the research findings, they may also have an interest in 'owning' the data and in disseminating or using the findings. Community-based research depends on trusting relationships among partners who have diverse reasons for being involved, who vary in their knowledge and understanding of research processes, and who may experience different burdens and benefits from the findings. Research that involves multiple, multilayered, and often long-term partnerships requires more than the traditional approach to ethics approval from an ethics review board. It requires open lines of communication and ongoing discussion among the partners, as well as clear mechanisms for averting problems before they arise and for resolving problems if they do.

Community-based research partnerships often link researchers and community members over many years. These networks of relationships can have different implications for researchers than for participating individuals, agencies, institutions, and communities. For example, a program evaluation that results in practice recommendations for a youth service organization may have ripple effects on the work climate of service providers, by increasing the effectiveness of their services, by increasing case loads or by suggesting that new types of services be delivered.

Community-based research represents a shift in the processes by which knowledge is produced, legitimated, and disseminated. Partners delineate the questions to be asked and interpret and vet the results before they are disseminated. As an approach to knowledge production, community-based research links the scientific expertise of researchers with the local and practical wisdom of community members. In an information age in which communication technologies are ubiquitous and part of daily life for most people, community-based research furthers the exchange of ideas in ways that reach beyond the traditional monopolies over knowledge production by schools and universities.

Ideally, community knowledge is integrated into the research process, rather than merely reflected by it (Fisher & Masty, in this volume; Weijer, Goldstand & Emanual, 1999). The knowledge and concerns of local communities blend with the canons of knowledge production that are grounded in empirical rules of inquiry. One challenge facing community-based research relates to the debate surrounding the very nature and value of the knowledge produced by such partnerships. Reconciling the differences between a scientific approach to knowledge production and an approach that emerges from the wisdom of practice itself can be a challenge to these research alliances. Scientists' concerns about validity, reliability, and rigour may be less important for community members, whose strategies for knowledge use are grounded in practical and taken-for-granted ways of knowing and in demands for action.

Researchers and community members may experience tension arising from these perceived gaps in epistemology. Values, and the partnership itself, can be derailed if such differences are not addressed. At the intersection of these scientific and practical approaches to knowledge production, researchers and community members also struggle with how best to define ethics in research, how to produce knowledge as equal partners with shared interests, and how to accord mutual respect to their diverse and sometimes divergent interests and epistemologies. To meet these challenges we must acknowledge that there are multiple ways of knowing and recognize the need for forms and strategies of knowledge translation that will allow shared understandings to develop. Identifying and clarifying the ethical dimensions of collaborative, community-based research projects can create a solid foundation on which to build those understandings. This book aims to advance that dialogue.

The challenges for ethical practice that can be generated by community-based research addressing sensitive social issues are numerous. To introduce these challenges, we identify some of the complexities in ethics in community-based research that are related to, but inadequately dealt with by, existing ethics guidelines, including those relating to (1) obtaining informed consent, (2) assessing the competence of vulnerable populations, (3) engaging in dual roles as research-practitioners, (4) reporting suspected child maltreatment or harm to self or others and (5) ownership of data and the dissemination of research findings on sensitive social issues.

The Ecology of Informed Consent

Existing ethics guidelines require researchers to gain written consent from individuals (or their authorized representatives), who must be fully informed about the potential risks and benefits to them of participating in the research project. This model is derived from the Western democratic tradition that emphasizes the importance of the individual. Doctor–patient relationships are based on it, and so is research designed to test drugs, treatments, and other clinical interventions. Contemporary research guidelines and university ethics review boards adhere to this tradition when evaluating the risks to an individual relative to the benefits. But this model does not map well onto community-based research, where community, school, family, and individual interests may be in conflict. The focus on the rights of individuals and the principle of reducing harm to them can overlook the fact that the risks and benefits of community-based research may be unequally distributed among the many stakeholders. For example, children may benefit from research on bullying, but school administrators, worried about parent complaints, may decline to participate (Fisher & Masty; Riecken & Strong-Wilson; and Underwood, Mayeux, Risser & Harper, in this volume). Yet research guidelines have only begun to address the complexities of obtaining consent in situations where there are multiple stakeholders (for example, see Weijer et al. 1999). Moreover, an emphasis on individual rights and on the development of ethics principles can underestimate the importance of processes and of individuals' relationships with other stakeholders.

When guidelines for community-based research are being developed, the community's views of risks and benefits must be considered. But what constitutes a community, and who can legitimately speak for it? The individuals who are being surveyed, interviewed, or observed will not be the only stakeholders in a given research project. Others will have concerns about the risks and benefits, including families, community partners, service agencies, schools, and even whole communities (for example, when small rural communities or Aboriginal bands are the participants). They may well have worries about what the research will reveal about their families, their staff, the functioning of their institutions, and the sustainability of their programs. Communities may fear that the research will strenghten the social stereotypes and value judgments imposed on them by others.

In the context of a long-term, community-based research project, a possible benefit to one of the stakeholders may constitute a risk to another. To illustrate, a needs assessment might identify individuals in need but that same assessment might harm a particular community if it suggests that it is a dangerous or undesirable place to live. In such a research environment, the complexities of consent are many. As the chapters that follows will illustrate, the solutions to ethics dilemmas of this sort are often arrived at only after long consultation and debate among the groups affected.

The research described in this volume points to the need for an ecological approach to establishing informed consent, one that identifies and communicates with these sometimes hard-to-identify or hidden interest groups. The following chapters also describe processes for reaching agreements with agencies, schools, and youth regarding the protection of privacy and the ownership of data. Some projects use advisory groups to negotiate and oversee these agreements. Others work to establish long-term relationships with service agencies, school personnel, or elders of Aboriginal communities for the purpose of opening avenues for ongoing discussion of risks, interests, and protections for both research participants and the groups or communities to which they relate or belong.

In youth participation models of research, young people play a central role in developing research questions, collecting data, and disseminating knowledge (Riecken & Strong-Wilson, in this volume). When young people are involved and their concerns are reflected, the resulting educational materials can be highly relevant to them; but this approach can also generate multilayered issues relating to informed consent. It may be necessary to obtain informed consent not only from the youth themselves, but also from others involved in these projects. Ethical issues, including obligations relating to informed consent, voluntary participation, and the minimization of risks, need to be introduced, openly discussed, and carefully monitored. Youth researchers require ongoing and systematic supervision directed at anticipating, uncovering, monitoring, and creating processes for addressing ethics concerns that may arise in the course of their work. Protocols need to be co-developed to guide youth in following research ethics.

Competence to Consent for the Participation of Vulnerable Persons

Community-based research often deals with complex and sensitive social issues that are sometimes also high-profile. Examples include maltreatment, bullying, and sexual exploitation. Such research seeks to include high-risk or marginalized groups and often utilizes a variety of qualitative and quantitative methods that carry with them their own ethical issues (Corbin & Morse, 2003; Van Den Hoonaard, 2002). The competence of the individuals consenting to participate in a research project is a concern of all ethics review boards, especially when the research involves vulnerable populations. The question, basically, is whether the individual participants are competent to give consent or assent. This in turn raises questions about the appropriate gatekeepers or guardians who can give consent or speak on their behalf.

Competence is defined by the *Tri-council Policy Statement* as 'the ability of prospective subjects to give informed consent in accord with their own fundamental values. It involves the ability to understand the information presented, to appreciate the potential consequences of a decision and to provide free and informed consent.' The same state-ment goes on to contend that competence is not an all-or-nothing, all-encompassing, or once-and-for-all condition; rather, it is specific to the participation of a particular participant in a particular research project. For those who are deemed not competent to give informed consent, the ethics considerations must 'seek to balance 1) the vulnerability that arises from their incompetence with 2) the injustice that would arise from their exclusion from the benefits of research' (section 2, E Consent, page 2.9).

The complexity of the problem and the lack of specific ethics guide-lines are particularly apparent when research involves youth. People who have not reached the age of majority, as defined by the jurisdiction in which they reside, are often not allowed to give consent on their own behalf to be involved in research. This is so even when they are devel-opmentally and even legally competent to understand both the re-search and the consequences of their decision to participate in it. The Tri-council guidelines are silent on the specific case of adolescents or youth; however, page 2 of the tutorial accompanying the section on competence states that in research involving a child under the age of majority, 'the child's parent or legal guardian is usually required to provide consent (although in some situations adolescents can be re-garded as competent and provide their own consent).' These situations are left unspecified.

It is rarely questioned that consent from a guardian should be at-tained for young children. Guidelines for determining the competence of thirteen- to seventeen-year-olds are more problematic. In the absence of specific legislation, determinations of the age of competence resort to provincial or state laws specifying the age of majority. However, when applied uniformly, this can result (and has resulted) in the exclusion of youth when the research deals with sensitive topics they might choose not to discuss with their parents or legal guardians (for example, sex-ual exploitation and maltreatment; sexual knowledge, orientation, and practices; engagement in illegal activities; attachments to parents and parenting practices; religious beliefs), or when the research involves the participation of youth who are in foster care or who are living indepen-dently or on the street (see Jansson & Benoit; Walsh & MacMillan, in this volume).

The World Health Organization (November 2004) offers guidelines for research on reproductive health involving adolescents. These guidelines take a strong position against restricting the use of consent given by competent youths in the absence of specific legislation denying them decision-making authority. This document argues: 'In general the law does not grant parents veto power over decisions of mature (that is, competent) adolescents who decide to participate in research on their reproductive health. In such cases where adolescents are or are about to be sexually active, investigators commit no legal offence in undertaking research that promises a favorable benefit–risk ratio. However, when the law specifically denies decision making authority to mature or competent adolescents below a given age, that provision must be respected' (www/who.int/reproductive-health/hrp/guidelines_adolescent.en.html).

There is considerable variability and conflict, particularly in Canada, regarding the age at which youth are deemed legally competent to give informed consent. (See Table 1.1 for a sampling of Canadian statutes, and Table 1.2 for American ones.) In many jurisdictions, youth under the age of majority are deemed legally competent to understand the responsibilities of having a driver's licence. They can also give their consent to employment or to receive mental health or medical treatment.

Research on juveniles' competence to stand trial as adults is one of the few areas where empirical research has begun to directly assess the effects of development on legal competence directly. A recent study (Steinberg et al., 2003) suggests that while two thirds of eleven- to thirteen-year-olds would be considered competent (compared to standards used for mentally ill adults), these youth are 'more likely to comply with authority figures and are less likely to recognize the risks inherent in the various choices that they face or to consider the long term consequences of their legal decision making' (2003, p. 1). However, instead of suggesting that these immaturities should automatically prevent youth from being tried as an adults, the authors suggest that in some instances, protections and periods of special instruction may be used to address matters that youth do not understand before determinations of their competence are made.

The legal and developmental competence of youth involved as research participants or as participant-researchers needs to be better understood. Assessing competence will remain a complex and difficult task in many situations; discussions about and delineations of situations where youth can be regarded as competent to give their own consent are increasingly needed to ensure that all adolescents are repre-

TABLE 1.1
Variations in age of majority and age of consent in selected provinces of Canada

Province	Issue	Age	Source	Year
British Columbia	Age of majority	19	Age of Majority Act	1996
	Working age	15	Employment Standards Act	1996
	Health care	19	Health Care (Consent) Act	1996
	Marriage	19	Marriage Act	1996
	Mental health	16	Mental Health Act	1996
	Driver's licence	16	Motor Vehicle Act	1996
Manitoba	Age of majority	18	Age of Majority Act	2003
	Working age	16	Employment Standards Code	1999
	Mental health	16	Mental Health Act	1998
	Marriage	18	Marriage Act	1988
	Driver's licence	16	Highway Traffic Act	2000
Ontario	Age of majority	18	Age of Majority & Accountability Act	1990
	Working age	14*	Occupational Health & Safety Act	1990
	Health care	16	Health Care Consent Act	1996
	Marriage	18	Marriage Act	1990
	Driver's licence	16	Highway Traffic Act	1990
Nova Scotia	Age of majority	19	Age of Majority Act	1989
	Working age	14*	Labour Standards Code	1989
	Health care	19	Medical Consent Act	1989
	Marriage	19	Solemnization of Marriage Act	1989
	Driver's licence	16	Motor Vehicle Act	2001
Canada-wide	Sexual consent	14**	Criminal Code	1997

*Youth in these provinces may work only in designated low-risk industries until the age of majority.
**Unless it takes place in a relationship of trust or dependency, in which case sexual activity with persons over fourteen but under eighteen can constitute an offence, notwithstanding their consent.

sented in research. Without this, the likelihood that sensitive research will be undertaken will continue to be determined ad hoc by private interests, including not only parents but also gatekeepers in schools, health care, and social service agencies. These gatekeepers can also – sometimes unintentionally – limit the right of participants to fair access to the benefits of research. The quality of the research can also be restricted by requests to exclude sensitive questions. This in turn can lead to conflicts between gatekeepers as well as to arbitrary practices that can prevent needed research from proceeding. For example, in some settings university ethics review boards agree that fourteen-year-olds can give consent to participate in research designated low risk (for

TABLE 1.2
Variations in age of majority and age of consent in selected states the United States

State	Issue	Age	Source	Year
California	Age of legal consent	18	Labor Code	2003
	Driver's licence	16	Vehicle Code	2003
	Medical consent	15	Family Code	2003
	Marriage	18	Family Code	2003
	Sexual consent	18	Penal Code	2003
Oklahoma	Age of majority	18	Office of the Oklahoma Attorney General	2002
	Marriage	18	Marriage Law	2002
	Driver's licence	16	Department of Public Safety	2002
	Medical consent	18	Office of the Oklahoma Attorney General	2002
	Sexual consent	18	Penal Code	2002
Florida	Age of majority	18	Children's Statute	2003
	Driver's licence	16	Motor Vehicle Act	2003
	Mental health	18	Mental Health Act	2003
	Marriage	18	Domestic Relations Act	2003
	Legal consent	17	Labor Act	2003
	Sexual consent	18	Crimes Statute	2003
Texas	Age of majority	18	Family Code	2002
	Health care	18	Consent to Medical Treatment Act	2002
	Marriage	18	Family Code	2002
	Driver's licence	16	Vehicles & Traffic Act	2002
	Sexual consent	17	Penal Code	2002
Maine	Age of legal consent	16	Criminal Code	2001
	Driver's licence	16	Bureau of Motor Vehicles	2003
	Health care	No Law	State Statutes	2001
	Marriage	18	Domestic Relations	2001
	Sexual consent	16	Criminal Code	2001

example, they can fill out anonymous questionnaires that are non-psychologically or socially invasive), while the school principals or school boards require written parental consent for all youth under eighteen for any data collection for non-school, research purposes. In other settings, university boards adhere to laws designating the age of majority as the age at which youth can give consent for themselves, while school boards deem younger youth competent to give consent (Sippola, in this volume).

Consent issues interact directly with methodological concerns and can enhance or compromise the quality of research and the benefits that can be derived from it. Young people typically bring a strong interest and vibrant energy to research participation. Typically, studies report that more than 80 per cent of school-based youth agree to participate in research when they give consent themselves; generally in these situations, parents are notified and are encouraged to phone the school or researcher only if they do not want their child to participate. When written parental consent is required before youth can be invited to participate in a school-based research project, participation drops to an average of 60 per cent of the available population. Moreover, high-risk youth – who may be the target of the research – are often poorly represented in these reduced numbers. There are many reasons for this discrepancy in levels of participation that do not relate to youth competence: contacting and motivating parents to give written consent is often difficult; consent forms sent home with students are returned at a low rate; older youth may be unwilling or reluctant to ask permission from parents; information about the potential benefits of the study can be inadequate; and review boards often reqire long and complex consent forms. Lack of school support, demands on teachers' time, and the disorganized or stressed family contexts of some high-risk families also limit participation.

We cannot, however, merely assume that youth of a certain age are competent to give informed consent without assistance. Confidentiality issues, as well as decisions to give consent, may generate difficulties for youth when they are asked to reveal potentially harmful information about their involvement in illegal activities (Lowman & Palys, 2001). Also, there are specific research data collection methods that challenge the competence of youth to give informed consent. For example, group interviews can yield rich and interactive data from participants. However, despite well-documented advantages (Morgan, 1997), group interviews create risks for participants, who may reveal more than they would in, for example, an individual interview (Banister & Daly, in this volume; Owen, 2001). In particular, young people may lack sufficient experience to anticipate the consequences of revealing their private thoughts in a group setting, especially as they come to believe that they can talk safely in an ongoing group. Participants may need to discuss the possible risks related to confidentiality in such interviews; they may also need to be reminded that they can choose what to disclose as the discussion progresses. Disclosing highly personal information is not necessarily harmful, and indeed may have a therapeutic effect for some participants if such disclosures are handled sensitively; even so, researchers facilitating group interviews require special training to ensure that the data collection process discourages unplanned and inappropriate overdisclosure (see Banister & Daly; Moretti, Leadbeater & Marshall, in this volume). Because the researchers cannot ensure confidentiality, early group sessions need to devote time to developing group rules relating to safety and trust, and these should be revisited in subsequent sessions (Banister & Daly; Marshall & Shepard, in this volume). Risks may increase as groups continue over time, or when the participants know one another, or when involvement in illegal or high-risk behaviours is discussed. On the other hand, groups that are closed to new members, that have little attrition, and that have met over a long period of time may develop a strong bond of trust that can protect confidentiality.

Managing Dual Roles and Conflicting Interests

Earlier practices for evaluating interventions and programs in the social sciences took a hands-off approach that clearly separated the roles and responsibilities of the researcher or evaluator from the program being evaluated. However, participant-research approaches used in community-based research projects may have advantages in facilitating access to hard-to-reach populations or in ensuring that innovative programs are implemented by highly trained professionals who have both a commitment to the research and experience with the populations served (Banister & Daly; Riecken & Strong-Wilson, in this volume).

In community-based approaches to evaluating interventions, researchers can gain valuable information about the integrity of the intervention and the processes of change, but they can also encounter role conflicts if they are in addition responsible for delivering the intervention, identifying the service needs of participants, or treating problems that become apparent during the intervention. Therapeutic roles and authority or power relationships can become blurred. For example, if teachers are involved as community partners, the students participating in research projects for course credits may feel that they cannot withdraw without incurring serious negative consequences. Involving practitioners as researchers or researchers as practitioners can lead to situations where researchers' roles overlap with their roles as therapists, teachers, caregivers, supervisors, or members of the targeted community.

The Tri-council guidelines advise that 'if the researcher is acting in dual roles, this fact must always be disclosed to the subject' (page 2.8). However, other protections may also be needed, especially when the relationship involves an inherent power differential – for example, when the voluntary nature of the participant's involvement could be compromised by his need to maintain the approval of the teacher or therapist who is also conducting the research. If the researcher is at the same time a service provider (such as a teacher or counsellor), her research interests may influence her judgment regarding the client's well-being.

The *Tri-council Policy Statement* addresses the ethics concerns that can arise when organizations (such as corporations, governments, or political parties) or institutions (such as schools or jails) are approached to be involved in research and are in a position of power over the individuals being invited to participate (for example, students or prisoners). When the authority has an interest in the research, researchers are advised to develop relationships that do not compromise free and informed consent or an individual's privacy, and that make the authority's views known to potential participants (Article 2.2).

Similarly, when researchers' roles overlap with their service roles, additional protections may have to be put in place to monitor ethical research practices. This may require that a third party – one who is independent of the research – assume a role in gaining informed consent and in handling any ethics concerns that arise (Edwards & Chalmers, 2002). The integrity and professional conduct of researchers holding dual roles is vital in such situations (Corbin & Morse, 2003). At a minimum, researchers with dual roles need to disclose potential conflicts of interest to the participants before beginning data collection.

Child Protection Laws: Reporting Obligations in Research Samples Where High Levels of Abuse and Neglect Are Expected

In both Canada and the United States, researchers have a legislated duty to report children who are in need of protection; they must do so to the government agency responsible for investigating reports of suspected abuse or neglect. This legislation is intended to ensure that children are offered the help and assistance they need, when they need it. Intervention is much more likely for younger children than for youth, particularly youth who are living independently. However, youth involved in research also need to be told clearly that if they divulge that they are or have been abused or neglected, the researchers are required by law to notify the appropriate authority. However, it may not be enough to inform youth of reporting requirements, since few can be expected to anticipate the consequences of a report, either to themselves or to their families. Unless they are provided with an additional clear explanation of the purpose and potentially good and harmful consequences of child-protection reports, high-risk participants may withdraw from the research. This problem is avoided when the researchers delete questions that could yield knowledge of abuse. However, this avoidance strategy creates problems when it comes to understanding and making recommendations for dealing with socially sensitive issues relating to youth well-being; it can also lead to underestimations of the role of abuse and neglect in such problems as teenage pregnancy, depression, aggression, and delinquency. When researchers avoid asking difficult questions about abuse or neglect, victimization, or suicidal intentions or behaviours, questions arise about the ethics of missed opportunities to provide children or youth with needed services and protections (Yuile, Peplar, Craig & Connolly; Underwood et al.; Walsh & MacMillian; Viallancourt & Igneski, in this volume).

Alternative strategies are badly needed. Jansson and Benoit (in this volume) conducted research with street-involved youth, some of whom were involved in the sex trade. From the onset of the project, they worked closely with representatives from the B.C. Ministry of Children and Family Development to educate themselves about the purposes, processes, and limits of child protection legislation and to develop strategies to maximize the probability that youth in need of protection (or their siblings) would receive assistance. The discussions that ensued informed the researchers about what kinds of reports were appropriate and what kinds of actions could be taken. Often the street youth were living independently, or were known to the reporting agencies and were already receiving services. In this situation, concerns about siblings still living at home were paramount. Lines of communication were established at the beginning stages of the project, and a contact person was designated at the reporting agency, who would act as a liaison to the research project and who could be approached when questions of reporting arose. All this having been done, the researcher could proceed with confidence in creating a protocol to instruct interviewers and the youth themselves on the potential benefits and risks of revealing that they had experienced abuse.

Disseminating Research in the Community

Community-based research involving multiple levels of relationships among community partners, university researchers, research participants, the media, and the general public can facilitate the timely transfer of empirically based knowledge. Moreover, when partners are involved in developing the research program, they become invested in knowing, using, and distributing the findings. However, there are ethics issues directly related to the dissemination of findings from academic–community collaborations, and these must be anticipated and discussed (Fisher & Masty; Riecken & Strong-Wilson, in this volume). While ethics review boards rarely consider the impacts of research beyond the individual participant, the dissemination of findings can raise specific ethics issues relating to the protection of privacy of communities, institutions, or individuals, to the ownership and use of the data and findings, and to authorship of research reports. Formal ethics guidelines are silent on the problems of dissemination. In the past, conflicts over research products and intellectual property have been conceptualized as conflicts among researchers (faculty and students) or between individual researchers and the universities that provided resources to support the research endeavour. The mechanisms for disseminating science-based knowledge produced by researchers are regulated by peer review systems, which are unrelated to the sites of knowledge generation or to the participants involved. Little attention has been paid to the rights of communities or institutions to disseminate the information, although researchers working with Aboriginal communities have begun to consider guidelines for dissemination agreements (see Fisher & Masty, in this volume).

In community–university research partnerships, conflicts over the dissemination of findings and unintended harms or burdens can arise from competing interests among stakeholders. Limited or different understandings of academic research designs, methodological approaches, interpretations of statistical analyses, generalizability of findings, and so forth, can lead to differences of opinion among partners and researchers regarding, for example, the adequacy or reliability of current findings and the need for further research. For example, program evaluations that only partially support or do not support program efforts may be a threat to funding for a specific program, but at the same time provide important knowledge for program development. When limited data are released in order to maintain or boost an agency's funding, the research project's overall findings may be distorted. Also, research findings can be taken out of context and sometimes misused, misrepresented, or (equally problematic) ignored as uninteresting. Findings that focus on marginalized populations can perpetuate myths and stereotypes, or they can be used to bring clarity and objectivity to the question at hand. Conflicts about the value of the findings may be compounded because academics submit their work to lengthy and competitive peer review processes; community partners may be more willing to readily accept information that is useful to seeking funding and support from members of the local community.

There is a related issue: Who ultimately owns the data that are collected in the course of the community–academic collaboration? Also, who owns and who can benefit economically from the intellectual property created by the project, such as videos, program manuals, and books (Riecken & Strong-Wilson, in this volume)? For example, can an individual program or researcher benefit from the sales of these products? Who are the actual owners of these products? Is it the research team (and university), the community partner, the wider cultural group (as in the case of Aboriginal peoples), or a mix of these owners? What are the responsibilities of the data owners to the other members of the collaboration and to the research participants? Are there circumstances when the data owners should not release the research findings? Are there conditions for their release that must be met?

The issue of authorship warrants consideration in advance of publication. How are community partners and researchers to be acknowledged for their contributions to the manuscripts, reports, and documents? When could these acknowledgments risk breaking the confidentiality that was negotiated at the outset of the project? What are the researchers' obligations with regard to producing press releases, general reports, and so on, and should these tasks be attended to before time and effort are focused on peer reviewed publications?

Solutions to ethics concerns over the dissemination of findings again emphasize the need to understand the development of ethical practices as part of an ongoing process in community-based research. Successful community–academic collaborations need to be able to bridge the divides between academic and community cultures for knowledge generation and validation and between their specific interests with regard to how to use and disseminate research findings. Graduate students' involvement in this research can create training opportunities, but it can also constrain those students' own research directions and raise issues concerning authorship and the independence of their contributions (Slattkoff, Corrin, Phillips, Rozeck-Allen & Strong-Wilson, in this volume). Discussion of who has the right to release the data, and when and under what conditions results may be released, need to be worked out in advance – possibly in formal agreements between community and academic partners. Clearly outlining the purposes of the research and the expectations of the different stakeholders, and how the findings will be used in the short and long term, may be essential to the dissemination phase of these projects.

The chapters in this book further illustrate these and other ethical concerns, as well as many solutions to these concerns that have been worked out in the course of conducting community-based research. It is unlikely that any list of guidelines could fully anticipate the ethics concerns generated by the university–community research partnerships, innovative methods, and the engagement of more vulnerable and marginalized participants. The chapters that follow demonstrate the need to create and maintain strong, open, and respectful relationships among all participants in the research process as well as a commitment to ongoing dialogue to ensure ethical practice.

NOTES

1 These review boards go by names that vary by country (Canada or the United States) or institution (university versus hospitals). Examples: institutional review boards (IRBs) and research ethics boards. These various terms are used interchangeably throughout the book.

REFERENCES

Benoit, C., Jansson, M., Millar, A., & Phillips, R. (In press). Community-academic research on hard-to-reach populations: Benefits and challenges. *Qualitative Health Research*.

Corbin, J., & Morse, J.A. (2003). The unstructured interactive interview: Issue of reciprocity and risks when dealing with sensitive topics. *Qualitative Inquiry*, 9(3), 335–54.

Edwards, M., & Chalmers, K. (2002). Double agency in clinical research. *Canadian Journal of Nursing Research*, 34(10), 131–142.

Janesick, V.J. (2000). The choreography of qualitative research design. In N.K. Denzin & Y.S. Lincoln (Eds.), *Handbook of qualitative research* (2nd ed.) (pp. 379–99). Thousand Oaks, CA: Sage.

Lowman, J., & Palys, T. (2001). The ethics and law of confidentiality in criminal justice research: A comparison of Canada and the United States. *International Criminal Justice Review*, 11, 1–33.

Morgan, D.L. (1997). *Focus groups as qualitative research* (2nd ed.). Thousand Oaks, CA: Sage.

Owen, S. (2001). The practical, methodological and ethical dilemmas of conducting focus groups with vulnerable clients. *Journal of Advanced Nursing*, 36(5), 652–658.

Petersen, A.C. & Leffert, N. (1995). Developmental issues influencing guidelines for adolescent health research: A review. *Journal of Adolescent Health*, 17, 298–305.

Steinberg, L., Grisso, T., Woolard, J., Cauffman, E., Scott. E., Graham, S. Lexcen, F., Repucci. N.D., & Schwartz, R. (2003). Juveniles' competence to stand trial as adults. *Social Policy Report*, 17, 3–15.

Van den Hoonard, W.C. (2002). *Walking the tightrope: Ethical issues for qualitative researchers*. Toronto: University of Toronto Press.

Weijer, C., Goldsand, G. & Emmanual, E. (1999). Protecting communities in research: Current guidelines and limits for extrapolation. *Nature Genetics*, 23, 275–283.

World Health Organization. (2004, 1 November). Guidelines for research on reproductive health involving adolescents. www/who.int/reproductive – health/hrp/guidelines_adolescent.en.html.

2 Through the Community Looking Glass: Participant Consultation for Adolescent Risk Research

CELIA FISHER AND JESSICA MASTY

In the United States, increases in adolescent risk-taking behaviours have renewed public anxiety about the adequacy of current social policies to promote their healthy development (Takanishi, 1993). In response, developmental scientists have been called on to generate the knowledge necessary to design intervention strategies that can reduce health-compromising behaviours jeopardizing the development of productive and adaptive life skills during the critical years of adolescence (Fisher & Lerner, in press and 1994; Haggerty, Sherrod, Garmezy & Rutter, 1996).

As the scientific study of adolescent risk has moved from the experimental laboratory to the community, the need to evaluate the costs and benefits of socially sensitive research has evolved from an abstract ethical issue to a collective community concern (Fisher, 2002; McGovern, 1998; Trickett, 1998). For example, surveys of community attitudes towards the risk behaviours and mental health problems of adolescents (such as suicidal ideation, drug use, sexual behaviours, and violence) can contribute to society's understanding of youth problems. The research findings can be applied to interventions, or they can inform therapeutic approaches aimed at decreasing these destructive behaviours. However, this research can have unintended negative consequences for participants – for example, by focusing teenagers' attention on emotionally charged issues, or by introducing them to forms of risk-taking about which they may have been naive (Fisher, 2002, 2003; Fisher & Wallace, 2000). Also, group or personal stigmatization can occur when specific populations of adolescents are recruited for research participation in public settings, thereby identifying them to others as 'at risk.' Additionally, recruitment efforts may be stigmatizing if they lead teenagers to believe that as members of the selected group, they are assumed to engage in health-compromising behaviours.

For example, focus-group discussions preceding a survey study to examine ways in which African-American culture and family support could buffer adolescents against peer pressure to use illicit drugs, revealed that some adults feared that endorsement of the study would suggest to youth that they were expected to engage in such behaviours (Wallace, 2002). Other research has shown that teens who participate in surveys of adolescent suicidality can inadvertently be led to believe that teen suicide is more common than it actually is or that it can be a logical solution to their own problems (Garland & Zigler, 1993).

Research is needed that places the integrity and adequacy of ethical procedures at the forefront. Federal regulations in the United States and Canada protecting the rights of adolescents involved in research require investigators to design studies that maximize benefits, minimize risks, and demonstrate a favourable balance of benefits over harms (DHHS 2001; Tri-Council Working Group, 1998). Regulatory language is written broadly to ensure generalizability across protocols that can vary in methods, settings, and participant demographics. Consequently, contextually sensitive interpretations of ethical guidelines are needed to ensure compliance of specific studies with federal regulations. Investigators studying adolescent risk typically base risk–benefit determinations on their own morals and values, advice of colleagues, and formal recommendations of institutional review boards (IRBs). However, reliance on scientific inference or professional logic can lead to research procedures that overestimate or underestimate the risk–benefit calculus as it is experienced by adolescent research participants and their guardians.

Community and Participant Consultation

Scientists, policy makers, and communities have begun to question the adequacy of ethical decisions made in the absence of consultation with members of the communities from which research participants will be recruited (De Jong & Reatig, 1998; Fisher, 1997, 1999; Melton, Levine, Koocher, Rosenthal & Thompson, 1988; Sugarman et al., 1998). Engaging communities as partners in the design and implementation of research can enhance understanding of the risks, benefits, and fairness of research procedures and increase the probability of community support and cooperation (Potvin, Cargo, McComber, Delormier & Macaulay,

2003; Sharp & Foster, 2002; Thomas & O'Kane, 1998). However, identifying the particular interest groups that should be consulted can itself be challenging (see Riecken & Strong-Wilson, in this volume).

A potential limitation of community consultation is that the concerns and values of community advocates may not reflect the views of the guardians and adolescents who will actually be recruited to participate in the research. Participants, especially if they are from high-risk environments, may be less powerful, more fearful, and more disenfranchised than community advocates, who are often invited by those who are in leadership positions or who have interests in conducting the research (Fisher, Hoagwood, Boyce et al., 2003). Adolescent participants and their guardians may view ethical issues through a different, more personal lens than community advocates, who may not themselves be prospective research participants (Fisher, 2002).

Fisher has proposed a co-learning model of participant consultation that views both scientists and participants as moral agents joined in partnership to construct ethical procedures that will produce knowledge carrying social value, scientific validity, justice, and care (Fisher, 1999, 2000, 2002). This co-learning model assumes that both investigators and participants come to the research enterprise as experts: the investigator bring expertise about the scientific method and current research findings, and the prospective participants and their family members bring expertise about the values, fears, and hopes they place on the prospective research (Fisher, 1999, 2002). Using co-learning procedures, scientists can share their views on how and why it is important to apply the scientific method to examine questions of societal import and to debate areas of current ethical concern. Prospective participants and their guardians can apply their own moral perspectives to critique the scientific and social value of a proposed study and can share with investigators the value orientations guiding their reactions to the planned procedures (Fisher, 1999, 2000, 2002; Fisher & Wallace, 2000).

In this chapter we describe research methodologies that are based on a co-learning model for gathering data in focus groups and surveys, with an emphasis on adolescent and parent perspectives on ethics in adolescent risk research. We also discuss the implications of these perspectives for decision-making by investigators and their IRBs. It is important to note that this research was conducted in the United States and that it focused on professional regulations that are key concerns in that country. We begin with a brief overview of three key ethical issues that can benefit from participant consultation in adolescent risk research – namely, research risks and benefits, guardian permission and adolescent assent, and confidentiality and disclosure policies.

Identifying and Evaluating Research Risks and Benefits

The processes of ethical justification must ensure that the potential benefits of research to participants or society outweigh the risks of participant or community harm. Teenagers' and parents' views regarding whether experimental procedures and the findings are beneficial or harmful are rarely considered. Views among researchers, participants, and community advocates can differ. For example, university-based investigators and IRB members may over- or under-estimate the degree to which survey questions about illegal and life-threatening behaviours are experienced as educational, intrusive, or distressing for youthful respondents. Teenagers and their parents can view recruitment into school-based risk prevention programs as an opportunity or a stigma. For example, communities can perceive research on adolescent drug use as a means to acquire assistance for neighbourhood youth or as a means of solidifying negative stereotypes.

Parental Permission

Federal regulations and professional codes in the United States generally state that a parent or guardian must give permission for a child or adolescent (under eighteen) to participate in research. Guardian permission serves as a protection against children's cognitive and social immaturities, which make them more vulnerable to researchers' misunderstandings, exploitation, and coercion. In recognition of children's developing autonomy, the child's active assent is also sought (APA, 1992; DHHS, 2001, 45 CFR 46.408 a and b). Under the U.S. Department of Health and Human Services regulations, guardian consent requirements may be waived by an IRB when the research involves no more than minimal risk to the subjects, when the waiver or alteration will not adversely affect the rights and welfare of the subjects, or when the research could not practicably be carried out without the waiver or alteration (DHHS, 2001, 45 CFR 46.116d). Guardian permission may also be waived if it is not a reasonable requirement to protect the adolescent research participant (for example, if the parents are abusive or neglecting), provided that an appropriate mechanism for protecting the child is in place, such as assigning a participant advocate to the subject (DHHS, 2001, 45 CFR 46.408c; Fisher, Hoagwood & Jensen, 1996).

Younger children have difficulty understanding the nature of research and their research rights. In contrast, adolescents generally have the cognitive capacity to make informed research decisions by about age fourteen, although their lack of experience with independent decision-making can continue to impede their understanding of the voluntary nature of participation (Abramovitch, Freedman, Thoden & Nikolich, 1991; Bruzzese & Fisher, 2003; Ruck, Abramovitch & Keating, 1998; Ruck, Keating, Abramovitch & Koegl, 1998). In survey or epidemiological research on adolescent risk behaviours, where research risks are minimal, investigators and IRBs often debate whether a waiver of parental permission is justified as a means to protect adolescent privacy and to obtain a sufficient sample size. Little is known about the reactions parents have to such waivers or about a waiver policy's effect on teenagers.

Confidentiality and Disclosure Policies

Illicit drug use and suicidality are experiences that adolescents often do not share with adults. Survey research on drug use and other risk behaviours may uncover evidence of these problems, bringing them to the awareness of the investigator and possibly of other adults who are concerned with a teenage participant's welfare. Whether to keep such information confidential or to disclose it to parents or professionals is a daunting ethical decision for investigators (Fisher, 1994, 2002; Brooks-Gunn & Rotheram-Borus, 1994; Vaillancourt & Igneski, in this volume). Investigators have long been reluctant to disclose information derived from survey research on adolescent risk out of concern that inferences drawn from such measures may lack diagnostic validity. Treatment or referrals precipitated by disclosures can cause methodological problems in the research that have the potential to threaten the internal validity of longitudinal designs, arouse feelings of betrayal in participants, or jeopardize study recruitment (Fisher, 1993, 1999, 2002; Fisher, Higgins-D'Alessandro, et al., 1996; Fisher, Hoagwood & Jensen, 1996; Palys & Lowman, 2001). However, while scientific validity is the foundation of the risk–benefit analysis in research, it cannot be privileged over the ethical evaluation of harms and benefits. A researcher must also consider that disclosures to school counsellors or child protection agencies may harm participants or their families if those informed react punitively or incompetently or entangle the family in criminal proceedings.

Confidentiality decisions are also complicated by ethnic variation and by differences in attitudes towards research among diverse cultural communities when the determinants of adolescent drug use and suicide are being examined (American Indian Law Center, 1994; Casas & Thompson, 1991; Fisher, Jackson & Villarruel, 1997; Fisher et al., 2002; Gibbs, 1988; Jenkins & Parron, 1995; Kilpatrick et al., 2000; Oetting & Beauvais, 1990; Range et al., 1999). Emerging evidence suggests that some teenagers may want investigators to actively assist them in obtaining help for drug or suicide problems (Fisher, Higgins-D'Alessandro et al., 1996; O'Sullivan & Fisher, 1997). Thus the extent to which information on adolescent risk behaviours should be kept confidential depends on the expectations of participants and their parents in addition to the responsibilities of the researcher (Beeman & Scott, 1991; Johnson, Cournoyer & Bond, 1995).

A research ethic that views adolescents and parents as partners in identifying ethical challenges in science can help ensure that risk–benefit evaluations, consent procedures, confidentiality policies, and recruitment efforts reflect the values of teenagers, families, and their communities. Fisher and her colleagues (Fisher 2002, Fisher & Wallace, 2003) used focus groups and grounded theory methodology to illuminate the rich and personal insights of prospective adolescent participants and their families regarding a range of adolescent risk research methods and topics. Drawing from these qualitative data, she then developed questionnaires to evaluate the extent to which these opinions reflected larger samples of adolescents and teenagers. Gender, generational, and cultural group attitudinal differences in concerns about adolescent risk research were also examined (Fisher, 2003). In the next section we describe the focus group and questionnaire methodologies. This is followed by a section summarizing key findings from these convergent studies.

A Qualitative Approach to Understanding Participant Perspectives on Research Ethics

Qualitative methods designed to uncover hitherto unexamined community attitudes are a necessary first step towards developing community-informed ethical procedures. Research using focus groups can provide in-depth analyses of community perspectives that can challenge current thinking about ethics in research and point to new directions for scientific inquiry and ethical awareness. The focus group approach described in this section was conducted as part of a multiyear investigation of adolescent and parent perspectives on ethical issues in adolescent risk research (Fisher, 2002; Fisher & Wallace, 2000). We explored adolescent and parent attitudes towards the three ethical challenges discussed above: research risks and benefits, the need for parental permission and use of passive consent procedures, and confidentiality and disclosure policies (Fisher, 2002; Fisher & Wallace, 2000). Parents and teenagers in the focus groups were asked to consider these ethical issues across different methodological approaches, including self-report and informant surveys, school-based intervention studies, research involving the drawing of physical samples (saliva, urine, blood tests), and research on the genetic basis of adolescent risk behaviours. Participants were also asked to consider ethical issues when research addressed different types of risk behaviours, including substance abuse, sexual activity, suicide and depression, violence, eating disorders, academic failure, and child abuse.

SAMPLE

Thirteen focus groups were conducted involving a total of 46 parents and 55 students from Grades 9, 10, and 11 who self-identified as African American, East or South Asian, Hispanic, Anglo-American, or multiracial. To encourage open discussion, the multiethnic research team met with small groups that were homogenous with respect to generation (separate teen and parent groups), teen gender (separate male and female groups), and neighbourhood (half were drawn from neighbourhood public schools in districts with high levels of crime and poverty, and half from an academically competitive magnet public high school serving students from lower-crime and middle-income neighbourhoods). All participants gave informed consent or parental permission and student assent, including permission to tape-record the sessions. To maintain confidentiality and encourage open discussion, each member wore a different-coloured nametag and was identified by nametag colour rather than by name during the sessions.

PROCEDURE

A detailed script was used to incrementally stimulate discussion of ethical issues across different research methods and adolescent risk behaviours. The focus groups began with 'ice breaker' conversations about benign topics such as where the teenagers got their news or the age and sex of the parents' children; this helped make the participants comfortable sharing ideas and opinions in a group setting. Participants were then asked to list the types of problems facing adolescents in their schools and communities as well as their experiences with research. The discussion then moved to research ethics issues related to perceived risks and benefits, informed consent, and confidentiality. Many had not directly participated in research but were familiar with media presentations of medical and social science studies. One parent had investigative experience.

Research was defined as 'how scientists go about finding out what teenagers do, why they do it, and whether programs, which are supposed to prevent teenagers from doing things that are harmful, actually work.' At various intervals participants viewed three very brief television news clips reporting on the findings of adolescent risk research conducted in schools and communities.

A grounded theory research approach was used in conjunction with content analysis to identify ethical themes emerging within each of the focus groups (Glaser & Strauss, 1967). Once these themes were identified, an independent pair of raters sorted the statements across each group into the identified content categories. Inter-rater reliability was high. These themes, along with illustrative quotes, were then hierarchically arranged in a thematic grid and analysed for frequency across generational, gender, and neighbourhood groups.

LIMITATIONS OF THE FOCUS GROUP METHOD

The need to keep group membership small to facilitate discussion, the non-random selection of participants, the unique community history of participants, and the interactive nature of focus group designs together mean that content analyses do not lend themselves to generalization beyond the particular discussants (Krueger, 1998). However, the format employed and the general themes that emerge should be transferable to other populations and research ethics questions. According to Guba and Lincoln (1982) in their work titled *Naturalistic Inquiry*, the concept of transferability in focus groups is parallel to the concept of generalizability except that it is the reader of a work – not the scientist who conducted the study – who decides whether the results can be applied to the next situation. Additionally, clinicians can examine how the general themes transfer from the group discussion to clinical practice. This type of qualitative exploration can be conducted across a range of academic and scientific disciplines, including research ethics. Detailed reports of the population, format, and content of focus group discussions on ethics in research can enable other investigators, community advocates, and IRBs to decide the degree to which ethical themes that emerge in one community are transferable to their own communities. Key findings are outlined below.

A Quantitative Approach to Understanding Participant Perspectives on Research Ethics

Qualitative analyses can suggest generational, ethnic, and gender differences in research ethics attitudes within communities; larger sample sizes and quantitative approaches are better suited to evaluating group differences in the opinions of potential participants and their guardians.

QUESTIONNAIRE DEVELOPMENT

A ten-member advisory board composed of scientists, IRB members, and adolescent and parent advocates commented on a working draft of the Ethics for Adolescent Research Questionnaire (EARQ). Items were drawn from a thematic grid that evolved from the focus group discussions described above (Fisher, 2002; Fisher & Wallace, 2000). Advisory board members provided judgments regarding the cultural and ethical validity of each item. They recommended that the final items specifically address the topics of adolescent drug use and suicide survey research because these drew considerable comment from focus group members and because they have been the focus of behavioural science and public attention. Separate versions of the EARQ were created for parents and teenagers, and to address issues encountered in drug use and suicide research. Four groups of ethnically diverse parents and teenagers, drawn from the original focus groups, also reviewed the EARQ instructions and items for content, clarity, and value (Fisher 2003). The final instrument included items related to perceived research risks and benefits, informed consent procedures, and confidentiality policies.

SAMPLE AND PROCEDURE

Three hundred twenty-two students from Grades 7 to 12 (44% female) and 160 parents (78% female) were recruited from the same neighbourhood and magnet public schools as the focus group participants. Approximately equal numbers of adolescents and parents self-identified as African American, Hispanic of Puerto Rican or Central/ South American descent, East Asian, or non-Hispanic white, with a small percentage indicating a South Asian, multiracial, or 'other' background. Non-Hispanic whites had significantly higher SES status than African Americans, Hispanics, or East Asians, and therefore SES was used as a covariate in ethnic group comparisons.

Teenagers whose parents gave written permission, and who signed assent forms themselves, completed the EARQ in their schools. Students also took home questionnaires for their parents to complete and return by mail. All received movie theatre gift certificates for their participation. Questionnaires were translated into Spanish for those who requested this. Only a subset of parents requested Spanish-language versions, and their responses did not differ significantly from those of English-language respondents of Hispanic heritage. Half the participants received the drug-use version of the EARQ and half received the suicide-research version. Participants were told that the study's purpose was to gather opinions about survey research on adolescent drug use (or suicide) to help scientists develop ethical procedures to protect participants' welfare. They were told that questionnaire items were based on diverse views expressed by teenagers and parents from their neighbourhoods.

Key Findings: Community Perspectives on Research Risks and Benefits

Many participants expressed the belief that their communities could benefit directly from research on adolescent risk. Within each focus group, some participants thought that survey research could help schools and parents better understand and cope with adolescent risk behaviours. Others felt that the research might help some teenagers know they were not alone in their concerns. Furthermore, many teenagers and magnet-school parents believed that including a no-treatment control group would protect the larger society from ineffective or harmful treatment, even though this benefit might come at the temporary expense of particular individuals who did not receive needed treatment.

Although parents and teenagers in the focus groups largely thought that research on the developmental course of youth problems could be of value, some distrusted the investigators' motives and questioned the ability of scientists to control how policy makers would use their data. For example, African-American parents from one public school in a disadvantaged neighbourhood expressed strong distrust of scientific and medical institutions, citing the Tuskegee syphilis study as evidence for their perspective. Some African-American individuals who felt disenfranchised from social policy makers viewed scientists as government agents conducting research to intentionally support racial stereotypes (Fisher & Wallace, 2000).

Both focus groups and questionnaire responses of parents and adolescents indicated concerns about the immediate and long-term impact of adolescent risk research on teenagers, their families, and their communities. Many voiced disappointment that past research had failed to help their communities and that in fact it had often stigmatized ethnic families who were from poor and disenfranchised neighbourhoods. Researchers who fail to identify this as a potential cost of research participation may be asking politically disadvantaged members of society to unjustly bear research risks (Fisher, 1999; Fisher & Rosendahl, 1990; McGovern, 1998; Sarason, 1984; Zuckerman, 1990).

COMMUNITY RECOMMENDATIONS
When asked to recommend ways to enhance the assessment of research risks and benefits, parents stressed that investigators should first confront their own ideas about race and cultural differences (Fisher & Wallace, 2000; Fisher, 1999; Helms, 1993). They should appreciate the injuries that minorities have suffered throughout history because of institutional racism and prejudice, and they should be sensitive the hesitation and distrust that some minority communities demonstrate when asked to participate in research (Essed, 1991; Fisher, Jackson & Villarruel, 1997; Hawley & Jackson, 1995; Heath, 1997; Jones, 1993). Additionally, investigators should accept responsibility for how research data are disseminated, to ensure that the research sample is not stigmatized. When considering the risk–benefit ratio for adolescent risk research, especially in minority populations, researchers must be willing to engage in an honest dialogue with participants about the potential benefits and harms a research study presents from the target community's cultural perspective, and reflect on how the results of the study could affect their daily lives.

Parents and teenagers also gave specific recommendations related to research design and procedures in adolescent risk research. For example, scientists sometimes anticipate that particular survey questions may cause distress or discomfort for the respondents. Parents and teenagers stress that this may not be the case and that potentially worthwhile procedures or questions may be rejected unnecessarily.

Community discussion about sensitive topics would greatly help the investigator discover which procedures or questions would or would not cause participant stress.

Parents and teens pointed out that investigators should also be wary of potential intergroup rivalries that can arise from various concerns – for example, from the perception that control groups are being deprived of established treatments; from gossip and ill-feelings that may result from breaches of confidentiality by teachers or other students when research is conducted at a school; and from concerns about whether the scientist can minimize potential risks. Parents and teenagers endorsed a process of community consultation during the design phase of a research study to help scientists protect participants from risk while optimizing their research designs.

ATTITUDES TOWARDS PARENTAL PERMISSION

Focus group members and survey respondents expressed remarkably similar opinions about the value of requiring parental consent for adolescent survey research. In focus groups, teenagers as well as parents commented that asking for parental permission indicates a respect for parental decision-making and values. Discussants stressed that parents are legally responsible for their children and, consequently, have the right to know about their children's activities. Adolescents worried that failure to ask for parental permission might leave the parent susceptible to harm in situations where teenagers divulge something damaging to the family's reputation. Parental permission can reduce harm by allowing the parent to be an advocate, protecting adolescents from coercion, deceit, invasions of privacy, and involvement in peer-induced negative behaviours (Fisher, 2002). In the questionnaire responses comparing senior high school students and their parents to junior high school students, the younger students were more likely to endorse parental permission policies based on parental rights, respect for parents, and child protections. Male students placed a higher value on respect for parents than did females. African-American youth were significantly more likely than teenagers from other cultural groups to affirm the importance of parental monitoring of adolescent participation in surveys on youth problems (Fisher, 2003).

Parents and adolescents also indicated that in some instances, parental permission could be waived if it was the only means by which important information about adolescent risk could be acquired. When responding to the EARQ, a majority of respondents across generations indicated that teens also have a right to decide about research participation and that they are old enough to make the decision themselves (Fisher, 2003). As one would expect of individuals who are eagerly anticipating the independence of adulthood, adolescents gave higher endorsements than parents for items reflecting adolescent autonomy and the right to privacy. Senior high teenagers and parents were more concerned than their junior high counterparts about these issues. Female students more than males thought that teens have the right to decide for themselves whether they want to answer survey questions. Students, but not parents, were concerned that permission forms could raise undue parental suspicion about adolescent risk behaviour.

Although many teenager and parent questionnaire respondents endorsed a universal policy of parental permission, parents and adolescents raised the possibility that permitting a waiver of parental permission for research with adolescents could increase the sample size and validity of the study results (Fisher, 2002, 2003). Teenagers were more likely than parents and senior high respondents were more likely than junior high respondents to assert that teenagers might feel more comfortable responding honestly about risk behaviours if parental permission were waived. African Americans were less favourable towards parental permission waivers than other ethnic group adolescents (Fisher, 2003). This raises the disquieting possibility that guardian consent waivers, when not preceded by discussions with families from different cultural communities, inadvertently communicate to teenagers that scientists and school administrators do not value local norms regarding parental decision-making.

RECOMMENDATIONS

During focus group discussions, the use of passive consent procedures (sending a letter home to parents giving them an option to withhold their child's participation) raised strong negative emotions. Both parents and teenagers thought that passive consent procedures are deceptive and do not encourage good research ethics. Adolescents were familiar with this procedure and reported that they often did not bring forms home to their parents, fearing that peers would stigmatize them if they were the only students whose parents refused to allow them to participate. Teens and parents also suggested that scientists take steps to ensure that parents receive consent forms and that they should be watchful of forged signatures. Consent forms should also be written so that it is clear that parents can withdraw their child from the study, complain about the study, or confront the investigator if they believe he or she is guilty of misconduct (Fisher 2002).

Community Attitudes towards Confidentiality and Disclosure Procedures

Parents and adolescents struggled – as investigators do – with the fine line between researchers' moral obligations to respect teenagers' privacy and also to protect their welfare. Many parents expressed the belief that disclosing information about a teen participant's risk behaviours is not the role of the scientist. They felt that maintaining confidentiality upholds family autonomy, especially in situations where it may be a cultural practice for the adolescent not to share certain types of information with his or her parents. As one parent said: 'This idea of telling a parent is, sometimes ... cultural. I came from a society in which you don't just talk about everything, so no matter how close I am with my mother, my daughter ... there are certain things that you don't talk about' (Fisher, 2002, p. 32). Others expressed the idea that permitting investigators to disclose personal information gives them too much power. Adolescents often endorsed the idea that they should be responsible for their own welfare (Fisher, 2002). Both parents and adolescents were concerned that responses given by teenagers on surveys would not be truthful if they knew the investigator could divulge the information. In response to the EARQ, a majority of parents and teens endorsed items indicating that assurances of confidentiality would increase the validity of self-reports. This statement was most strongly endorsed by adolescents and senior high school students. Ethnic group differences were apparent in the disclosure perspectives as well. For example, African Americans were less likely to see a relationship between confidentiality and the honesty of teen responses than Hispanics, East Asians, or whites.

In the focus groups, parents and teenagers expressed concern about the potential harm that could befall a family if an investigator were to disclose information about, for example, physical abuse that is not really occurring. Parents and teenagers worried that Child Protective Services could be called and that families would unnecessarily be torn apart. 'If you send for BCW [child welfare] or somebody on your family ... you're not fixing the problem' (Fisher, 2002, p. 37). Close to half of all respondents to Fisher's survey (2003), especially teenagers, agreed there was a danger that investigator disclosures might be based on inaccurate or incomplete self-reports. Participants from Fisher's focus groups (Fisher, 2002) were also concerned that requiring scientist disclosure yokes investigators to a responsibility to disclose when it may not be appropriate, either because the researcher does not know the right person to tell or because he or she is not competent to handle the problem. Teens often feel betrayed when confidentiality is broken.

At the same time, many parents and teens felt that investigators are obligated to protect children from harm and should disclose information if it is in the interest of the participant. One parent explained: 'You're trying to protect the person when you keep something confidential, but in a case like this [i.e., life threatening] you wouldn't be protecting the person, you're causing more damage' (Fisher, 2002, 35). Teenagers and parents were convinced that many times adolescents disclose their problems to investigators in order to get help. In both focus group and questionnaire responses, teens and parents indicated that investigators who failed to report teen problems would be responsible if the problem got worse. Not surprisingly, the legal responsibility of researchers was perceived to be greater for suicide research than for drug research (Fisher, 2003). There were ethnic group differences on this issue as well. African-American teens were most likely, and East-Asian teens least likely, to want information disclosed to a parent rather than to a school counsellor or independent physician.

RECOMMENDATIONS

There are no simple answers to the ethical ambiguities tied to confidentiality and disclosure policies for adolescent risk research. For each project, the most appropriate policy will emerge from a dialectical exchange between investigators and communities that focuses on (1) the effect of confidentiality procedures on the honesty of self-reports (2) whether risk assessments, based solely on the data collected, are sufficiently accurate to justify disclosure or referral, (3) expectations and concerns of participating youth and their families regarding the legal and social harms and benefits of disclosures, and 4) the adequacy of neighbourhood referral sources (Fisher, 1999, 2000, 2002).

When asked how investigators might improve their confidentiality and disclosure procedures, teenagers and parents suggested that teenagers and guardians should be informed about the researcher's confidentiality and disclosure policies at the beginning of a study. Before initiating a study, researchers who anticipate the need to disclose information should ensure that the research team is trained to assess levels of risk requiring assistance and that the legal ramifications of disclosures for teenagers and families are adequately understood by all (see Jansson and Benoit, in this volume).

VALUING OF COMMUNITY PERSPECTIVES IN RESEARCH DESIGN

Applied developmental scientists have a dual obligation: to produce scientifically sound research to increase our understanding of the development of today's youth, and to generate socially relevant findings that can inform social policy, programs, and legislation for the betterment of society (Fisher, 2002). Consideration of the attitudes, ideas, and opinions of adolescents and parents for whom today's social problems and social policies are most relevant is necessary to inform the selection of appropriate topics for discussion, accurate risk-benefit analysis, suitable parent permission policies, and confidentiality and disclosure policies (Fisher & Wallace, 2000; Fisher, 2002, 2003). The investigator who utilizes participant perspectives to inform the ethical design and execution of research studies is implicitly encouraging the healthy development of adolescents and families through open discussion and community engagement. Culturally sensitive research with real-life relevance can have a more positive impact on social policy.

REFERENCES

Abramovitch, R., Freedman, J.L., Thoden, K., & Nikolich, C. (1991). Children's capacity to consent to participation in psychological research: Empirical findings. *Child Development*, 62, 1100–1.

American Indian Law Center. (1994). *The model tribal research code: With materials for tribal regulation for research and checklist for Indian health boards.* Albuquerque, NM: American Indian Law Center.

American Psychological Association. (1992). Ethical principles of psychologists and code of conduct. *American Psychologist*, 47, 1597–1611.

Beeman, D., & Scott, N. (1991). Therapists' attitudes toward psychotherapy informed consent with adolescents. *Professional Psychology: Research & Practice*, 22, 230–4.

Brooks-Gunn, J., & Rotheram-Borus, M.J. (1994). Rights to privacy in research: Adolescents versus parents. *Ethics & Behavior*, 4, 109–21.

Bruzzese, J.M., & Fisher, C.B. (2003). Assessing and enhancing the research consent capacity of children and youth. *Applied Developmental Science*, 7, 13–26.

Casas, J.M., & Thompson, C.E. (1991). Ethical principles and standards: A racial-ethnic minority research perspective. *Counseling & Values*, 35, 186–95.

De Jong, J., & Reatig, N. (1998). SAMHSA philosophy and statement of ethical principles. *Ethics & Behavior, 8*, 339–43.

Department of Health and Human Services. (2001). Title 45 Public Welfare, Part 46, *Code of Federal Regulations, Protection of Human Subjects.*

Essed, P. (1991). *Understanding everyday racism: An interdisciplinary theory.* Newbury Park, CA: Sage.

Fisher, C.B. (1993). Integrating science and ethics in research with high-risk children and youth. *SRCD Social Policy Report, 7*, 1–27.

Fisher, C.B. (1994). Reporting and referring research participants: Ethical challenges for investigators studying children and youth. *Ethics & Behavior,* 4, 87–95.

Fisher, C.B. (1997). A relational perspective on ethics-in-science decision making for research with vulnerable populations. *IRB: Review of Human Subjects Research, 19*, 1–4.

Fisher, C.B. (1999). Relational ethics and research with vulnerable popula-tions. *Reports on research involving persons with mental disorders that may affect decision-making capacity.* Vol. 2 (pp. 29–49). Commissioned Papers by the National Bioethics Advisory Commission. Rockville, MD.

Fisher, C.B. (2000). Relational ethics in psychological research: One feminist's journey. In M. Brabeck (Ed.), *Practicing feminist ethics in psychology* (pp. 125–42) Washington, DC: American Psychological Association.

Fisher, C.B. (2002). Participant consultation: Ethical insights into parental permission and confidentiality procedures for policy relevant research with youth. In R.M. Lerner, F. Jacobs & D. Wertlieb (Eds.), *Handbook of applied developmental science,* vol. 4 (pp. 371–96). Thousand Oaks, CA: Sage.

Fisher, C.B. (2003). Adolescent and parent perspectives on ethical issues in youth drug use and suicide survey research. *Ethics & Behavior, 13*, 302–31.

Fisher, C.B., Higgins-D'Allesandro, A., Rau, J.M.B., Kuther, T., & Belanger, S. (1996). Reporting and referring research participants: The view from urban adolescents. *Child Development, 67*, 2086–99.

Fisher, C.B., Hoagwood, K., Boyce, C., Duster, T., Frank, D.A., Grisso, T., Macklin, R., Levine, R.J., Spencer, M.B., Takanishi, R., Trimble, J.E., & Zayas, L.H. (2002). Research ethics for mental health science involving ethnic minority children and youth. *American Psychologist, 57*, 1024–40.

Fisher, C.B., Hoagwood, K., & Jensen, P. (1996). Casebook on ethical issues in research with children and adolescents with mental disorders. In K. Hoag-wood, P. Jensen & C.B. Fisher (Eds.), *Ethical issues in research with children and adolescents with mental disorders* (pp. 135–238). Hillsdale, NJ: Lawrence Erlbaum Associates.

Fisher, C.B., Jackson, J., & Villarruel, F. (1997). The study of African American and Latin American children and youth. In W. Damon (Editor-in-Chief) & R.M. Lerner (Vol. Ed.), *Handbook of child psychology: Vol. 1. Theoretical models of human development*, 5th ed. (pp. 1145–1207). New York: Wiley.

Fisher, C.B., & Lerner, R.M. (1994). Foundations of applied developmental psychology. In C.B. Fisher & R.M. Lerner (Eds.), *Applied developmental psychology* (pp. 3–20). New York: McGraw-Hill.

Fisher, C.B., & Lerner, R.M. (2005). *Encyclopedia of applied developmental science*. Thousand Oaks, CA: Sage.

Fisher, C.B., & Rosendahl, S.A. (1990). Risks and remedies of research participation. In C.B. Fisher & W.W. Tryon (Eds.), *Ethics in applied developmental psychology: Emerging issues in an emerging field* (pp. 43–59). Norwood, NJ: Ablex Publishing.

Fisher, C.B., & Wallace, S.A. (2000). Through the community looking glass: Re-evaluating the ethical and policy implications of research on adolescent risk and psychopathology. *Ethics & Behavior*, 10, 99–118.

Garland, A.F., & Zigler, E. (1993). Adolescent suicide prevention: Current research and social policy implications. *American Psychologist*, 48, 169–181.

Gibbs, J.T. (1988). Conceptual, methodological, and sociocultural issues in Black youth suicide: Implications for assessment and early intervention. *Suicide and Life-Threatening Behavior*, 18, 73–89.

Glaser, B.G., & Strauss, A.L. (1967). *The discovery of grounded theory: Strategies for qualitative research*. New York: Aldine.

Guba, E.G., & Lincoln, Y.S. (1982). Epistemological and methodological bases of naturalistic inquiry. *Educational Communication & Technology Journal*, 30, 233–252.

Haggerty, R.J., Sherrod, L.R., Garmezy, N., & Rutter, M. (Eds.). (1996). *Stress, risk, and resilience in children and adolescents: Processes, mechanisms, and interventions*. New York: Cambridge University Press.

Hawley, W.D., & Jackson, A.W. (Eds.). (1995). *Toward a common destiny: Improving race and ethnic relations in America* (pp. 205–36). San Francisco: Jossey-Bass Publishers.

Heath, S.B. (1997). Culture: Contested realm in research on children and youth. *Applied Developmental Science*, 1, 113–23.

Helms, J.E. (1993). White racial identity influences White researchers. *Counseling Psychologist*, 21, 240–41.

Jenkins, R.R., & Parron, D. (1995). Guidelines for adolescent health research: Issues of race and class. *Journal of Adolescent Health*, 17, 314–22.

Johnson, H.C., Cournoyer, D.E., & Bond, B.M. (1995). Professional ethics and parents as consumers: How well are we doing? *Families in Society*, 76, 408–20.

Jones, J.H. (1993). *Bad blood: The Tuskegee syphilis experiment* (rev. ed.). New York: Free Press.

Kilpatrick, D.G., Acierno, R., Saunders, B., Resnick, H.S., Best, C.L., & Schnurr, P.P. (2000). Risk factors for adolescent substance abuse and dependence: Data from a national sample. *Journal of Consulting and Clinical Psychology*, 68, 19–30.

Krueger, R.A. (1998). *Analyzing and reporting focus group results.* Thousand Oaks, CA: Sage.

McGovern, T.F. (1998). Vulnerability: Reflection on its ethical implications for the protection of participants in SAMHSA programs. *Ethics & Behavior*, 8, 293–304.

Melton, G.B., Levine, R.J., Koocher, G.P., Rosenthal, R., & Thompson, W.C. (1988). Community consultation in socially sensitive research: Lessons from clinical trials of treatments for AIDS. *American Psychologist*, 43, 573–81.

Oetting, E.R., & Beauvais, F. (1990). Adolescent drug use: Findings of national and local surveys. *Journal of Consulting and Clinical Psychology*, 58, 385–94.

O'Sullivan, C., & Fisher, C.B. (1997). The effect of confidentiality and reporting procedures on parent-child agreement to participate in adolescent risk research. *Applied Developmental Science*, 1, 185–197.

Palys, T., & Lowman, J. (2001). Social research with eyes wide shut: The limited confidentiality dilemma. *Canadian Journal of Criminology*, 43, 255–67.

Potvin, L., Cargo, M., McComber, A.M., Delormier, T., & Macaulay, A.C. (2003). Implementing participatory intervention and research in communities: Lessons from the Kahnawake Schools Diabetes Prevention Project in Canada. *Social Science & Medicine*, 56, 1295–306.

Range, L.M., Leach, M.M., McIntyre, D., Posey-Deters, P.B., Marion, M.S., Kovac, S.H., Banos, J.H., & Vigil, J. (1999). Multicultural perspectives on suicide. *Aggression & Violent Behavior*, 4, 413–30.

Ruck, M.D., Abramovitch, R., & Keating, D.P. (1998). Children's and adolescents' understanding of rights: Balancing nurturance and self-determination. *Child Development*, 64, 404–17.

Ruck, M.D., Keating D.P., Abramovitch, R., & Koegl, C.J. (1998). Adolescents' and children's knowledge about rights: Some evidence for how young people view rights in their own lives. *Journal of Adolescence*, 21, 275–89.

Sarason, S.B. (1984). If it can be studied or developed, should it? *American Psychologist*, 39, 477–85.

Sharp, R.R., & Foster, M.W. (2002). Community involvement in the ethical review of genetic research: Lessons from American Indian and Alaska Native populations. *Environmental Health Perspectives Supplements*, 110 (suppl. 2), 145–9.

Sugarman, J., Kass, N.E., Goodman, S.N., Parentesis, P., Fernandes, P., & Faden, R. (1998). What patients say about medical research. *IRB: A Review of Human Subjects Research*, 10, 1–7.

Takanishi, R. (1993). The opportunities of adolescence – Research, interventions, and policy: Introduction to the Special Issue. *American Psychologist*, 48, 85–7.

Thomas, N., & O'Kane, C. (1998). The ethics of participatory research with children. *Children & Society*, 12, 336–49.

Trickett, E.J. (1998). Toward a framework for defining and resolving ethical issues in the protection of communities involved in primary prevention projects. *Ethics & Behavior*, 8, 321–38.

Tri-council Working Group. (1998). *Tri-council policy statement: Ethical conduct for research involving humans* (with 2000, 2002 updates). Retrieved 11 March 2004 from www.pre.ethics.gc.ca/english/policystatement/policystatement.cfm.

Wallace, S.A. (2002). Cultural resilience: An examination of parent, peer, and cultural factors associated with Black teenage attitudes toward delinquency and substance use (doctoral dissertation, Fordham University, 2002). *Dissertation Abstracts International*, 63, 1592.

Zuckerman, M. (1990). Some dubious premises in research and theory on racial differences: Scientific, social, and ethical issues. *American Psychologist* 45, 1297–1303.

3 At the Edge of Consent: Participatory Research with Student Filmmakers

TED RIECKEN AND TERESA STRONG-WILSON

Traditional Pathways to Health is an ongoing project that is unlike most research on Aboriginal health and wellness. It is a participatory action research project conducted with First Nations teachers and youth in Victoria, British Columbia. Using digital video technology, the youth themselves identify the questions and issues relevant to them, gather footage in the form of interviews, images, songs, and text, and use digital video editing technology to produce short videos. These videos are then viewed by members of the university and the wider community, in homes, classrooms, and the offices of Aboriginal community organizations. While the project was being carried out in two First Nations high schools and one community adult education program, two ethical dilemmas emerged. One related to conducting a participatory action research project with adolescents, the other to who owned the videos and the First Nations knowledge represented in them. One way to conceptualize these dilemmas is to focus on the complex layers of consent involved in working with youth, teachers, and the community in the context of university–community research collaborations. Below, we examine issues of data ownership, the roles of youth participant researchers and their teachers in participatory research, and the challenges inherent in a participatory research framework.

'The edge of consent' is a metaphor that expresses the thin line the participants (youth, researchers, teachers) have walked in negotiating ethical dilemmas produced by these multiple layers of consent. Although the students were of age to participate, their consent represented the edge of consent. For instance, the students were leaders within their First Nations programs and were being taught to see themselves as speakers for themselves and for their community and families

(Frank Conibear, personal communication, April 2002). However, their giving of consent indirectly involved the entire Aboriginal community, and this community also expected to be consulted. In this chapter, we identify those ethical issues which we have found to be central when it comes to involving Aboriginal adolescents, especially in a community–university research project. The students' involvement possibly meant opening leadership opportunities for them in Aboriginal health and wellness; nevertheless, they were participating at the edge of consent.

Description of the Project

Traditional Pathways to Health is one of six projects within the Healthy Youth in a Healthy Society Community Alliance for Health Research, described in the preface to this book. The Traditional Pathways to Health project invited two classes of senior high school Aboriginal youth and their teachers and one class of high school completion students to identify and investigate issues affecting youth health and well-being. The classes were a First Nations Leadership class that focused on preparing youth to be leaders in their own communities and the Aboriginal community as a whole; a First Nations Career and Personal Planning class, in which students were learning career preparation within a First Nations framework; and a First Nations high school completion program in a local adult education centre, also taught through an Aboriginal lens.

A participatory and learner-centred approach works well in the context of First Nations pedagogy. After several sessions with the students during which we discussed the kinds of things that affect the health and well-being of young people, the students, individually or in small groups, selected their topics and began considering how best to investigate them: how to collect information and images, which people to interview and where, what kinds of questions to ask, and so on. The injury prevention topics that students explored included the following: suicide, drug and alcohol abuse, diabetes, eating disorders, discrimination and racism, the protective effects of involvement with one's culture, and the benefits of sports for healthy living. However, these research topics – indeed, the research project as a whole – were outcomes of a much broader political and social context – one that we as researchers became increasingly aware of as the students carried out their research. Those broader contexts are discussed in the following section.

Historical and Geographical Contexts of the Study

Traditional Pathways to Health is being conducted in one of the most culturally diverse regions of North America. The University of Victoria is located on the traditional territory of the Coast Salish people of Vancouver Island. Vancouver Island is only a small part of the province of British Columbia but is the traditional territory for 46 of the 198 First Nations in the province. Over the years it has drawn the attention of ethnographers and linguists from around the world. The three suburban school districts in the city of Victoria, located on the southern tip of Vancouver Island, enrol students from nine different First Nations: Beecher Bay, Esquimalt, Pacheedaht, Pauquachin, Songhees, T'sou-ke, Tsartlip, Tsawout, and Tseycum. Most of the students participating in the Traditional Pathways project came from the Esquimalt and Songhees nations, although students from other First Nations in B.C. and from across Canada were also enrolled in each of the classes. Thus the partnership on which this project was founded has provided rich opportunities but also challenges for the researchers. We have learned to work with the Aboriginal youth of long-resident cultures, each with its own history, traditions, and protocols.

Health and Wellness in First Nations Communities

Colonialism and the failure of educational systems to ensure success for all First Nations learners have resulted in ongoing difficulties for many First Nations communities. The most obvious manifestions of these difficulties are high unemployment, below-average income levels, and low rates of entry into postsecondary institutions that provide training in key professions such as law, education, and health care. In combination, these factors have resulted in the marginalization of many First Nations communities, and poor overall levels of health is one consequence. With regard to health, First Nations communities are much less healthy than Canadians as a whole. Data from Health Canada demonstrate this. In 1999, infant mortality was 1.5 times higher among First Nations people; life expectancy for both males and females was significantly lower; infection rates for tuberculosis were eight to ten times higher; and dental decay rates for Aboriginal children were two to five times higher. The same year, suicide accounted for 38 per cent of all deaths among Aboriginal youth aged ten to nineteen, and for 23 per cent of all deaths among young Aboriginal adults. Between 1990 and 2001, the proportion of AIDS cases among Aboriginal people climbed from 1 per cent of all cases in Canada to 7.2 per cent – an alarming rate of increase by any measure (Health Canada, 2003)

The Traditional Pathways to Health project focuses on the poor health of First Nations communities relative to other segments of Canadian society. That it focuses on youth is particularly important, given that 35 per cent of Aboriginal people in Canada are under fourteen, compared to 19 per cent for the general population (Statistics Canada 2003). When we consider that the birthrate for Aboriginal people in Canada is 1.5 times the rate for non-Aboriginals, the population pyramid promises to retain this shape for some time. From a First Nations perspective, young people are the hope of the next generation, and this hope was reflected in the leadership focus of the First Nations classes in which Traditional Pathways to Health was conducted. The history of research into Aboriginal community health has been, to say the least, troubled, and the complexities of consent demonstrate that these troubles are far from over.

The Ethics of Research with First Nations Communities

The history of research among Aboriginal communities around the world has, for good reason, led many Aboriginal peoples to be wary of researchers. In B.C., past interactions with anthropologists, photographers, collectors, and government officials often led to outcomes that were less than favourable for Aboriginal communities. In the last century, for example, valuable ceremonial regalia were removed from coastal First Nations communities to become part of museum collections. Furthermore, misrepresentations of potlatching ceremonies by researchers from outside the community led governments and churches to prohibit this key element of many First Nations cultures in the first half of the twentieth century. Members of those cultures who attempted to carry on this tradition were persecuted through fines and prison sentences, and potlatching traditions are still being followed today only because of a stalwart resistance to regulation by outsiders. First Nations communities are thus understandably cautious when it comes to accepting outsiders (Deloria, 1997; Smith, 1999).

In Canada, the First Nations Information Governance Committee of the Assembly of First Nations has developed principles relating to the ownership of, control over, and access to (OCA) information developed through research. These principles are designed to facilitate decision-making in First Nations communities regarding proposals for research. They pose the following questions (the last of which holds particular meaning for our research project):

- Is the research project a priority issue for First Nations?
- Will this project build First Nations' capacity and capability in research and data collection?
- Is the proposed research potentially harmful to First Nations?
- Do the principles of ownership, control, and access apply?
- Are the data available from other existing sources?
- Does the research project respect community tradition, values, language, and politics, and the individual and collective rights of the community?
- Has there been full disclosure of the partnership and management of the research project, including the data collection process and methodology, interpreting the data, dissemination of the research results, and publication of results?
- What are the ethics of the project and the accountability of the researcher to the community? (Day, 2001)

Besides the OCA principles, two other documents have guided our approach to the ethics of this research project. One is the Protocols and Principles for Conducting Research in an Indigenous Context. This document is published by the Faculty of Human and Social Development at the University of Victoria and is designed to be a supplement to the university's research ethics board (REB) approval process. It was developed by members of that faculty, with strong input from faculty of the graduate-level Indigenous Governance Program. The document begins with this statement: 'Researchers are knowledge brokers, people who have the power to construct legitimating arguments for or against ideas, theories or practices. They are collectors of information and producers of meaning, which can be used for, or against Indigenous interests' (Faculty of Human and Social Development, 2003). It provides researchers with a set of principles organized around the themes of partnership, protection, and participation. It also discusses the importance of informed consent, control over the results of research, and the need to incorporate Indigenous values into the research design and methodology.

The other document we have used as a guide is the *Tri-council Policy Statement*, specifically 'Section 6: Research Involving Aboriginal Peoples.' The statement acknowledges that this section is a work in progress and only a starting point for discussions with Aboriginal communities; however, it does include a list of 'good practices' (www.pre.ethics.gc.ca/english/policystatement/policystatement.cfm). We have used these as guideposts against which to compare our own practices in the planning and implementation of this project.

A concern that is raised in each of these sets of guidelines is whether the research project gives something back to the Aboriginal community, in the form of increased local capacities, employment skills, or knowledge that is useful at the community level. This issue was raised indirectly during the course of the project by one of the students when she asked us to provide additional training for possible career opportunities, or at least inform students of places where they could find such training.

In developing the project, we worked diligently to respect and apply the various principles expressed in these documents. Our use of the methodologies of participatory action research, with their orienting frameworks that position research as a collaborative process between equal partners, has meant many of these principles have been addressed. Traditional Pathways to Health is already giving back to the participating communities an increased expertise in digital technology, which the student participants learned to use during the project. For example, several students who graduated after the project was launched are still using their video production skills to document community life. Another concrete legacy for the communities has been the videos themselves. As creators and owners of the videos, students are in a position to work within their families and communities to disseminate the health knowledge they acquired through this aspect of the research process. In a recent follow-up study designed to examine the ethical dimensions of the project, a student participant commented that the project contributed to healing within the community (Batten, 2003). This student believed that as researchers and film makers, the students were raising topics for discussion and analysis that might not otherwise be considered within the community. The same study broached ethical issues about consent that are important when participatory research is carried out with Aboriginal youth.

Key Ethical Issues

Layers of Consent

The meaning of consent in this project is layered. Different levels and types of involvement require different protocols relating to informed consent and voluntary participation. Section 6 of the *Tri-Council Policy Statement* acknowledges how complex research can be when it involves individuals who are representing not only themselves but also perhaps their communities and culture. It goes on to suggest that research ethics boards need to consider this dimension when reviewing research proposals: 'The central issue for discussion is when it is legitimate for researchers to interview individuals in their own right as individuals, without regard to the interests of the group as a whole and without seeking permission from any group authority or spokesperson, conversely, when the approval of the community as a whole should be required' (*Tri-Council Policy Statement* 1998, 6.3).

As we moved through the various levels of approval needed for this project, we were mindful not only of the different constituencies represented by the individuals we met, but also of the different processes and protocols they had to embrace as members of their particular group or agency. In obtaining approval to conduct this research, the first layer of consent involved the school districts. Before contacting First Nations teachers, we sought approval from the Director of First Nations Education within the local school district. This individual acts as gatekeeper for the First Nations staff and screens research projects for their respectfulness to the First Nations community. After an initial meeting with the principal investigator, Ted Riecken, the director asked him to provide a written description of the project to present to her teaching staff. After attending a staff meeting to discuss the proposed research, two teachers contacted Riecken for more information. He met with these teachers and explained the project's purpose and methodology to them. They agreed to participate and to invite their students to participate as well. The director then transferred her role as gatekeeper to the First Nations teachers.

A second layer of consent involves school boards. In both school districts where this project was conducted, protocol requires that researchers submit a written application to the Superintendent of Schools, who reviews the application on behalf of the school board. For research with Aboriginal students, the superintendent relies on the recommendations of the First Nations director.

The students and their teachers were the project's main research partners and coparticipants; they represented the third layer of consent. As key participants, they were asked to sign letters of informed consent that had been approved by the university's REB (in effect, another layer of consent). The principal investigator discussed the contents of the REB-approved letter with the students and teachers and answered their questions about its contents and the implications of their agreeing to participate. All of this involved a double-layer of translation: (1) from academic language to language that youth could readily understand, and (2) from the language of Western research institutions to that of classrooms run according to First Nations principles and protocols.

The challenges inherent in this seemingly straightforward task of ensuring informed consent should not be underestimated. The number of considerations that must be addressed when obtaining informed consent have increased considerably over time. Increasing attention to the ethical dimensions of research, and a corresponding increase in the level of specificity required by REBs, have meant that letters of informed consent are now longer and more complicated than they have ever been. This increasing attention to the ethics of research with human subjects represents a protection for research participants. But at the same time, for those working with participatory research models, REB consent forms can be cumbersome and unwieldy and can require long explanations. The process of getting them signed can sometimes present universities as exceedingly bureaucratic and bound by complex and legalistic procedures. Which perhaps they are, as one of our community partners wryly noted while reviewing the letter of informed consent. In fact, some sections of the letter are there to protect the university. The point is that at times, the process can make both parties feel more encumbered than protected.

Under the guidelines of the University of Victoria, given their age (sixteen years and over), the students involved in this project were able to give consent on their own behalf. In other words, students signed letters of participant consent, but parents were not asked to sign letters to allow their children to participate in the project. This veers from what is typical in the school district: usually, researchers are required to obtain signed parental consent for *any* school-age children involved in research. (see Jansson et al., in this volume)

A fourth layer of consent arose for this project when the Aboriginal students conducted interviews with individuals who might eventually appear in their videos. The individuals who were included in the students' videos were informed that the videos would be shown publicly, that as interviewees they might be identifiable through their presence in the video, and that the videos were being made as part of a joint school–university project on health and wellness among young people. Questions of trust of the research institution were latent, and could be inadvertently hidden behind the youth participant, who was positioned as connected to the Aboriginal community but who, as a researcher, was also affiliated with the University of Victoria. As we discuss below, some students fell back on Indigenous values relating to ownership and control of cultural knowledge, and refused to participate until their relatives were informed of who would have control over the video's content and dissemination. They would not collect footage, or disclose footage already collected, until these matters were clarified.

Depending on their role and status, individuals could be giving consent not only on their own behalf but also as representatives of an institution, a family, or a culture. Because this project was working across cultures and also across institutions – including the university, the school, and the school district – the consent given by certain individuals had cultural and political dimensions. For instance, the Director of First Nations Education provided a form of consent at the individual, school system, and cultural levels; her job was to be a link between outside institutions and the First Nations communities represented in the school district. In addition, when one of the hereditary chiefs granted consent to appear in a student video, he was consenting not only at an individual level but also at a cultural and political level because of his role and status within his community. As members of First Nations communities, students who chose to participate were providing consent at both the individual and the cultural levels. Many Aboriginal youth felt a primary responsibility to their community, one that both motivated and constrained their actions. For some students, existing ways of properly approaching elders, chiefs, and family members overrode the university's protocol of procuring written informed consent. The students' teachers, working in a bicultural context as agents linking school and community, also provided a consent that had individual (self), institutional (school), and cultural (First Nations) dimensions. The Superintendent of Schools, although not a participant in the study, provided a central component of the institutional consent required for the study to proceed through his role as representative of the school board. He also indirectly endorsed the cultural support required, having been apprised that the Director of First Nations Education would

TABLE 3.1
Level of consent provided by those involved with the study

Agent	Individual	Institutional/ System	Cultural	Family
Director of First Nations Education		X	X	
Superintendent of Schools		X		
Teachers	X	X	X	
Students	X		X	X
Subjects in students' videos	X		X	X

play a consultative role in the initial recruitment phase. Table 3.1 summarizes all of these different levels of consent.

Data ownership

The video projects rightfully belonged to the creative producers, the students. Once we had shifted ownership of the data to the student researchers, we were placed in a vulnerable position: we might not be able to freely use the videos as examples of student-driven research. We built a relationship of trust within the study. Having been given free rein in creating their videos, the students came to believe that both the videos and the research process belonged to them. Our responsibility as researchers then became an ethical one of respecting and extending that relationship of trust. This had the potential to conflict with conventional modes of using the videos – that is, as data to analyse and to help disseminate study results.

'Researchers working with Aboriginal communities need to be aware that discussion of Indigenous knowledge is practical, personal and contextual and needs to be respected as such' (Pideon & Hardy Cox, 2002, p. 99). Another layer of the ownership question arose when the student, in belonging to an Aboriginal community, carried the responsibility of making sure the research was used in a manner consistent with the protocols and expectations of that community. These expectations could rub against conventional understandings of data ownership within the university community. Students asked us questions such as: 'What will the videos be used for and how will they be used?' These questions reflected the desire of the students and their communities that the information gathered by the students and presented in their videos be treated in respectful and non-exploitive way, and that the ownership of the Aboriginal knowledge represented in the videos be retained by its producers, the youth themselves. Indigenous researchers and communities are deeply concerned about how Indigenous knowledge is used (Smith, 1999; Steinhauer, 2002; Weber-Pillwax, 2001), and such issues are also a central concern in the ethics guidelines, referred to earlier in this chapter (Day, 2001; Faculty of Human and Social Development, 2003; *Tri-Council Policy Statement*, 1998). Questions of ownership of research in the context of Indigenous knowledge unavoidably involve intellectual ownership (Greaves, 1994). Central to discussions of intellectual property rights is First Nations' interest in sovereignty, which has clashed in the public domain with traditional Western notions of private property and ownership.

Voluntary Participation and Course Credits

The students' video projects were embedded in a school context in which teachers needed to evaluate student work and assign grades. Evaluations, like attendance and participation, are taken-for-granted elements of school settings. In this study, with its methodologies of participatory research, the teachers' desire to perform a more collaborative research role with the students could conflict with their responsibilities as teachers. From a university perspective, participation in research must be completely voluntary. However, in the classroom, teachers had the authority to compel students to participate in what was essentially a classroom assignment (that is, one that could be evaluated). The teachers in the study needed to find creative ways to navigate between these conflicting expectations, and they did. They agreed on evaluative strategies such as negotiating the grade with the student and providing a grade of completion rather than one in which the teacher alone was placed in the position of judging student learning. Also, the students took ownership for their learning by speaking about their own video productions in front of an audience of peers, family and community members, and university representatives.

Measuring Success within a Participatory Research Approach

A hallmark of participatory research is that all involved collaborate in its processes. Providing a space in which students could develop a sense of ownership and control of the project meant that as a research team, we had to step back and let the process unfold in ways in which the students could feel comfortable. Cognizant of our role not only as representatives of the dominant culture, but also as individuals trained in particular conceptions of what it means to do research and produce knowledge, we worked hard at holding in check our own expectations for the project. We aimed instead to see the project's progress reflected in the growth of the students' abilities and understandings. A deepening of our own understanding of the students' experiences within a school system – one that in many ways fails to recognize their culture and heritage – followed from allowing that process to unfold.

Successful Approaches to Ethical Dilemmas

'Deciding what to do about what we know requires having an ethical standpoint' (Frank, 2000, p. 363). Solutions to the ethical dilemmas that emerged during the study were often situation specific. As problems emerged, decisions needed to be made and ethical approaches discussed. Many decisions happened collaboratively, through conversations between researchers and teachers or researchers and students. Several decisions, such as those relating to ownership of data, were based on what felt right and, conversely, on knowing what would feel wrong. A knowledge of what felt right emerged against a backdrop of developing relationships of trust between researchers and students, respecting the right of Indigenous communities to self-determination of their knowledge, and a participatory action research framework that prioritized the participants' ways of knowing, being, and learning. We also based our decisions on the evolving guidelines described earlier in this chapter. The decision to distinguish between different kinds of data – some would belong to the researcher, others to the student – addressed the ethical dilemmas of data ownership. For their part, the teachers respected the students' need to participate freely in the study. They offered students the choice of an alternative assignment, or the same project but done on their own terms, if they chose not to participate in the research.

Now that several student video projects have been completed, new ethical questions have arisen. In response to a groundswell from the broader community, which is keenly interested in showing the videos to youth, teachers, and professionals, we are reopening the question of whether we can share the students' videos in contexts that promote healing, or whether we need to seek the student's prior consent for every occasion. Involving students in creating videos on topics of health and wellness was intended to solicit from those youth an aspiration to promote wellness for others. That goal also exists within a larger context of university–community collaborative research projects intended for all youth. The goals of dissemination by well-intentioned university researchers and instructors compete with issues of student ownership and informed consent – issues that within Indigenous contexts of research are strained by arguments of good intentions. The challenge for us is to balance the research community's interests of knowledge translation and dissemination with the Aboriginal communities' concerns about ownership and control of the cultural knowledge represented in the students' videos.

Implications for Community-Based Research with Adolescents

When working with Aboriginal youth, the implications of the research for Aboriginal communities need to be borne in mind at all times. Throughout this chapter we have used the notion of layers of consent to convey the idea that individuals do not operate or give consent as social isolates. Rather, they act as members of families, institutions, or cultures, and such membership entails accompanying obligations and responsibilities. Many Aboriginal students carried into the project knowledge and ways of accessing that knowledge that were guided by long-standing cultural traditions. However, the students differed in their relationships with their communities: some had close ties to a particular community, while others felt dislocated or disconnected. These differences influenced the kinds of projects that students could and/or wanted to do. One-size-fits-all solutions often do not work. Researchers working with Aboriginal youth need to be aware of and open to these differences.

Researchers working within the school system also need to be sensitive to the many issues Aboriginal youth face as they attempt to succeed in their classes. Bazylak (2002) has listed a number of factors that contribute to school failure for Aboriginal students, including contrasting world views, lack of an engaging curriculum with cultural content, and teacher intransigence. At the sites where we conducted this research, the First Nations teachers concentrated on creating a welcoming space within the school in which the students could be themselves. The classroom settings presented an alternative to the classroom environments we were accustomed to seeing. Through the participating First Nations teachers' patience, role modelling, and actions as coparticipants in the research, we as researchers learned how best to work with the students. This was in many ways a learning experience for us as researchers and educators, as we often worked outside our familiar peda-gogical and cultural contexts.

The purpose of the Traditional Pathways project is to promote wellness among youth as they investigate topics relevant to themselves; para-doxically, however, project topics have the potential to create situations of risk or harm to the students. Students often begin with topics that affect youth generally. They then narrow their focus to an issue directly affecting them. The student's investigations of personal health issues have made the project more meaningful and more relevant to their own circumstances, but have also placed them at risk if they have chosen a topic they are struggling with themselves, such as suicide or an eating disorder. The video project may assist some students in overcoming a problem, but it also poses risks. The counselling services made avail-able to the students have provided a counterweight to this dilemma; both teachers are also former First Nations counsellors. From the researcher's point of view, the outcome of the student involvement is unknown and presents a risk that, from an ethical point of view, needs to be continuously evaluated through communication with the teacher and follow-up interviews with selected students.

Ideas for Future Research on Ethical Questions Involving Aboriginal Youth

Pigeon and Hardy Cox (2002) offer the following guidelines based on their review of cultural sensitivity protocols developed by Kowalsky and colleagues (1996). These protocols arose out of their experiences with health research in Aboriginal communities: a) To be prepared for uncertainty; b) to recognize that Aboriginal people are in charge; c) to be honest about the researcher's motives; d) to be oneself and be pre-pared for the unexpected; e) to allow for time; f) to show sensitivity, respect confidence, and guard against taking sides; and g) to maintain ongoing consultation (Pigeon & Hardy Cox, 2002). These guidelines reflect many of the principles we have endeavoured to put into play throughout Traditional Pathways to Health.

REFERENCES

Batten, S.L. (2003). 'Ethical practices with First Nations youth involved in participatory action research.' Unpublished masters thesis, Department of Educational Psychology and Leadership Studies, University of Victoria.

Battiste, M., & Henderson, S. (Eds.). (2000). *Protecting Indigenous knowledge and heritage: A global challenge*. Saskatoon, SK: Purich.

Bazylak, D. (2002). Journeys to success: Perceptions of five female Aboriginal high school graduates. *Canadian Journal of Native Education*, 26(2), 134–51.

Day, L. (2001). *Ethics in Aboriginal research*. AFN Health Conference, First Nations Information Governance Committee. 2003. www.fnchc.ca/_pdf/Ethics-presentation-FNinfo-GovCmt.pdf.

Deloria, V. (1997). Anthros, Indians and planetary reality. In T. Biolsi & L.J. Zimmerman (Eds.), *Indians and anthropologists* (pp. 209–21). Tucson: University of Arizona Press.

Faculty of Human and Social Development. (2003). *Protocols and principles for conducting research in an Indigenous context*. University of Victoria, February 2003 (final revision).

Frank, A.W. (2000). The standpoint of the storyteller. *Qualitative Health Research*, 10, 360–365.

Greaves, T. (Ed.). (1994). *Intellectual property rights for Indigenous peoples: A sourcebook*. Oklahoma City, OK: Society for Applied Anthropology.

Health Canada. (2003). A statistical profile on the health of First Nations in Canada. Retrieved 11 November 2004 from www.hc-sc.gc.ca/fnihb/sppa/hia/publications/statistical_profile.pdf.

Kowalsky, L.O., & Verhoef, M.J., et al. (1996). Guidelines for entry into an Aboriginal community. *Canadian Journal of Native Studies* 16(2), 267–82.

Pigeon, M., & Hardy Cox, D. (2002). Researching with Aboriginal peoples: Practices and principles. *Canadian Journal of Native Education* 26(2), 96–106.

Smith, L. (1999). *Decolonizing methodologies: Research and Indigenous peoples*. New York: St Martin's Press.

Statistics Canada. (2003). *2001 Census: Aboriginal people of Canada*. Ottawa: Government of Canada.

Steinhauer, E. (2002). Thoughts on an Indigenous research methodology. *Canadian Journal of Native Education*, 26(2), 69–81.

Tri-council policy statement: Ethical conduct for research involving humans (1998, with 2000, 2002 updates). Medical Research Council Canada, Natural Sciences and Engineering Research Council of Canada, and Social Sciences and Humanities Research Council of Canada. www.pre.ethics.gc.ca/english/policystatement/policystatement.cfm.

Weber-Pillwax, C. (2001). What is Indigenous research? *Canadian Journal of Native Education*, 25, 166–74.

PART TWO

Longitudinal Samples: Protecting Privacy and Maintaining Consent

4 A Youth Population Health Survey

MIKAEL JANSSON, WAYNE MITIC, TRACEY HULTEN,
AND MANDEEP DHAMI

Along with an increasing number of surveys that collect data for various purposes are resources that describe and guide this data collection process (see for example, Gilbert, 2001; Robson, 2002). These publications range from short guidebooks to extensive and detailed commercial and non-commercial products, such as the Total Design Method (Dillman, 1978). Most writing in this area has focused on maximizing the reliability and validity of the analyses that are conducted. While emphasizing the importance of research design, sample selection, and survey construction, the literature places less emphasis on the ethical issues that may arise and how they may be resolved.

In this chapter we identify some of the salient ethical issues involved in conducting research with a youth population in a large-scale, longitudinal survey, and we describe how we resolved them. We argue that, as with issues of reliability and validity, ethical issues should be viewed on a continuum rather than as a simple right–wrong dichotomy. In adopting this perspective we seek to achieve the highest level of ethics possible in the context of our research rather than merely an acceptable level of ethics as judged by available policies and guidelines.

We present the ethical issues encountered and the resolutions utilized during a population-based survey of 664 young people aged twelve to eighteen years from a medium-sized Canadian city with a population of approximately 325,000.

Survey Method Used in the Healthy Youth Survey (HYS)

The HYS was designed to examine the relations among risk factors (such as individual health-compromising behaviours, family stresses, and community/social adversities), protective factors (such as individual health-promoting behaviours, family strengths, and community/social capital), and physical injury. The youth were interviewed once in 2003, and again in 2005. The HYS project included youth who provided feedback on the survey and consultation with professionals who work with youth in various capacities. In addition, some members of the research team sought opinions from youth in their own families. The process of involving youth during survey development proved invaluable in terms of becoming familiar with language, concepts, and formats that youth would relate to in the survey.

The research team contracted a telephone market research company to undertake the original recruitment, using a script developed by the team. The company contacted and screened a random sample of telephone numbers in a three-step process that (1) identified households with eligible youth, (2) presented the study to parents or guardians and, with their consent, (3) presented the study to the youth. The company also scheduled the in-person interviews, which were conducted by a trained member of the university research team. Interviewers met with the youth in their homes or in a location that offered a safe, private environment in which to respond. Most of the answers to the questionnaire were recorded by the interviewer, with the youth recording answers to more 'sensitive' questions independently.

We chose in-person interviews over a telephone/mail-out data-collection procedure for a number of reasons: active parental consent would be difficult to obtain without personal contact; a lengthy survey administered by phone could result in youth becoming fatigued; telephone interviewing posed the risk that a parent or other family member might overhear the youth's responses, either by eavesdropping or by listening on another phone, thus breaching confidentiality. This same risk exists during in-person administration in the youth's home; however, the interviewers strove to identify, monitor, and maintain a private space to reduce the chances of others overhearing the youth's responses. When the interviewer felt that there was a lack of privacy in the home, a radio or television was turned on to introduce background noise and thereby increase privacy of responses.

The interviewer presented formal letters of consent to both the youth and the parent or guardian before starting the interview. Youth and parents signed two copies, one copy for the research team's records and another for the family to retain.

Ethical Issues Faced by Research Team

A survey planning committee developed the survey instrument and devised a research plan. We discussed ethical issues, keeping in mind the potential risks (or negative effects) to youth while balancing these against the potential benefits. We reviewed ethical guidelines, if they existed, and consulted authorities with expertise in legal and ethics matters. The ethical issues we discussed fell into five broad areas: gaining informed consent in a large-scale survey that straddled a wide age range; maximizing confidentiality and anonymity; including all groups of youth, including those not in the regular school system; respecting participants; and minimizing the probability of causing harm to participants. We describe each of these in detail below.

Gaining Informed Consent from Parents and Youth

Given our recruitment of young people aged twelve to eighteen years, we considered two levels of consent to participate in the research project: consent from parents/guardians, and consent from youth and adolescents. The primary resource on research ethics for academic research in Canada is the *Tri-council Policy Statement: Ethical Conduct for Research Involving Humans*, coauthored by the Medical Research Council Canada, the Natural Sciences and Engineering Research Council of Canada, and the Social Sciences and Humanities Research Council of Canada (Canadian Institutes of Health Research et al., 1998). The *Tri-council Policy Statement* discusses at considerable length whether an individual possesses the competence to give consent. Competence 'refers to the ability of prospective subjects to give informed consent in accord with their own fundamental values' (page 2.9). In practice, 'competence' is generally equated with age; however, legislation in British Columbia provides limited guidance regarding the youngest age at which people are considered competent to give consent and is silent on the competence of adolescents. While age is, strictly speaking, not a determinant of ability to provide consent, concern about competency becomes more important with younger adolescents than with older ones. Formal regulations vary in relating age with competency. In British Columbia, the most relevant statute that addresses the age at which people can consent to treatment is the Child, Family and Community Services Act (RSBC 1996 C.46) (CFCSA). The CFCSA states that persons twelve and older must have their views solicited and taken into account when a plan of care is developed for them; that the wishes of persons twelve and older who are in continuing custody must be considered when granting access to a person who has appealed to the court for access; and that persons twelve and older can give consent to make custody or supervision orders. In addition, the CFCSA states that before voluntary care agreements can be signed, the views of the child must be solicited and taken into account if possible. However, in this section, the age of the child is not specified; the implication is that this must occur regardless of the age of the child.

In contrast, the B.C. Mental Health Act (RSBC 1996 c.288) declares that only those sixteen and over can apply for voluntary admission to a provincial mental health facility. Those under sixteen can be voluntarily admitted at the request of a parent or guardian; however, the person so admitted must be discharged if they so request after turning sixteen years of age (section 20).

While legislation is silent on the age at which youth can give consent to research, these two pieces of legislation suggest that youth might be considered competent to give their own consent to be interviewed in a survey. Nevertheless, we decided to obtain parental/guardian consent in all cases, instead of requiring interviewers to determine the capacity of the youth to provide informed consent. Some of the benefits of obtaining parental consent include increased transparency of the study as well as parents' ability to explain the study to young participants and to show their support for it. Moreover, when parents are involved in the recruitment process and are informed of the potential risks and benefits to participants, longitudinal follow-up interviews may be easier to conduct (since the parent has already consented to the first survey). Informing the parent about the study is also respectful, particularly since most interviews were administered in the home.[1]

The questionnaire included a small number of questions about sexuality, and we feared that parents might withhold consent because of these questions. The team considered producing two different questionnaires and allowing the parent or guardian to choose, at the first telephone contact attempt, between a version including questions about sexuality and a version excluding these questions. However, we dismissed this option because we believed that this strategy would increase the number of parents who would exclude these questions from the youth's survey beyond the anticipated small number who would do so if they previewed the whole questionnaire before signing the consent form. We instead chose to inform the parent or guardian of the survey's content and provided them with the opportunity to have the questions about sexuality removed from their youth's questionnaire. In the end, a very small minority of parents requested that questions about sexuality be excluded from the survey. Nineteen questionnaires (4 per cent) out of the 490 administered to youth fourteen and over had missing values for all questions in this section, indicating that either the youth refused to answer these questions or that the parent asked that these questions be excluded.

Maximizing Confidentiality and Anonymity

Researchers collecting longitudinal data are faced with the difficult task of meeting two contradictory goals: maximizing the confidentiality of participants, and maximizing the probability of maintaining contact with them over time. On the one hand, keeping as little identifying information as possible reduces the possibility that respondents could be identified. On the other hand, keeping as much identifying information as possible – including contact information – increases the possibility that respondents can be identified and contacted for the follow-up interviews. Researchers manage this balancing act with the knowledge that if respondents feel that the data they provide are confidential and that their responses are anonymous, the accuracy of their responses improves and the social desirability response bias diminishes (Bradburn, 1983). Therefore, increasing anonymity and confidentiality can enhance reliability, validity, and response rates.

To protect identifying information in the HYS, respondents were assured that two databases would be maintained. Their contact information, in one database, would only be accessible to those who needed to arrange for the follow-up interview. The respondent's survey responses would be in a separate database that could not be accessed by interviewers. In addition, respondent names were not placed on any survey materials or envelopes; only the respondent ID, interviewer name, and date of the interview were noted. The only materials that contained the youth's name were a signed consent form and contact information, both of which were placed in a sealed envelope with the respondent ID, separate from the completed survey. The contact information was subsequently retained in a separate filing system in the research office.

The HYS was administered in two parts to increase privacy for responding to sensitive questions while preserving a standardized administration and reducing reading demands. Part 1 included demographic and less sensitive questions, and the interviewer completed this part based on the answers supplied by the participant. Part 2 included questions of a more sensitive nature such as the youth's engagement in risky behaviours and questions about their sexuality. The interviewer read items in this section aloud, and the youth completed it without assistance unless he or she explicitly requested help. This section concluded with a page of questions about sexuality that the youth both read and answered independently. The interviewer placed the youth-completed section in an envelope, which – in front of the participant – was sealed and placed within a larger envelope that included the remainder of the survey materials.

The interviewers were trained extensively in the administration procedures and in how to maintain the privacy and confidentiality of participating youth. The interviewers were required to sign an oath of non-disclosure and confidentiality; this specified that survey information must not be shared with anyone outside the research team. In addition, interviewers could not interview respondents known to them because this might reduce the youth's privacy.

Managing Reporting Requirements

The CFCSA limits the level of confidentiality that researchers can offer youth respondents in that all British Columbia residents are obligated to report any suspected physical, sexual, or emotional harm to child protection officials. This limit to the promise of confidentiality was explicitly described in the consent forms that the youth and their parent or guardian signed.

Since the HYS aimed to explore the relationship between risk and injury in youth, we anticipated a substantial risk for uncovering scenarios in which a youth needed protection. While developing the questionnaire, we carefully scrutinized all questions to determine the likelihood that they would reveal child abuse and, ultimately, compel a breach of the confidentiality of the youth's survey information. Besides deliberating as a group, we consulted with an expert in the CFCSA and worded questions and response categories to reduce the likelihood that abuse would be revealed unintentionally due to suggestive questions. For example, the sexual health questions that the youth read and completed independently received special consideration. Since fourteen is the age of consent to participate in sexual activity according to the Criminal Code (R.S. 1985, c. C-46), only youth fourteen and older were asked to answer these questions. An initial question asked whether the youth participant had ever had sex, and subsequent questions asked about sexual behaviour; for example, a question about when the youth first had sex. The lowest response category on this scale was 'younger than 15.' This reduced the possibility that a youth would declare that he or she had had sex before the age of fourteen without an understanding that this answer could result in the researchers notifying the child protection agency about this response.

A large part of the training of interviewers consisted of a discussion of the relevant sections of the CFCSA that legislate the reporting requirement. Several scenarios were discussed with the interviewers that emphasized the importance of reporting youth in need of protection to the Ministry of Children and Family Development (MCFD) so that youth would receive the help they needed. Interviewers were also instructed that even an unsolicited disclosure by the youth that alluded to abuse or harm would require reporting to child protection officials. For example, if while answering a particular question about parental support, the youth alluded to serious parental neglect in a spontaneous remark, it would be the duty of the interviewer to make a report to the principal investigator, who would facilitate the contact with the MCFD. In cases of immediate need, the interviewers were asked to phone the provincial Helpline for Children, which is open twenty-four hours a day. Besides this, information gleaned from the in-person visit to the family's home by the interviewer could warrant reporting – for example, the physical, emotional, and living conditions of the youth and family. A member of the research team had developed cooperation with a contact person at the MCFD while working on a different research project (see Jansson & Benoit, in this volume), and this person agreed to serve as the contact person for this project also. Despite these conservative guidelines, we made only one report to the ministry while interviewing 664 youth.

Inclusion of Youth in Unconventional Education and Living Situations

Young people are most at risk for social exclusion. Youth marginalized by, for example, school leaving and non-standard living situations are unlikely to be involved in consultative processes involving issues that affect them (McAuley and Brattman, 2002). Rather than a school-based sample (which excludes, by definition, youth who are not attending school, because they are home schooled or for some other reason), the HYS sample was a random sample drawn by a company that maintains a database of all White Pages listings. This sampling strategy systematically excludes youth who live in households that are not in the phonebook because the number is unlisted or because there is no phone in the home.

We did, however, aim to include and accommodate youth with varying needs in the HYS. For instance, the telephone recruiters gathered and relayed to the interviewers pertinent information concerning a potential participant's literacy level or disabilities. As a result, interviewers could tailor their approach to administering the survey to meet the unique needs of youth with special needs. In addition, conducting individual home-based interviews allowed youth without access to transportation to participate.

Respect for Participants

We endeavoured to treat youth who were involved in the survey with respect. Respect for their living situation, background, and opinions was demonstrated in a multitude of ways and permeated many of the ethical decisions that were made. For example, during the hiring process, potential interviewers were asked how they would place youth participants at ease. This invoked comments about how they might dress and what type of language they might use. Interviewers were trained to utilize a language and tone that was accepting, non-judgmental, and non-patronizing.

We acknowledged the contribution that youth made in terms of their time and sharing of information by providing a small honorarium. Remuneration provides an explicit recognition of youth as experts or quasi-consultants as well as an incentive and a sign of appreciation. This is not as straightforward as it sounds; some believe that youth do not or should not expect remuneration, that it could be perceived as manipulative, and that it undermines the spirit of volunteerism (White, 2001). A $25 honorarium was provided to participants in the belief that this modest amount would not unduly coerce participation even for economically disadvantaged youth. An explicit statement was included on the consent form stating that the youth should not participate if the only reason was to receive the honorarium.

We debated the form of the honorarium at length. On the one hand, cash honorariums would provide the maximum benefit because the recipients could use them however they chose. On the other hand, they might spend the cash on unhealthy choices (perhaps drugs or cigarettes), which would be counter to the spirit of the survey. We decided to offer a choice of gift certificates – movie theatre, music store, sports store, or grocery store – instead of cash. All four choices were popular among the youth.

Minimizing the Probability of Causing Harm to Participants

In working with minors of any age, it is important to consider their safety at all times. It is the primary concern of researchers to avoid causing harm to participants during the course of any study. Since HYS interviewers were to survey youth in private settings, the screening process for interview staff was an important consideration for the research team. In addition to formal job interviews and reference checks, a criminal record check was considered for screening applicants.

In British Columbia, the Criminal Records Review Act (CRRA) (RSBC 1996, c. 86) requires that those who work with children and youth under nineteen have a criminal record check conducted if they are employed by, licensed by, or receive funding from the province. This act applies to a broad range of professionals who work with young people, such as dentists and optometrists, beyond the obvious groups such as teachers and daycare staff.

Federally funded programs, such as the HYS research project, are not referred to in the CRRA. Nevertheless, the HYS research team wished to ensure youths' safety and asked for recent copies of criminal record checks. Nine out of eleven interview staff were already working in fields that required criminal record checks, and the other two were known assistants who had worked in related research projects; hence, criminal record checks were omitted in the interest of time and costs.

The authors of this chapter – who were part of the original HYS research team – believed in hindsight that their decision to not require criminal record checks of interview staff may not have been the most ethical choice. We now believe that the research team should have required interview staff to undergo criminal record checks, and have done so for the second wave of the study, in the interest of increasing child and youth safety.

Conclusions

The language traditionally used to frame discussions of ethics invites us to structure our thoughts dichotomously: studies are either ethically acceptable or they are not. In the HYS, the process of establishing ethical research practices took the form of ongoing consultation and debate. Despite the stories that abound about the difficulties researchers face before ethics review boards, our collaborative experiences were very positive. Indeed, the research team and the board members worked in tandem to achieve a high level of ethical acceptability. Difficult issues were discussed and resolutions were developed through interactions among researchers, community partners, and board members.

This kind of negotiation and discussion also occurred among interdisciplinary members of the University of Victoria's Community Alliance for Health Research (CAHR) research team. The current research effort was guided by the expertise that the research team had acquired during past work with children, youth, and vulnerable adult populations. The youth studied in the HYS straddle the divide between those individuals in our society who may not fully understand the consequences of their participation in research projects and those who do understand. These youth also straddle the age at which legislation attempts to define and limit rights and obligations that separate adults from children (see Leadbeater et al., in this volume).

We did not always reach consensus around decisions that concerned ethical issues in the survey. Even now, discussions are lengthy as we reconsider the decisions described above in anticipation of subsequent surveys. However, we realize that continued dialogue is essential if we are to maintain a high standard of ethical practice in this ongoing research project.

NOTE

1 Given the option of being interviewed in their home, at the university, in a downtown office, or in any other location that offered sufficient privacy, most youth chose to be interviewed at home. This setting allowed for consent to be easily obtained from the parents or guardians, while giving families the choice to participate in a location away from the home. This may have excluded those living in poverty or those who were uncomfortable inviting the interviewer to their home for some other reason.

REFERENCES

Bradburn, N.M. (1983). Response effects. In P.H. Rossi, J.D. Wright & A.B. Anderson (Eds.), *Handbook of survey research*. New York: Academic Press.

Canadian Institutes of Health Research, Natural Sciences and Engineering Research Council of Canada, Social Sciences and Humanities Research Council of Canada. 1998. *Tri-council policy statement: Ethical conduct for research involving humans* (with 2000, 2002, 2005 amendments). www.pre.ethics.gc.ca/english/policystatement/policystatement.cfm.

Dillman, D.A. (1978). *Mail and telephone surveys: The total design method*. New York: Wiley-Interscience.

Gilbert N. (Ed.). (2001). *Researching social life* (2nd ed). London: Sage.

McAuley, K., & Brattman, M. (2002). *Hearing young voices*. Dublin. Open Your Eyes to Child Poverty Initiative. www.youth.ie/research/hearing.pdf.

Robson, C. (2002). *Real world research* (2nd ed.). Oxford: Blackwell. National Commission for the Protection of Human Subjects of Biomedical and Behavioral Research (1979). *The Belmont report: Ethical principles and guidelines for the protection of human subjects of research*. Washington, DC: Department of Health, Education, and Welfare.

White, P. 2001. *Local and vocal: Promoting young people's involvement in local decision-making: An overview and planning guide*. London: Save the Children/ National Youth Agency.

5 The Ethics of Peeking behind the Fence: Issues Related to Studying Children's Aggression and Victimization

AMY YUILE, DEBRA PEPLER, WENDY CRAIG, AND
JENNIFER CONNOLLY

Over the past fifteen years our research group has been involved in multimethod research into children's and adolescents' experiences of bullying, victimization, and related problem behaviours. Bullying is a relationship problem in which one person uses power aggressively to cause distress to another (Pepler, Craig, Yuile, & Connolly, 2004). As bullying interactions are repeated, the relative power of the aggressive child over the victimized child becomes increasingly differentiated. Bullying encompasses a wide range of verbal, social, and physical forms of aggression such as name-calling, social exclusion, gossiping, spreading rumours, hitting, issuing threats, and confinement. Bullying is most often short-lived, verbal, and difficult to detect. Bullying most often unfolds in the context of a peer group, and the 'audience' for bullying can play a role in exacerbating or stopping bullying interactions (Hawkins, Pepler & Craig, 2001; O'Connell, Pepler & Craig, 1999). Teachers, on the other hand, seldom intervene to stop bullying (Atlas & Pepler, 1998; Craig & Pepler, 1997). Children appear to understand that bullying is wrong and to recognize where and when they can engage in these negative behaviours without adults being aware of it.

The covert and sensitive nature of bullying presents a challenge to researchers. In our work we have recognized the immense privilege we have been afforded to 'peek behind the fence' to view children's and adolescents' lives and to study inter- and intra-personal processes that are often hidden from adults (Pepler & Craig, 1995). If we hope to learn more about these covert and often distressing behaviours, we must pay close attention to the manner in which we gather information from youth about their experiences of being bullied, bullying others, or witnessing bullying. In this chapter we relate some the lessons we have learned and are still learning through our program of research on bullying.

Our research program started with naturalistic observations of children's interactions on the school playground and in the classroom, and has recently extended to observations of adolescents interacting with their best friends, romantic partners, and parents. In addition, we have conducted longitudinal surveys of children's and adolescents' experiences of bullying, victimization, and related problems. More than three thousand Canadian children and adolescents from a range of cultural and socio-economic backgrounds have participated in the research program and assisted us in gaining an understanding of bullying problems.

We have used a combination of observational and survey research methods to unravel the complex and often covert nature of aggression and victimization. The observations comprised part of the evaluations of two school-based interventions: social skills training (Pepler, Craig, & Roberts, 1995) and an antibullying intervention (Pepler, Craig, O'Connell, Atlas & Charach, 2005). We identified a subsample of children at the participating elementary schools and used videotaping with remote microphones to capture the children's interactions in the classroom and during unstructured time on the school playground. We supplemented the observations with questionnaires for children, teachers, and parents to assess the prevalence and nature of bullying problems (Craig, Pepler & Atlas, 2000).

Our observations of elementary schoolchildren's naturalistic interactions raised concerns for the lessons about power and aggression that might carry forward into adolescence (Craig & Pepler, 1999). The next step in our research program was to examine how bullying diversifies in form and context in adolescence and to assess the behaviour problems associated with using aggression to gain or maintain power and control over others. As part of our Teen Relationships Project, we followed three cohorts of adolescents over seven years, as they progressed from Grades 5, 6, and 7 to Grades 11, 12, and 13 at several schools in Toronto, Canada. The students completed annual surveys about various forms of aggression, victimization, and developmentally relevant behaviours and relationships. Observational data were collected for a subset of adolescents who met criteria related to bullying involvement and for a comparison group of non-involved adolescents. For these observations, we invited adolescents to complete a number of structured activities: plan a party together, discuss two issues that sometimes caused problems in their relationships, and play a game together. We videotaped the adolescents engaging in these activities with their best friends, mothers, and romantic partners. By highlighting the developmental and systemic nature of bullying problems, our research has provided direction for prevention and intervention efforts to reduce bullying and victimization among children and youth.

In this chapter we discuss several ethical themes that emerged throughout our research program to illustrate the complex issues arising in research on children's and adolescents' aggression and victimization. The Canadian ethical guidelines for research involving human subjects identified in the *Tri-Council Policy Statement* (1998) provided an important foundation from which the researchers engaged in principle-guided discussion, debate, and decision-making. King and Churchill (2000) have articulated how understanding and recognizing key ethical principles brings reasoned discussion into decision-making in research. When research with children and adolescents is being conducted, the importance of this process cannot be overstated. For example, in our work examining aggression and victimization, the questions are complex and the outcomes bear both scientific and social implications. Thus researchers must apply particular care and reflection to ensure that above and beyond a process of principled reasoning, the context of the research and of the young participants is taken into account in the methodology of the study (King & Churchill, 2000).

The discussion focuses on the value of adopting developmental and systemic perspectives in research with children and adolescents. We consider how to ensure participants' well-being through consent and confidentiality procedures. We draw on our own experiences in providing examples of ethical considerations for vulnerable youth and in reinforcing the importance of training and support for research staff. Using case examples from the survey and observational research, we illustrate the ethical dilemmas we have faced and how we resolved them.

Applying a Developmental Perspective in Research

A developmental perspective is essential in research with children and youth in order to evaluate their level of understanding of the research process and also in order also to anticipate the potential impact, risks, and benefits of their involvement at different developmental stages (Thompson, 1990). We have relied heavily on a developmental perspective in implementing our research on bullying. Bullying and forms of interpersonal aggression result from highly complex interactions between child, family, peer, school, and other ecological factors (Sroufe, 1997). Exploring the topic of bullying can arouse difficult emotions for some children, particularly those who are victimized. As children approach adolescence, during which friendships are especially important (Youniss, 1980), questions about relationships with peers can arouse troubling feelings among youth who are friendless or who have strained peer interactions. Research on adults generally shows that when asked about past traumatic experiences, most adults do not suffer from an overwhelming emotional response (Putnam, Liss & Landsverk, 1996). There is, however, limited understanding about how children and adolescents respond to sensitive questions, particularly when the bullying and/or victimization is ongoing. In addition to feeling discomfort when answering questions about this form of abuse at the hands of peers, youth may be fearful that reporting victimization will have negative social repercussions, especially if peers learn about the reports and retaliate. Compared to youth in high school, children in elementary school may be more willing to discuss with adults their experiences of bullying. This is because of the shame and fear associated with experiences of victimization in adolescence. In our research we have recognized the importance of approaching these issues sensitively and have been challenged to facilitate alternative opportunities for youth to connect with researchers to discuss these troubling issues.

A Systemic Approach: Consent, Confidentiality, and Compensation

A developmental perspective is embedded in a broader systemic framework. As others have argued (e.g., Christakis, 1992; Jensen, Hoagwood & Fisher, 1996), a systemic approach is invaluable in navigating the relationship between research science and ethical considerations. Our experiences of working with children and adolescents around issues of aggression in relationships have encouraged us to look not only at the characteristics and history of individual students, but also at factors related to peer groups, family, school, and sociocultural background, when designing appropriate steps to ensure the well-being of all participants. The challenge for researchers is to create a context that students perceive as safe and supportive and in which they can share their experiences, concerns, and feelings. In developing ethical protocols to address issues of consent, protection of confidentiality, and incentives for participation in longitudinal designs, it is important to consider both the developmental capacities of the participants and the social sensitivities and influences in the salient systems in their lives.

Obtaining Parental Consent and Maintaining Confidentiality

Our longitudinal and intervention studies were conducted in the school context; this presented challenges when it came to obtaining parental consent for the child and adolescent participants. Since we did not have access to students' addresses, we relied on students to deliver and return the parental consent forms. Elementary school–age children, compared to high school students, were more reliable about delivering forms to their parents and returning them. The lack of adolescents' follow-through in obtaining their parents' consent for participation may coincide with increasing autonomy at this stage. Although Canadian adolescents are able to consent to medical treatment at a younger age, the age of majority in our provincial jurisdiction (Ontario) is eighteen; thus it was essential that we obtain parental consent for participation in research. Some older adolescents admitted to forging their parents' signatures in order to participate. To ensure that parents were actually aware of their children's participation and to obtain their initial verbal consent, we followed up with a telephone call to parents of students who were interested in participating and who were willing to provide us with a contact phone number. We explained the process to the parents; to those who gave verbal consent for their children's participation, we mailed consent forms in an addressed, postage-paid envelope.

In the context of longitudinal research, it is essential to link an individual's data over time; this raises additional ethical concerns relating to the balance between protecting participants' privacy and linking their data over time. As is customary, a unique identification number was assigned to each student. As the children entered adolescence, we asked questions about illegal activities; this heightened our concerns about confidentiality of the youths' reports. To provide additional protection for potentially sensitive information, our codebook that linked the names with the numbers was held by a lawyer under a client-confidentiality agreement. With this arrangement, we were able to reassure students that their information would remain confidential and would not be used against them. Below we discuss situations in which we returned to students to ask for permission to disclose information about situations were of concern to us.

Concerns about confidentiality extended to the requests of a few parents throughout the research process. Some parents asked to review the questionnaires prior to giving consent. These parents were invited to view a copy of the document, which was maintained in each school office. Several parents indicated that they would only permit their elementary school-aged child to complete a survey if they were allowed to see their child's responses. The issues of confidentiality were explained to these parents, and it was made clear that they could not have access to their children's responses. Children of the parents who were not willing to provide consent under these conditions did not participate in the research. Following survey administration, a few parents asked whether they could see their children's responses. Again, we explained confidentiality and encouraged these parents to initiate some general discussions with their children about their experiences at school and experiences with bullying and victimization. In presentations at the schools, we emphasized to parents that learning about children's experiences at school, particularly with respect to a sensitive issue like bullying, requires a gentle and balanced approach rather than high-pressure questioning. We provided guidelines for parents to pose open-ended questions about their child's day, such as asking him about the best thing and worst thing of their day and with whom did the child play? In the context of supportive communication, children may feel more comfortable in sharing with their parents troubling experiences with peers. In approaching parental requests in this way, we were trying to protect the privacy of children's survey responses and at the same time to address parents' concerns for understanding their children's experiences.

Payment for Participation

There has been a trend in research over the past decade to provide some form of compensation to participants appropriate for the time and effort involved in participation (Attkisson, Rosenblatt & Hoagwood, 1996). At this point, however, there are no clear guidelines as to what constitutes a fair honorarium. Careful thought about fair compensation is necessary to ensure that incentives are respectful of the time and effort expended by the participants, but not so high that their sense of power and control is jeopardized. For children and adolescents, a large and attractive honorarium carries a risk of coercion if participants are placed in a vulnerable position – that is, if they are persuaded not by the project, but by the prize (Thompson, 1990).

For our longitudinal study, we struggled to find a balance: we wanted to pay an honorarium in appreciation of students' participation, but we also wanted to avoid creating a coercive or overly attractive context for participation. We believed that providing a small honorarium for completing the survey each year would ensure that students recognized our appreciation; we also felt that the gesture would help lower attrition, especially considering that the surveys were to be administered annually for seven years. Distribution of the compensation varied across participating schools. In some schools, students chose to donate the money to a charity. At other schools, the money went towards field trips for the students. In some schools, compensation was given directly to the participants, and this compensation quickly became associated with the project, with students referring to it as 'the $5 Survey.'

The issue of payment was salient for the adolescents because most of them were eager to earn some money. We did not inform students that they would be receiving compensation for completing the surveys until we had received signed parental consent and the youth's assent to participate. This was to ensure that students made an informed decision that was not motivated by a financial gain. Adolescents who were asked to participate in the observations were informed before agreeing to participate that there would be compensation. We recognized that the demands on students' time, effort, and involvement for the observations were significant, so letting students know they would be financially compensated was important for recruitment. After completing the observations, some participants and their partners commented that they had enjoyed the experience and would have done it even if they had not received compensation. Other students often mentioned how much they appreciated the compensation, which demonstrated that we valued their time and participation.

Creating a Comfortable Context for Participation

In conducting our observational and survey research, we have come to recognize the importance of a safe and comfortable context for the data collection. By developing strong lines of communication between participants and the researchers as well as strategies for monitoring the research administration, we have endeavoured to address young people's concerns and gain their trust in the research process. Next we highlight the strategies we have used through examples from our research.

Surveys: A Context for Further Victimization

As the peer group takes on increased importance in middle childhood, bullying increasingly occurs as part of a group process (Craig & Pepler, 1999). In conducting research on the sensitive issues of bullying and victimization, we have been concerned about providing youth with the opportunity to share their experiences without creating a context for further victimization. An example of how this can happen occurred at one participating school. When the survey was administered, privacy folders were provided to allow students to complete the survey without others being able to view their responses. These privacy folders consisted of file folders, opened into a V, to shield the survey. One of our research assistants noticed that several male students had written sexually demeaning comments about another student on a folder. The comments were derived from specific questions in the survey about sexual harassment and were displayed for others in the room to read.

When the research assistant alerted senior researchers about the harmful messages, the senior researcher approached the boys, took the privacy folders, and dispersed the small group by reassigning seating. The senior investigator passed the folders on to the school principal and met with school staff to discuss what had happened so that staff could be vigilant for signs of aggression, harassment, and victimization. Additional instructions were given to research assistants to alert them to subtle behaviours that might be generated from the survey material. Careful monitoring ensured that students completed the survey without talking with one another and that the task was taken seriously.

Facilitating Comfortable Participation

In collecting observational data with adolescents, we considered how contexts for the interviews might compromise confidentiality or place them in an uncomfortable position. Some students had friendships or romantic relationships that they did not want to reveal to their families. We offered a range of safe and comfortable spaces for observations. Providing youth with options enabled greater participation by reducing their reservations about participating.

The issue of diversity of relationships arose several times during our research program. Some students reported circumstances that differed from the planned methodology, such as having a same-sex romantic partner or requesting to film with a father because their mother was deceased. An ethical decision was made to include adolescents who had alternative relationships so that they too felt supported and involved. We recognized that these data might not fit logically into our general data set, but planned to examine them perhaps as case studies to enrich our understanding of the divergent relationships in the lives of adolescents.

Ensuring Well-being and Reporting Responsibilities

When students provided information that required us either ethically or legally to notify someone, we sought to strike an ethical balance between respecting confidentiality and the duty to report (see also Jansson & Benoit, in this volume). For example, perhaps the youth was at risk of harm from others or at risk of harming him/herself or someone else. The likelihood of learning that peers were victimizing a child arose in the context of our studies. To allow for possible follow-up of these concerns, the consent form was carefully worded to communicate to parents and potential participants what the conditions of disclosure would be. The consent form for parents read as follows: 'Your child's responses will be confidential and his/her name will not appear anywhere on the questionnaires. Sometimes, however, children choose to speak to the researchers about these questions (this can be indicated on the questionnaires) and sometimes the researchers choose to speak to a child about his/her responses.'

Gaining permission to reveal a situation of victimization required us to consider that we risked making the problem worse rather than better. Children reported that telling an adult about being bullied does not always result in getting help, but can serve as another reason for the other children to bully him/her (O'Connor, Pepler & Craig, 1999). Especially in schools where an established policy for bullying is not in place, teachers and parents may not know how to handle reports of bullying or how to conduct adequate follow-up. Despite having good intentions, adults may not be sufficiently prepared to deal with the complexities of supporting youth in ongoing negative social interactions. To ensure that revealing a situation of victimization would help rather than harm the student, we found it necessary to provide support for the adults (including the principal and teachers) in dealing with bullying. Senior members of our research team were available for consultation with school staff with regard to bullying issues. The investigators also offered workshops for teachers, students, and parents on the issues of bullying and victimization.

Within the research program itself, we also examined the context in which aggressive behaviour occurs by asking about a constellation of problem behaviours that adolescents may have engaged in. The students' responses created a picture of how aggressive behaviours, delinquent activities, substance use, gang involvement, and externalizing and internalizing symptoms may cluster. To a certain extent, experimentation with deviant behaviours is normal in adolescence; however, serious levels of engagement in problem behaviours can signify substantial risk to an adolescent's well-being.

Although all survey information was considered confidential, each survey was screened after completion for the presence of high-risk problems such as severe depression or illegal activities. When a student with severe problems was identified, a senior member of the research team contacted the youth confidentially and individually. The senior researchers made every effort to maintain privacy by contacting students individually, by meeting with students one-on-one in a private space, and by not disclosing to either the teacher or the classmates the specific reason for the interview. When the research team was in the school, requests to withdraw students from classes were quite frequent and related to a variety of issues such as providing another consent form, finishing an incomplete survey, or providing information for students' projects. If the youth was interested in seeking assistance, the researcher provided contact information for support services. This solution acknowledged the need to ensure adolescents' well-being but did not breach confidentiality or interfere with the validity of the research, since the researchers did not assume a clinical role in providing assessment or intervention. As researchers in the school context, we were occasionally involved in a consultative capacity. Consistent with principle-guided ethical practice (King & Churchill, 2000), minimizing harm was the chief responsibility and concern of the research team; providing any direct benefits to the young participants was a secondary outcome.

Developing and Evaluating Ethical Initiatives

Although members of the research team do not assume a clinical role while conducting a study, researchers bear significant responsibility for ensuring that adolescents understand the process and for supporting their well-being throughout their participation in the research. Incorporating precautionary measures into research design and evaluating the usefulness of those measures affords a better understanding of which ethical procedures are effective in research with youth.

In the course of our research program, surveys about bullying and victimization were administered to several thousand elementary and high school students. To ensure that children and adolescents, who might be troubled by the research process, could receive some support, we included a 'Talk Box' at the end of each survey form. Participants were invited to check the box if they wanted to discuss any issues raised in the survey, privately, with a researcher. Students' indications in these boxes were reviewed within a day of the administration. A protocol was developed for the steps to be taken when a 'Talk Box' was checked.

Each year, between 1 and 3 per cent of students indicated that they wished to talk with a member of the research team. When we met with them individually, some youth revealed that they were being bullied; others wanted to talk about family problems; still others had comments or suggestions about the questionnaires. When students revealed concerns about victimization, we acted as consultants to help them voice their concerns and connect with the appropriate resources in the school or community. In our interviews we followed a specific protocol to assess whether the bullying was ongoing, what students had done to try to stop it, whether these responses had been effective in stopping it, and whether the students had told an adult about it. When the victimization was ongoing and the students were not receiving support, we indicated our concern and support and asked the student whether we could speak to the school principal about the problem. We had an agreement with a designated person at the school (typically, the principal or a student counsellor) that we would share this information if the student gave us permission and that we would support the school in intervening to help victimized students effectively. In almost all cases, students agreed; when this happened, to have the concerns shared with school staff. In several cases, however, the students did not agree; when this happened, we returned to talk to them a week later in a similarly private interview to determine whether they were still being victimized, what they had tried to stop the bullying, how effective their responses had been, and how we could provide support for them.

We ask ourselves whether asking students to indicate that they wanted to speak to a researcher actually connected the research team with those students who were at particular risk for psychosocial problems and victimization. A review of the data for youth who selected the Talk Box revealed that they were at risk in several ways. Early adolescents (Grades 6 to 8) were more likely to check the Talk Box than older students

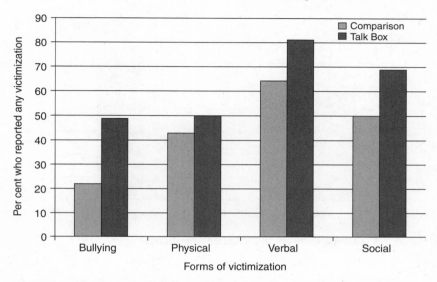

Figure 5.1. Reports of forms of victimization

(Grades 9 to 12). This difference may reflect developmental changes in the prevalence and forms of bullying. With age, bullying appears to diversify into other developmentally salient forms of aggression, most notably sexual harassment and dating aggression. Reports of bullying decline in early adolescence, whereas reports of sexual harassment and aggression with dating partners increase (Pepler, Yuile, Craig, Connolly & McMaster, 2002). Thus high school students may be less likely to select the Talk Box because they may not regard these more sophisticated forms of aggressive behaviour as bullying, although we understand these forms of aggression to fall under the broad rubric of bullying – the combined use of power and aggression. Furthermore, younger students may regard asking an adult for assistance as more acceptable; older students may feel that they should be able to handle difficulties on their own.

We compared youth who selected the Talk Box (n=84) to a grade- and gender-matched sample of those who did not select the box (n=84). Adolescents who selected the Talk Box were more than twice as likely to be victims of bullying than those who did not. They reported significantly more physical, verbal, and social victimization than other students (see Figure 5.1). In addition, youth who selected the Talk Box

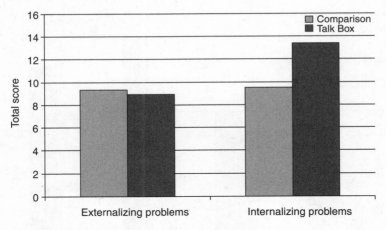

Figure 5.2. Externalizing and internalizing problems

reported higher levels of internalizing problems, including anxiety, depression, withdrawal, and somatic complaints. Beginning in early adolescence (Grade 6), youth who selected the Talk Box also reported higher levels of externalizing problems (delinquent activities, aggressive behaviour) than youth who did not select the box (see Figure 5.2).

Students who asked to speak with a researcher were more vulnerable in terms of experiences of victimization and behavioural problems. These data provide some validation of the utility of this tool for enhancing ethical research practices. These data also reflect how distressed some adolescents must have felt that they wanted to reach out to adults for help around problems with peers. What does this mean for research with adolescent participants? The willingness of some youth at risk to come forward suggests that it is important to provide young people – especially those who are highly victimized – with opportunities to discuss and gain support.

It is important to recognize that only some adolescents who are having difficulties have the courage to identify themselves and reach out to adults. The challenge for researchers is to create a context that students perceive as sufficiently safe and supportive that they can voice their concerns and feelings. Part of this challenge may be met by establishing positive and considerate relationships between the research team and adolescent participants. Longitudinal research offers this benefit: researchers have time to become familiar with students and foster connections with them. This can encourage vulnerable youth to view the researchers as a resource for support.

Awareness of Concerns for Aggressive/Victimized Youth

Several ethical considerations for youth-based research are constant across many of fields of study. Some are related to the specific focus and methodology of the research. We now turn to discuss the ethical challenges encountered during naturalistic observational research in order to illustrate the complex issues faced by researchers working with children involved in aggressive interactions.

Naturalistic Audiovisual Observations of Children

In naturalistic observations of elementary schoolchildren's interactions on school playgrounds and in classrooms, we used remote microphones and video cameras to peek into children's social worlds (Pepler & Craig, 1995). The ability to view what actually occurs when children interact led to unexpected ethical concerns. Bullying among children was observed about every seven minutes on the playground. Teachers seldom intervened to stop bullying, and peers were present in 85 per cent of the episodes (Craig & Pepler, 1997). These insights heightened our understanding of the complexities of bullying and helped generate awareness about how serious a problem bullying was. An ethical protocol was developed to ensure the safety and well-being of children participating in the study while maintaining the integrity of the research (Pepler & Craig, 1995). In research involving naturalistic observation, several factors require close attention, including the nature of the activities observed, the setting, and the means of recording (TCPS, 1998). Despite careful planning to ensure the safety and privacy of the children, additional ethical challenges emerged during the research that required significant deliberation.

In particular, it was essential to decide when to intervene when aggressive interactions were observed among children. Due to the remote filming, we observed negative incidents among children that were sometimes out of view of the adults (such as duty teachers and monitors) on the playground. It surprised us how much verbal cruelty we witnessed, and how many physical and social acts of aggression. As researchers, we were somewhat constrained from actively intervening when we observed aggression: we had no authority in the school, we had agreed with the school community to be unobtrusive in our observations, and we were concerned about the integrity of our naturalistic observations. Nevertheless, we were troubled by the severity of some of the aggressive exchanges and wondered how to protect children's safety without directly intervening.

An ethical protocol for handling these aggressive situations was developed to ensure the safety of the children without directly involving the research team. One member of the research team was based on the playground, equipped with a two-way radio to communicate with the researcher(s) monitoring the audiovisual equipment. When a harmful or dangerous event was observed, the researchers informed supervising school staff, who then intervened.

In our study with adolescents, we observed aggressive interactions during semistructured conversations involving the youth and three partners (mother, best friend, or boy/girlfriend) with regard to 'hot topics' they identified in their relationship. It was not uncommon for participants to work through difficult feelings in talking about conflict in their relationships. For example, one mother verbally berated her son, who appeared increasingly uncomfortable during the discussion. Negative verbal exchanges like these raised concerns about whether and how to debrief conflict between an adolescent and his/her parent or partner. For each session, the researcher left the room to allow greater privacy; however, we were able to monitor the interaction by drawing the audio and video feed to outside the testing area. Researchers took steps to regulate the tone of the experience by checking in with the participants to ensure their comfort with the interactions and by addressing any negative emotions through supportive discussion. The research team attempted to model a positive and constructive context for the activities. As we debriefed with the adolescent and partner, we acknowledged that they had been asked to discuss some difficult issues and checked to ensure that they felt comfortable about what had happened. The majority of participants were receptive to engaging in a constructive follow-up discussion with the researcher about the interactions in the session and their reactions to the experience.

Training and Support for Research Personnel

The challenges research personnel face when gathering data, recruiting subjects, and conducting observational research in schools and youths' homes must be recognized. Research staff must be properly trained, supervised, and supported in their role of working with young people, who may be experiencing a range of socio-emotional and behavioural difficulties. The impact of interacting with high-risk youth must not be underestimated, especially because frontline research personnel often include students who are relatively inexperienced and who are involved in a formative learning process (Attkisson, Rosenblatt & Hoagwood, 1996). Components of our research protocol specifically addressed the needs of research personnel, including thorough debriefing, training, and procedures to ensure the staff's safety.

Working with high-risk youth facing sensitive issues can elicit an array of feelings and responses among the members of a research team. Data collection personnel who work directly with the participants require ongoing supervision and debriefing to improve their understanding of their role in the process, as well as to ensure the implementation of the research protocol and ethical procedures (ibid.). It is important for senior investigators to be cognizant of their ethical obligations to recognize the emotions that research staff may experience when observing or participating in challenging interactions with high-risk youth. Providing adequate training and resources, and facilitating open discussions between staff and investigators, provide an opportunity for research staff to gain support in working through their experiences.

The safety of the research personnel was also paramount in our research, especially when it came to observations of adolescents, which often involved entering unknown home environments in unfamiliar neighbourhoods to meet unknown individuals. To protect the well-being of the personnel, it was arranged for two individuals to attend each observation, and for them to carry a cell phone. Public emergency telephone numbers, as well as contact information for the research coordinator and investigators, was kept in a binder carried by the data collection personnel. Observation sessions were never scheduled to begin after seven p.m. so that personnel would not be required to travel to and from the location when it was late at night. This simple protocol was effective in ensuring the safety of the research team and promoting the confidence of staff who were entering situations where risk could be encountered.

Disseminating and Communicating the Research

It is understandable that violence among young people has captured the attention of schools, communities, governments, and the media. As researchers, we are committed to sharing our findings with the participants, the community, other researchers, concerned media, and government officials. Our paramount concerns are to preserve the confidentiality of the participants (particularly for observational data) and to ensure the integrity of the research on conflict. It is a challenge to balance these concerns with our desire to offer a revealing look into the social lives of children and youth to promote understanding and positive social actions and policies. During workshops with children, teachers, and parents, besides providing an educational service to participants and the larger society, we have gained new perspectives on what our data may portray. These new insights, in turn, inform the research process. Research on children's aggressive social interactions can elicit a range of emotional responses. We have found it essential to be aware of the potential responses of parents and teachers to data on levels and forms of aggressive behaviour. We are careful to discuss these problems in such a way as to promote healthy development as well as an understanding of the circumstances in children's lives that place them at risk.

The process of providing feedback to the students themselves has been both challenging and enlightening. The problems of bullying are complex; therefore, finding ways to communicate our results on this difficult social issue to large groups of young people in a meaningful and effective way provides a constant challenge to us. Opportunities for new insights arise when students reflect on our findings as they relate to their own experiences and understanding. Essential feedback loops are created when researchers and participants exchange knowledge, ideas, feelings, and experiences.

Bullying in schools has garnered a significant amount of attention over the past decade. As researchers in this area, we have been asked by a range of community groups and agencies to help them develop initiatives. When helping organizations address a complex problem such as bullying, the researcher assumes an ethical responsibility to ensure that the messages and strategies implemented are founded on solid empirical bases. For example, a number of groups have been interested in developing public service announcements for television that would provide a message to children about bullying. The developmental appropriateness of some of these messages and the potential inadvertent harmful consequences that may result from them are not always adequately assessed. Considering that these messages will reach hundreds of thousands of children, the stakes are high, and the role of researchers in this process is not always clear. Nevertheless, researchers can play an important role in knowledge transfer and translation; both processes are highly relevant for issues such as bullying, which can affect a significant number of children and families.

Summary

Principle-guided approaches to ethical decision-making, including the TCPS guidelines for Canadian research, provide a useful base for researchers as they prepare for and respond to ethical challenges. However, there is no static set of guidelines for conducting research with children and youth on sensitive social issues. Rather, ethical practice requires a dynamic understanding shaped by children, youth, families, and schools as well as by the research context in which the process takes place. The importance of developmental considerations in research ethics cannot be overlooked. Ethical practice may depend on ongoing dialogue among parties involved in the research. Working with young people has taught us that although we can anticipate and develop solutions to address many ethical issues, additional concerns emerge as the research unfolds. The concerns of children and youth are expressed in a variety of ways, both verbal and non-verbal. Our young participants ask us and challenge us, as researchers, to respond to and support them in respectful and meaningful ways. The responsibility of researchers is, ultimately, to pay attention to the subtle messages that youth communicate about what they need in order to feel comfortable in sharing intimate aspects of their lives with us. The view of research as a collaboration between parties will serve to promote understanding of adolescents' experiences.

NOTE

This research was supported in part by a doctoral fellowship from the Social Sciences and Humanities Research Council of Canada awarded to the first author. The investigators acknowledge the support from the Ontario Mental Health Foundation, the National Health Research and Development Program, the Social Sciences and Humanities Research Council of Canada, and the LaMarsh Centre for Research on Violence and Conflict Resolution. The authors extend their appreciation to the children, adolescents, schools, and parents who participated as well as to the graduate students and research assistants and the research coordinator, Arland O'Hara, for their contributions and dedication to the research program.

REFERENCES

Atlas, R.S., & Pepler, D.J. (1998). Observations of bullying in the classroom. *Journal of Educational Research, 92,* 86–99.

Attkisson, C.C., Rosenblatt, A., & Hoagwood, K. (1996). Research ethics and human subjects protection in child mental health services research and community studies. In Christakis, N.A. (1992). Ethics are local: Engaging cross-cultural variation in the ethics for clinical research. *Social Science Medicine, 35,* 1079–91.

Christakis, N.A. (1992). Ethics are local: Engaging cross-cultural variation in the ethics for clinical research. *Social Science Medicine, 35,* 1079–91.

Craig, W.M., & Pepler, D.J. (1999). Children who bully: Will they just grow out of it? *Orbit, 29,* 16–19.

Craig, W.M., Pepler, D., & Atlas, R. (2000). Observations of bullying in the playground and classroom. *School Psychology International, 21,* 22–36.

Craig, W.M., & Pepler, D.J. (1997). Observations of bullying and victimization in the school yard. *Canadian Journal of School Psychology, 2,* 41–60.

Hawkins, D.L., Pepler, D., & Craig, W. (2001). Peer interventions in playground bullying. *Social Development, 10,* 512–27.

Jensen, P.S., Hoagwood, K., & Fisher, C.B. (1996). Bridging scientific and ethical perspectives: Toward synthesis. In K. Hoagwood, P.S. Jensen & C.B. Fisher (Eds.), *Ethical issues in mental health research with children and adolescents* (pp. 287–98). Hillsdale, NJ: Lawrence Erlbaum Associates.

King, N.M.P., & Churchill, L.R. (2000). Ethical principles guiding research on child and adolescent subjects. *Journal of Interpersonal Violence, 15,* 710–21.

O'Connell, P., Pepler, D., & Craig, W. (1999). Peer involvement in bullying: Issues and challenges for intervention. *Journal of Adolescence, 22,* 437–52.

Pepler, D., & Craig, W. (1995). A peek behind the fence: Naturalistic observations of aggressive children with remote audiovisual recording. *Developmental Psychology, 31,* 548–53.

Pepler, D., Craig, W., O'Connell, P., Atlas, R., & Charach, A. (2005). Making a difference in bullying: Evaluation of a systemic school-based program in Canada. In P.K. Smith, D.J. Pepler, & K. Rigby (Eds.), *Bullying in schools: How successful can interventions be?* Cambridge: Cambridge University Press.

Pepler, D.J., Craig, W.M., & Roberts, W.R. (1995). Social skills training and aggression in the peer group. In J. McCord (Ed.), *Coercion and punishment in long-term perspectives* (pp. 213–28). New York: Cambridge University Press.

Pepler, D., Craig, W., Yuile, A., & Connolly, J. (2004). Girls who bully: A developmental and relational perspective. In M. Putallaz & J. Kupersmidt (eds.), *Aggression, antisocial behaviour, and violence among girls: A developmental perspective.* New York: Guilford Press.

Pepler, D., Yuile, A., Craig, W., Connolly, J., & McMaster, L. (2002). A developmental perspective on bullying and aggression. Paper presented at the Biennial Meeting of the Society for Research on Adolescence, New Orleans, April.

Putnam, F.W., Liss, M.B., & Landsverk, J. (1996). Ethical issues in maltreatment research with children and adolescents. In K. Hoagwood, P.S. Jensen, & C.B. Fisher (eds.), *Ethical issues in mental health research with children and adolescents* (pp. 113–34). Hillsdale, NJ: Lawrence Erlbaum Associates.

Sroufe, L.A. (1997). Psychopathology as an outcome of development. *Development and Psychopathology, 9,* 251–68.

Thompson, R.A. (1990). Vulnerability in research: A developmental perspective on research risk. *Child Development, 61,* 1–16.

Tri-council policy statement: Ethical conduct for research involving humans. (1998). Medical Research Council Canada, Natural Sciences and Engineering Research Council of Canada, and Social Sciences and Humanities Research Council of Canada.

Youniss, J. (1980). *Parents and peers in social development.* Chicago: University of Chicago Press.

PART THREE

Weighing Benefits and Preventing Harms

6 The Ecstasy and the Agony of Collecting Sociometric Data in Public School Classrooms: Challenges, Community Concerns, and Pragmatic Solutions

MARION K. UNDERWOOD, LARA MAYEUX, SCOTT RISSER,
AND BRIDGETTE HARPER

Most children care deeply about fitting into their peer group, getting along, and making friends. Many children want to have someone to sit with at lunch, play with at recess, hang around with after school, make sure they never are picked last for a team, and commiserate with when they are feeling left out and excluded. Researchers seeking to understand social development have been powerfully motivated to discover what enables children to initiate peer interactions and maintain friendships. This question is central to the subarea of developmental and child clinical psychology that focuses on children's peer relationships, which has burgeoned since the mid-1980s in both the United States and Canada (see Rubin, Bukowski & Parker, 1998, for a review).

For more than a decade our research group, located in one region of the southern United States, has been fascinated with how children manage strong emotions in their peer relationships – that is, with what they understand about display rules for anger (Underwood, Coie & Herbsman, 1992), how they cope with angry provocation (Underwood, Hurley, Johanson & Mosley, 1999), how they manage emotions in interactions with same- and other-gender peers (Underwood, Schockner & Hurley, 2001), and how girls (and likely boys, too) express anger and pursue their social goals through subtle hurtful behaviours that we call social aggression (Galen & Underwood, 1997; Paquette & Underwood, 1999; Underwood, 2003). With the help of extraordinarily talented students and research assistants and the patient cooperation of many families, we have used a variety of methods to address these questions. These have included sociometric testing in which peers nominate one another for specific descriptors, questionnaires asking children to respond to vignettes, semistructured interviews in which children describe their peer experiences, and a variety of observational tasks designed to induce mild degrees of negative affect in order to allow us to observe children's responses.

Almost any research method for studying children's negative emotions raises ethical challenges. The ecological validity of research on these issues depends on either inducing negative affect in children by exposing them to a mildly aversive experience or, at the very least, asking them to recall experiences of stress or victimization. Research on these issues requires investigators to think carefully about issues of parental consent, children's assent, deception, voluntary participation, withdrawing without penalty, and debriefing. To make matters even more complicated, if the goal is to understand how children's efforts to manage strong emotions relate to the quality of their peer relationships, it becomes important to use state-of-the-art methods to assess children's standing in the peer group. This has led us to use sociometric methods to get valid measures of children's peer relations at school.

In other forums we have described the challenges involved in experimental, observational studies of children's anger and aggression (Underwood, 2003) and their understanding of their research rights (Hurley & Underwood, 2002). In this chapter we will focus on the challenges involved in sociometric data collection, which involves going into public school classrooms and asking children to nominate peers whom they like, whom they dislike and who engage in a variety of positive and negative behaviours. We will review the small but growing body of research on the impact of sociometric testing on children who participate. The chapter will also offer solutions for pragmatic dilemmas, such as the need to protect and respect children while collecting these data and to respond sensitively to parents' and educators' concerns. The chapter will conclude with guidelines for conducting research on the impact of sociometric testing as perceived by children, parents, and teachers.

Sociometric Data Collection: Competing Goals

Researchers who seek to understand children's peer relationships have compelling scientific reasons to collect sociometric data in public school classrooms. Sociometric testing involves asking children to nominate peers as liked, as disliked, and as engaging in various positive and negative behaviours, or asking children to rate individual peers on similar types of items. Collecting these data in school classrooms is advantageous because school is a critically important context for children's social adjustment, and because studying children in public schools provides scientists with the most representative samples possible.

Sociometric data are valid measures of peer behaviours that can be difficult for adults to see. The subtle ways in which children harm one another by damaging the friendships or social status of others has left us convinced that peer nomination data are our best hope for measuring who engages in these behaviours and who does not. Researchers interested in predicting and preventing adolescent psychopathology have found that sociometric nominations for variables such as peer rejection and physical aggression are strong predictors of later negative outcomes (delinquency, substance abuse, and teen parenthood; for reviews see McDougall, Hymel, Vaillancourt & Mercer, 2001; Parker & Asher, 1987). Although a technical analysis of the validity and reliability of various sociometric methods will not be our focus here, the science of sociometry has flourished as investigators have devised more and more sophisticated methods of using peer ratings and nominations to obtain fine-grained information about children's social standing in the peer system (Bukowski & Cillessen, 1998; Cillessen & Bukowski, 2000).

Regardless of how sophisticated, such data require the cooperation of public school systems, whose administrators, teachers, and counsellors may have very different concerns from those of the researchers. Although public school educators share researchers' goals of reducing harmful peer behaviours and helping all children feel a sense of belonging and acceptance, it can be difficult for them to understand how the path to these goals requires asking aggressive children whom they like and whom they do not, who fights, and who spreads ugly rumours. Understandably, they are likely to view sociometric testing as contradicting everything they are trying to teach about building positive communities. They may also fear that the testing will hurt children's self-concepts and result in those with peer problems experiencing even higher levels of peer maltreatment. Finally, they worry about time away from instruction, and fear that extreme negative reactions from even a small number of parents could have serious consequences for their schools and for their teaching or administrative careers.

One Research Group's Nightmare

Recently our research group embarked on a large, longitudinal study of the developmental precursors and outcomes of social aggression – that is, behaviours that harm others by hurting their friendships and social status (see Underwood, 2003). The design of the study required that we collect detailed information about children's peer interactions from multiple sources: parents, teachers, the children themselves, and observations in the laboratory. Because we were particularly interested in getting accurate information about children's peer status and the extent to which individuals engaged in social aggression with peers, an important part of the project was yearly sociometric testing in school classrooms, beginning when the sample was in the third grade and continuing through to the eighth grade.

For the past five years our research group has been working cooperatively with a large public school district in our metropolitan area in the southern United States (whose policies require they go unnamed), inviting families to participate in laboratory-based, observational studies of social aggression. Our research group goes by the name 'The Friendship Project' in interactions with schools and families, and our group had successfully recruited more than four hundred families for previous studies, without a single complaint from children, parents, or school personnel. When it was time to begin the new longitudinal study, we approached this same district, carefully followed their review procedures, provided them with detailed information about all measures and procedures, and included a cover letter highlighting the sociometric component to make sure they understood what this would involve. The project was approved by the district-level research director. The principal investigator met with eleven different elementary school principals and presented them with sample sociometric materials (including rosters with false names), so that principals would understand all of the mechanics of what they were agreeing for us to do (ten of the eleven we contacted agreed).

Sociometric testing began in February and was conducted successfully with more than four hundred children until parent letters went home at a school in an affluent neighbourhood with a large contingent of parents who are heavily involved in school affairs. One mother became furious that the school and the district had approved of our doing sociometric testing. She met with the principal, expressed disappointment that the principal supported our project and its goals, and then urged several of her friends to join her in contacting an associate superintendent directly. These parents were terrified that sociometric testing could harm their individual children by making them feel socially rejected and by inciting peers to treat one another badly. They were also convinced that we were coercing families and teachers and even the district to participate by paying them large sums of money (in actual fact, compensation was modest and went only to participating families and teachers who completed our questionnaires). The associate superintendent was horrified that the sociometric testing had ever been approved, claiming that it violated district policies against releasing rosters and time away from instruction, and suspended the project entirely.

To this outstanding school district's credit, having determined that all aspects of our project had been conducted within their guidelines and that the vast majority of the community had responded positively, they have agreed that all components of the study should go forward, except for the sociometric testing. They have continued to cooperate extensively with us in recruiting participants for this large, federally funded project. We believe this was possible for several reasons: we had a long relationship with them and a track record of being sensitive to their needs and concerns, we were up front from the beginning about our plans, and they shared our goal of understanding why some children are mean in various ways. Most importantly, this project is continuing because we showed sensitivity to the ethical issues involved in sociometric testing from the beginning. We explained consistently how we planned to collect these data within our ethical responsibilities, and we immediately proposed a follow-up study to assess the impact of the sociometric data collection already completed when that component of the project was halted.

An Ethical Analysis of Sociometric Testing

What exactly are our ethical responsibilities as investigators who seek to use sociometric methods to understand children's status in their peer groups? This analysis will focus first on the new ethical guidelines for psychologists formulated by the American Psychological Association (APA, 2002) and second on the available empirical evidence for the effects of sociometric testing on child participants.

Application of the Ethical Principles of Psychologists and
Code of Conduct to Sociometric Testing

The APA's ethics code (2002) contains both general standards ('aspirational goals to guide psychologists toward the highest ideals,'

p. 2) and ethical standards ('enforceable rules for conduct as psychologists,' p. 2). Contrary to the strong contentions of some parents and educators, ethical principals for psychologists contain no strict prohibitions against sociometric testing. However, as pointed out by Bell-Dolan and Wessler (1994) with reference to the older version of the ethics code, both the principals and the standards provide helpful guidance with direct relevance for sociometric data collection. The aspirational principles provide the highest standards to which sociometric or any data collection procedures should be held, and applying them leads to specific methodological choices.

Principle A, *beneficence and non-maleficence*, reminds us that we should collect sociometric data only when this method is necessary for research that has the ultimate goal of helping children and that we should use every available strategy to protect children from possible harm. The empirical evidence for the effectiveness of these strategies will be discussed later, but briefly, these include practical efforts such as the following: explaining to children what confidentiality means and persuading them to refrain from discussing their responses to sociometric measures; providing manila folders so that children can shield their responses from peers; and scheduling testing before a structured activity so that children will have fewer opportunities to discuss their nominations or ratings.

Principle B, *fidelity and responsibility*, urges us to establish cooperative, trusting relationships with those with whom we work, by holding ourselves to the highest professional standards, by respectfully resolving conflicts when they arise, and by donating a proportion of our professional time. When collecting sociometric data, this principle reminds us to be honest in explaining what we want to do and why, to respect schools' and parents' concerns, and to do what we can in return. For example, we can offer to give community presentations at the school or to lead faculty in-service sessions for no fee.

Principle C, *integrity*, cautions us to follow through with our commitments and to correct any misunderstandings or perceived harm that results from our work. In practical terms for our research group, it was this principle that motivated the principal investigator to respond immediately to the associate superintendent's request to write a letter to all parents at the large elementary school where a few were outraged, to withdraw the study from that school, to apologize for any distress, to thank them for their feedback on our project, and to express our willingness to listen to more of their concerns.

Principle D, *justice*, urges psychologists to be fair and equitable in ensuring that everyone has the opportunity to benefit from work done by psychologists. For our research group, this principle is applied when we invite all children in the grade level to participate, when we make an effort to send parents letters in their native language, when we offer children incentives for returning our letter whether or not the parent provides consent, and when we provide packets of fun activities for children whose parents do not give consent so that they can be happily occupied while we are doing the testing and are not stigmatized for non-participation.

Principle E, *respect for people's rights and dignity*, urges psychologists to 'respect the dignity and worth of all people' (APA, 2002, p. 4) and to remember that special safeguards are needed for vulnerable populations, including but not limited to children. This principle inspires sociometric researchers to seek children's assent even after obtaining parents' permission, to be sensitive to the fact that children do not always feel empowered to decline, to try to assure children that their participation is indeed voluntary, to communicate children's research rights to them in understandable terms, and to remember that sociometric testing might be more upsetting for children who are lonely or who experience rejection on a daily basis.

The more specific ethical standards also contain important guidance for researchers collecting sociometric data. This discussion will highlight only those standards that are most directly relevant.

Standard 2, *competence*, requires that investigators who oversee sociometric data collection be properly trained (2.01) and that collecting sociometric data be delegated only to those who have received sufficient training and are adequately supervised (2.05). This standard also requires that sociometric researchers use only methods that have been developed on the basis of scientific knowledge in the discipline of psychology (2.04).

Standard 4, *privacy and confidentiality*, requires that we explain to parents and to children in understandable terms that confidentiality will be maintained and that we need their help in keeping responses private – this is why we ask them not to discuss their nominations. Given that the content of sociometric items focuses on peer interactions, the measures typically do not require researchers to explain the limits of confidentiality (2.02) as they relate to our responsibility to report child abuse or neglect or suicidality. However, researchers who administer other questionnaires in classrooms along with sociometric measures may need to explain these limits if the other measures assess psychological adjustment or parent–child relationships.

Standard 8, *informed consent*, requires sociometric researchers to explain clearly to parents and children the purpose of the study, their right to decline or withdraw, what will happen if they decline or withdraw, the benefits of the research for the participants themselves or for others, and the limits of confidentiality (8.02). Parents must be informed about whom to call with questions about the research and their rights as participants. Although Standard 8 permits dispensing with informed consent 'where research would not reasonably be assumed to create distress or harm ... or where otherwise permitted by law or federal or institutional regulations' (APA, 2002, 11), we believe that sociometric researchers would be extremely unwise not to obtain informed consent from both parents and children. Given that most of us ask children to nominate one another for negative items, we must acknowledge that there is at least some likelihood of this procedure causing distress and harm. In the current conservative climate in many regions of North America (including our research site), we urge sociometric researchers to obtain active rather than passive consent, for the long-term health of their collaborative relationships with school districts and families.

Standard 8 also requires debriefing (8.08). For sociometric researchers, this means explaining again briefly the purpose of the study, reminding children that we keep responses confidential, reminding them not to share responses with others, giving them an opportunity to ask questions, and correcting any misconceptions that become apparent. This standard also requires sociometric researchers to take reasonable steps to minimize harm that may have occurred as a result of the classroom testing. Although it happens rarely, when our research group administered sociometric testing last spring with grade three students, one girl left a testing session in tears. A friendly volunteer with whom we had a relationship helped her teacher comfort her immediately. The principal investigator on the project was promptly informed and sent e-mails to the volunteer, the teacher, and the school counsellor, saying that we were sorry that a child had become upset during our testing and asking if there was anything we could do to help. All three adults involved responded immediately, stating that this girl's difficulties were ongoing and likely related to our testing only indirectly, and making it clear that they sincerely appreciated our noticing her distress and offering to help. Although we would never wish to upset a child with our testing procedures, this sequence of events did serve to demonstrate to this school that we are concerned about children's welfare.

Empirical Research on the Impact of Sociometric Testing on Children

The ethical principles outlined above provide much helpful direction for sociometric researchers. However, our community partners and parents may care very little about these ethical ideals and standards and our strategies for meeting them. Some educators and parents oppose sociometric testing because they believe it hurts individual children and could change the overall tenor of the peer environment in the following ways: (Bell-Dolan & Wessler, 1994) by adults sanctioning children maligning one another (Asher & Hymel, 1981), by causing children to perceive and interact with rejected peers even more harshly (Foster & Ritchey, 1979), and by making social rejection even more salient and hurtful for children (Bell-Dolan, Foster & Sikora, 1989). Are these fears well founded? What does empirical research suggest about the impact of sociometric testing on the children who participate?

Compared to the large numbers of studies in which sociometric methods have been used, the number of investigations of the impact of sociometric testing on children has been small, with very few studies published recently (the most recent in 1996). This discussion will highlight the empirical investigations that speak most precisely to fears about sociometrics and present the highest-quality evidence; more exhaustive reviews of this literature and the issues involved appear elsewhere (Bell-Dolan & Wessler, 1994; Iverson & Iverson, 1996; Merrell, 1999; McConnell & Odom, 1986).

Overall, the results of several studies using a variety of methods suggest that children do not experience ill effects as a result of sociometric testing. In one study with preschoolers, researchers conducted behavioural observations five weeks before, ten minutes after, and five weeks after classroom sociometric testing to assess both short-term and long-term effects of sociometric testing on participants (Hayvren & Hymel, 1984). Although participating children did act more positively to well-liked peers than to disliked peers following testing, there were no differences in negative behaviours: children did not behave more negatively to disliked peers following the testing. Furthermore, although the children were overheard talking about positive nominations they had made (for example, saying things such as 'I put you down for "liking a lot" because you're my friend'), they were not overheard discussing negative nominations. The authors concluded that sociometric data collection seemed not to influence children's observed peer interactions.

In a similar study with Grade 5 students, researchers observed children's social interactions with preferred and non-preferred playmates before and after sociometric testing, and children also completed measures of mood and loneliness before and after providing positive and negative peer nominations (Bell-Dolan, Foster & Sikora, 1989). This study included a control condition, in which some children completed these same measures before and after nominating 'liked most' and 'liked least' academic subjects in school. The results showed no differences in children's responses to the sociometric and control tasks, and no pre- or post-test differences in children's peer interactions, moods, or self-reported loneliness. In another study, to assess the longer-term impact of responding to sociometric questions from the children's perspective, students completed sociometric testing at the end of their Grade 5 year, and then were interviewed at the beginning of Grade 6 (Iverson & Iverson, 1996). Children answered questions about whether they remembered the testing, how well they liked it, what they disliked about positive and negative nominations, and whether they discussed their nominations with peers. Almost all children remembered completing the sociometric measures. Most children said they liked the peer nomination procedures, but when asked to rate how much they liked positive and negative nominations, they reported liking negative nominations less. When asked why they disliked the sociometric techniques, the most common answer was difficulty choosing among liked and disliked peers (in this study, students were limited to three nominations for each item). Interestingly, one-third of the participants reported that they had talked with peers about their nominations. The children's responses showed no indications that they had been harmed by the procedures or by the ensuing conversations, and no differences in how children in different peer status groups viewed the impact of the testing.

When concluding that sociometric testing seems not to harm children, all of these investigators are careful to point out that these procedures seem not to hurt children when they are properly administered and when safeguards are in place. To gather information about the particular strategies investigators use to protect children when conducting sociometric testing, Bell-Dolan & Wessler (1994) surveyed 145 scientists who use sociometric methods, asking them to report in detail on the methods they use for testing. Seventy-five per cent of the researchers surveyed reported that they used both positive and negative behavioural nominations in their research, yet only 4.8 per cent of all researchers reported any kind of negative impact on their participants. Safeguards used to protect children and to respect parents' concerns included active parental consent, obtaining children's assent, individual administration, explicit instructions to children to keep responses confidential, scheduling sociometric testing prior to structured activities so that children would have fewer opportunities to discuss nominations, embedding sociometric questionnaires in large test batteries or using distracter tasks immediately following them, and allowing unlimited nominations for positive items. On the basis of the survey, Bell-Dolan and Wessler concluded that sociometric methods are in line with professional ethical standards of conduct and that 'the benefits of sociometric research clearly seem to outweigh the risks' (1994, 28). Although it is positive that sociometric researchers strive to meet ethical ideals and have sought to examine the impact of these procedures on children, it is unclear whether the concerns of troubled educators and parents will be assuaged by any of this evidence. For psychologists to argue that they have demonstrated that their procedures are not harmful would seem to outsiders to be a bit like foxes appointing themselves in charge of the henhouse (Hurley & Underwood, 2002); naturally they have an investment in showing that their procedures are ethical.

Experts in this field have found that this research evidence about the lack of harm from sociometrics persuades educators and parents to different degrees. One senior colleague described winning over a superintendent who was about to cancel a large longitudinal study that relied on sociometrics by showing him the articles described above and carefully explaining how sociometric testing seems not to hurt children according to this evidence (Coie, personal communication). In our large, metropolitan school district run by highly educated, research-oriented administrators, these findings were mostly unpersuasive, because they were deemed unlikely to convince outraged parents. As scientists, we care deeply about obtaining the highest-quality and most valid data on children's social adjustment, and we are reassured by the evidence described above, which suggests that sociometrics are not harmful. Parents are concerned that one single child might be hurt (usually their son or daughter), and school administrators fear having to defend procedures that seem on the face of things to be unkind.

Solutions for Balancing Researchers', Educators', and Parents' Concerns

Although these very different concerns of researchers, educators, and parents present serious obstacles to sociometric data collection, it is possible for researchers to work collaboratively with public school systems to study children's peer relations. Researchers and public school educators share concern about the ethics of collecting data from children – about issues such as parents' right to consent or not, children's voluntary participation, responses remaining confidential, children being treated respectfully at every step of the data collection procedure, and most importantly, conducting the research so that children are not harmed by participating. One important way that researchers can build collaborative relationships is by discussing ethical concerns explicitly when submitting proposals, when seeking principals' approval, when meeting with teachers to schedule the data collection, and when parents call to express their concerns. We would all be wise to consider the 'ecology of informed consent' (Leadbeater, in this volume) and 'process consent' (Marshall and Shepard, in this volume) and to remember that schools and parents are also stakeholders in our projects.

Although we all know that in order to do sociometric testing we must have the consent of the district and parents, as well as the children's assent, we might do well to consider even more levels of approval. For example, although principals typically give consent for sociometric testing in their schools without consulting teachers, many of us have learned the hard way that testing is successful only when classroom teachers are supportive of the process, or at least when they have had the opportunity to voice their concerns. Similarly, angry parents often report feeling shocked when they receive a parent consent letter for sociometric testing. Researchers may do well to place advance notices in newsletters, or to make a brief appearance in front of the parent–teacher organization to introduce themselves and the project and give parents a chance to ask questions in person. With all of these groups, it is important to explain why we do sociometric testing and what we hope to achieve, and to describe how children are protected in our research procedures. Last but not least, when concerns are raised about sociometric procedures that are underway, it can be very helpful to respond with a plan to immediately conduct a follow-up study to assess the impact of the sociometric testing that has already been completed.

A Research Agenda for the Ethics of Sociometric Data Collection

As researchers, when we conduct empirical research to understand the impact of sociometric testing in our local communities, we are demonstrating that we are willing to spend our time and money to address the concerns of our community partners, and we are also gathering evidence that might be persuasive with these same community collaborators in the future. As scientists, we thereby build a much stronger evidence base that ethical administration of sociometric measures is possible.

In studying the ethics of sociometric data collection, we could profitably be guided by several principles. First, it is important to continue using multiple measures. The pioneering studies in this field used behavioural observation before and after testing to assess whether participating in sociometric testing affected children's social behaviours, and it would be wonderful to see similar studies with larger samples and children of different age groups. However, because not all negative effects of sociometrics can be directly observed, it is important to augment observational methods with carefully designed questionnaires from the perspectives of children, classroom teachers, and parents. In the appendices we provide the questions we are using to assess children's and teachers' perceptions of the impact of sociometric testing; we present these as starting points for other investigators. It would be helpful to know more about both the short-term impact of sociometric testing and children's perceptions after longer periods of time.

Second, it is important to remember that the impact of sociometric testing may well depend on the developmental stage of the children (see Thompson, 1990, for a thoughtful discussion of the changing developmental calculus of the ethics of particular research procedures). Sociometric testing may be less hurtful for younger children, who have fewer concerns about peer status and who are less vulnerable to social comparison; and more harmful for children in middle childhood and early adolescence, who care desperately about fitting in and belonging to a group (Gottman & Mettetal, 1986).

Third, we might want to avoid arguing that sociometric testing is acceptable because it does not pose much greater risk than children's everyday peer interactions pose, because children often talk among themselves about whom they like and whom they do not. Such a position is questionable on ethical grounds: just because peers mistreat or judge one another does not make it ethical for scientists to do something that might lead to maltreatment (Thompson, 1990). Instead, we should ask ourselves whether particular sociometric procedures constitute decent treatment of children, the standards for which – again – could well depend on the children's developmental stage (ibid.).

Fourth, it seems critically important for us to examine the impact of sociometric testing on those who might be most vulnerable to its negative effects – that is, on children who are actively disliked. If many sociometric researchers begin to augment their studies with measures of the impact of testing on children, we will be in a perfect position to determine whether rejected children are more hurt by these techniques. We should also examine the impact of sociometric testing on other vulnerable groups: children who are members of ethnic minority groups, children with developmental disabilities, children who are socially anxious, and children with serious behavioural and emotional problems.

Publicly expressing our concern for the most vulnerable children and taking great care to study the impact of sociometric testing on these particular groups might be the ultimate way to join with those parents and educators who oppose peer nomination or rating procedures. Many of us choose professions serving children because we want to help those who feel excluded, who lag behind, or who are disadvantaged in some way. In an eloquent address to the American Psychological Association, the Reverend Jesse Jackson (2000) spoke to the question 'What Ought Psychology to Do?' He ended his talk with the parable of the lost sheep. In this parable, a shepherd calls for his flock of one hundred sheep at the end of the day, and ninety-nine come quickly when called. The shepherd starts looking for his lost sheep, and is chastised by his fellow shepherds for taking so much time for one sheep when all of the others came, and while they are arguing the sun goes down. Jackson pointed out that perhaps the lost sheep did not come when called because it was disabled, or had a hearing problem, or had been picked on, beaten up, or abused. He challenged: 'You, as good psychologists, as teachers, bring your light into dark places. Help us find all the lost sheep, and leave no one behind' (2000, p. 330). To understand the dark place that is social rejection in childhood, we will likely need to collect sociometric data, including negative nominations. To continue to be able to use these techniques, we will need to use a variety of methods to explain our motives and our methods to our community collaborators, and invest our time and energy in collecting the kind of data that will convince experts and lay people alike that we can conduct our research while protecting and respecting children.

Appendix A: Questionnaire to Assess Children's Perceptions of Sociometric Testing

We would like to know how you feel about the questions you answered for the Friendship Project when we visited your 3rd grade classroom back in the spring. Please think about the following questions and circle or write in your answers.

1) What did The Friendship Project team ask you to do when they visited your classroom?
2) What was the purpose of their questions?
3) How did you feel about answering The Friendship Project's questions?
   a. How much did you feel happy? (1 = not at all, 5 = a lot)
   b. How much did you feel sad?
   c. How much did you feel surprised?
   d. How much did it hurt your feelings?
   e. How much did you feel bored?
4) Did it bother you to vote for your classmates for different statements?
5) Did it bother you to answer questions about how others kids are nice and mean to you?
6) Did other kids act different toward you after The Friendship Project team left your classroom?
7) Did other kids act nicer to you after the Friendship Project team left your classroom?
8) Did other kids act meaner to you after the Friendship Project team left your classroom?
9) If you had wanted not to be in the Friendship Project, could you have said no even if your parents said yes?
10) If you had wanted to stop answering the questions, could you have stopped? How?
11) Who was going to find out the answers you gave during the classroom testing?
12) What was your favorite part of being in The Friendship Project?

13) What was your least favorite part of being in The Friendship Project?
14) Would you like to answer questions for The Friendship Project again if you had permission?
15) Would you recommend the Friendship Project classroom testing to a good friend?
16) Did answering the questions for the Friendship Project change the way you think about yourself? How?
17) Is there anything the adults working on the Friendship Project could do to make the classroom testing easier for the kids?

Appendix B: Questionnaire to Assess Teacher's Perceptions of Sociometric Testing

We would like to know how this child reacted to school visit we made earlier in the year. Please think carefully about the following question and circle or write in your answers. If any questions are not applicable to this particular student, please leave the rating blank.

1. Did this child appear upset about voting for their classmates for different items?
2. Did he/she appear upset after answering questions about their classmates being nice or mean to her/him?
3. Did other kids act different towards the child after the session ended or the Friendship Project team left the classroom?
4. Did other kids act nicer to her/him after the session ended?
5. Did other kids act meaner to her/him after the session ended?
6. Did he/she seem to understand he/she had the option of not participating, even when her/his parents said it was okay?
7. Did he/she seem to understand they could have stopped the session at any time?
8. Did he/she seem to understand her/his answers were confidential?
9. Did he/she appear to be open to more research participation?
10. Did he/she speak positively about the session or the Friendship Project team?
11. Did he/she speak negatively about the session or the Friendship Project team?
12. Did any children in this child's class speak about their responses to other students?
13. Is there anything else you would like to tell us about how this child responded to the classroom testing?

NOTE

This research described here was supported by NIH grants MH52110, MH55992, and MH63076. Please direct correspondence to Dr Marion Underwood, School of Behavioural and Brain Sciences, University of Texas at Dallas, PO Box 830688, GR 41, Richardson, TX, 75083. Dr Underwood may also be contacted by phone (972-883-2470), FAX (972-883-2491), or electronic mail (undrwd@utdallas.edu).

REFERENCES

American Psychological Association. (2002). Ethical principles of psychologists and code of conduct. *American Psychologist*, 57, 1060–73.
Asher, S.R., & Hymel, S. (1981). Children's social competence in peer relations: Sociometric and behavioural assessment. In J.D. Wine & M.D. Since (eds.), *Social Competence* (pp. 52–77). New York: Guilford.
Bell-Dolan, D.J., Foster, S.L., & Sikora, D.M. (1989). Effects of sociometric testing on children's behavior and loneliness at school. *Developmental Psychology*, 25, 306–11.
Bell-Dolan, D., & Wessler, A.E. (1994). Ethical administration of sociometric measures: Procedures to use and suggestions for improvement. *Professional Psychology: Research and Practice*, 25, 23–32.
Bukowski, W.M., & Cillessen, A.H. (1998). Sociometry then and now: Building on six decades of measuring children's experiences with the peer group. *New Directions in Child Development*, 80, 1–4.
Cillessen, A.H.N., & Bukowski, W.M. (2000). Recent advances in the measurement of acceptance and rejection in the peer system. *New Directions in Child Development*, 88, 1–10.
Foster, S.L., & Ritchey, W. (1979). Issues in the assessment of social competence in children. *Journal of Applied Behavior Analysis*, 12, 625–38.
Galen, B.R., & Underwood, M.K. (1997). A developmental investigation of social aggression among children. *Developmental Psychology*, 33(4), 589–600.
Gottman, J., & Mettetal, G. (1986). Speculations about social and affective development: Friendship and acquaintanceship through adolescence. In J.M. Gottman & J.G. Parker (Eds.), *Conversations with friends: Speculations on affective development* (pp. 192–237). New York: Cambridge University Press.
Hayvren, M., & Hymel, S. (1984). Ethical issues in sociometric testing: The impact of sociometric measures on interaction behavior. *Developmental Psychology*, 20, 844–9.

Hurley, J.C., & Underwood, M.K. (2002). Children's understanding of their research rights: Informed assent, confidentiality, and stopping participation. *Child Development*, 73, 132–43.

Iverson, A.M., & Iverson, G.I. (1996). Children's long-term reactions to participating in sociometric assessment. *Psychology in the Schools*, 33, 103–12.

Jackson, J. (2000). What ought psychology to do? *American Psychologist*, 55, 328–30.

McConnell, S.R., & Odom, S.L. (1986). Sociometrics: Peer referenced measures and the assessment of social competence. In P.S. Strain, M.J. Guralnick, & H.M. Walker (Eds.), *Children's social behavior: Development, assessment, and modification* (pp. 215–83). New York: Academic Press.

McDougall, P., Hymel, S., Vaillancourt, T., & Mercer, L. (2001). The consequences of peer rejection. In M.R. Leary (ed.), *Interpersonal rejection* (pp. 213–47). New York: Oxford University Press.

Merrell, K.W. (1999). *Behavioural, Social, and Emotional Assessment of Children and Adolescents*. Mahwah, NJ: Lawrence Erlbaum Associates.

Paquette, J.A., & Underwood, M.K. (1999). Young adolescents' experiences of peer victimization: Gender differences in accounts of social and physical aggression. *Merrill-Palmer Quarterly*, 45(2), 233–58.

Parker, J., & Asher, S.R. (1987). Peer acceptance and later personal adjustment: Are low-accepted children at risk? *Psychological Bulletin*, 102, 357–89.

Rubin, K.H., Bukowski, W., & Parker, J.G. (1998). Peer interactions, relationships, and groups. In N. Eisenberg (Ed.), *Handbook of child psychology* (pp. 619–700). New York: Wiley.

Thompson, R.A. (1990). Vulnerability in research: A developmental perspective on research risk. *Child Development*, 61, 1–16.

Underwood, M.K. (2003). *Social aggression among girls*. New York: Guilford Press.

Underwood, M.K., Coie, J.D., & Herbsman, C.R. (1992). Display rules for anger and aggression in school-aged children. *Child Development*, 63, 366–80.

Underwood, M.K., Hurley, J.C., Johansson, C.A., & Mosley, J.E. (1999). A experimental, observational investigation of children's responses to peer provocation: Developmental and gender differences in middle childhood. *Child Development*, 70, 1428–46.

Underwood, M.K., Schockner, A.S., & Hurley, J.C. (2001). Children's responses to provocation by same- and opposite-gender peers: An experimental, observational study with 8-, 10-, and 12-year-olds. *Developmental Psychology*, 37, 362–72.

7 Ivory Tower Ethics: Potential Conflict between Community Organizations and Agents of the Tri-council

LORRIE SIPPOLA

Recently, extreme negative outcomes of school-based peer victimization among adolescents have attracted substantial media attention in Canada. In British Columbia, the suicides of two adolescents, one girl and one boy, have been attributed to intense emotional and frequent physical abuse from their peers at school (Jiwa, 2000; McMartin, Fong & Skelton, 2000; Munro, 2000; Owens, 2000). In Alberta an adolescent boy, reported to be alienated and rejected by his peers, shot and killed a popular boy in his high school (Dimmock, 1999; Nagy, Stewart & Dudley, 1999). More recently, lawsuits have been brought against school administrators and teachers by individuals who claim that nothing was done to prevent the victimization they experienced from their peers during school hours on school property (Culbert & Steffenhagen, 2000; Tibbetts, 2002). In addition to all this, teenagers aggressing against other teenagers is a ubiquitous theme of popular television dramas and talk shows such as *Third Watch*, *Law and Order*, and *Oprah*.

Reports of these types of incidents, occurring among seemingly average adolescents, have caused students, parents, and teachers great concern. These reports have also contributed to demands for high school personnel to involve themselves more heavily in the social development of their students – specifically in terms of designing, implementing, and evaluating intervention and prevention programs for both offenders and victims. However, the efforts of frontline personnel are hampered by the lack of theoretically derived empirical research on victimization in adolescence. Effective programs must be developed from a solid foundation of trustworthy information and not from media representations of a problem.

In reviewing the published literature on the topics of bullying and peer victimization, it appears that researchers have focused primarily on the elementary school years (e.g., Camodeca, Goossens, Meerum-Terwogt & Schuengel, 2002; Coleman & Byrd, 2003; Stockdale, Hangaduambo, Duys, Larson & Sarvela, 2002). Much less empirical work has examined peer-based victimization in high school settings (see Rigby, Cox & Black 1997, Rigby, 1998, and Rigby, 1999, for exceptions). One possible explanation for this gap may be related to the unique ethical challenges associated with conducting community-based research on peer victimization in adolescence.

In this chapter I will examine three ethical issues I have encountered while conducting research in high schools. Although these ethical issues have emerged specifically in the context of peer victimization research, they are relevant to researchers who are generally interested in studying socially sensitive issues related to adolescent development. In Canada, developmental research is guided by the current standards outlined by the *Tri-council Policy Statement for Ethical Conduct in Research Involving Humans* (1998). Consequently, these issues will be examined from this particular perspective.

The first issue to be examined is the definition of competence and the tension created for researchers by the lack of clarity in determining the age at which individuals are considered competent to provide informed consent for participation in social science research. The current guidelines do not differentiate children from adolescents in the definition of vulnerable populations. Thus, variability exists across Canada in the ethical standards applied by various university research ethics boards (REBs). I will explore the implications of this variability for understanding socially sensitive issues relevant to normative adolescent development.

Related to this first issue, institutional REBs may rely too heavily on legalistic interpretations of ethical issues when making decisions regarding 'risk.' As noted by Lépine and Smolla (2000), seeking solutions to ethical issues through a single philosophical perspective, such as a legalistic lens, is dangerous. The law provides a basic framework for the protection of the institution, the researcher, and the participants. However, ethical problems are often more complex than the law allows. For the purposes of this chapter I will examine the issue of risk in peer victimization research from the justice and care perspectives.

The final issue I explore in this chapter concerns the limits of ethical liability of researchers. In view of the increasingly sensational media representations of school-based violence among adolescents, I will argue that researchers have a moral and ethical responsibility for how media and community organizations interpret and make use of research results.

My thoughts about these issues stem primarily from my experiences of negotiating the tension between the needs of the community and the demands of the university REB. So, before exploring the issues, I will describe a specific experience that contributed to the writing of this chapter.

Ethics in Community-Based Research: Conflicting Community Needs and REB Demands

In the spring of 2001 I was approached by a local school division to conduct a study on the prevalence of peer victimization in its schools. School personnel were facing a noticeable increase in pressure from parents to develop and implement programs to deal with a perceived problem of bullying in the schools. Administrators and school personnel believed that an accurate picture of the prevalence of the problem in their school system was needed before they could implement expensive programs. So they were eager to implement a program of research on this topic.

After consultation with the professionals from the schools and with division administrators, a research protocol was developed. We decided that the best strategy for determining the prevalence and nature of peer victimization was through the use of both self and peer reports. A passive consent procedure was proposed. This procedure would have involved informing parents of the goals and procedures of the study through a letter. Parents would then be asked to return the consent form only if they did *not* consent to their child's participation. Our decision to use this procedure was based on (a) the large number of parents who needed to be contacted (N > 1500) and (b) the difficulties previously experienced by school personnel in obtaining written consent from parents for other school activities. A research ethics application was submitted that included a letter from the Director of the School Division indicating his understanding of the procedures to be used and his support for the project. However, the REB refused to approve the protocol with the proposed passive consent procedure and expressed additional concerns regarding the methods to be used. The individuals in the community who had collaborated on the development of the protocol with me were upset by the REB's decision and suggested that they would conduct the study using their own resources (that is, without the author's involvement), and thereby circumvent the need for the REB's approval. A mutually agreeable solution was arrived at after lengthy negotiations between the REB and my community partners. I agreed to use an active consent procedure, but I would also be allowed to telephone parents subsequent to mailing out consent forms and to obtain consent verbally. Because the study is longitudinal, the REB has agreed to the use of passive consent procedures for subsequent follow-up data collection. Each year, I am required to mail out new consent forms to parents for their child's continued participation in the study. If they no longer consent to that participation, they are asked to contact the school or my research lab to withdraw their consent. Concerns about the methods proposed were addressed in numerous written responses to the REB to clarify and justify the methods selected. Some of these concerns are described in subsequent sections of this chapter.

Section I. Consent

The most contentious issue that emerged from the above example centred on the proposed consent procedures. A review of the literature on consent in research suggests that at least three important and connected concerns involving consent must be considered when conducting research on peer victimization among adolescents. The first of these is directly related to the fundamental question of who has the authority (that is, 'competence') to provide consent for participation in this type of research. The second and third concerns relate to the procedures for involving parents and school authorities in decisions about adolescents' participation in school-based research.

RESPECT FOR AUTONOMY: DETERMINING COMPETENCE TO
PROVIDE CONSENT IN RESEARCH WITH ADOLESCENTS
It is a generally agreed-upon principle that informed consent to participate in research can only be obtained from individuals who are autonomous and legally competent (King & Churchill, 2000). However, the Tri-council guidelines are notably vague regarding the age at which individuals are deemed 'autonomous and legally competent.' In preparation for this chapter, I conducted a Web search of the ethics protocols at ten universities across Canada.[1] Several observations about the guidelines provided to researchers by REBs regarding the age of consent can be made based on this search. First, many university REBs simply refer to the Tri-council guidelines for information regarding 'informed con-

sent.' This issue is addressed under Section 2E, 'Competence,' in the *Tri-council Policy Statement*. This statement recognizes that competence is a complex construct and that an individual's competence may vary across different tasks. Furthermore, the policy recognizes that the law on competence varies among jurisdictions. It is important to note that the guidelines do not distinguish between children and adolescents in identifying 'vulnerable' populations. That is, I could not find a clear definition of the age at which children were no longer considered 'vulnerable' or 'incompetent.' Four of the universities surveyed for this chapter have, however, made specific recommendations regarding age of consent (University of Waterloo, University of Toronto, University of Victoria, and, more recently, University of Saskatchewan).

University REBs often use a legal definition of competence that appears to be based on a statutory age of consent at which children have the right to consent to or refuse medical treatment. However, this statutory age varies considerably from province to province. For example, Saskatchewan sets the age of consent at eighteen.[2] In British Columbia and New Brunswick the age of consent is sixteen, while in Quebec it is fourteen (Hesson, Bakal & Dobson, 1993). (See the introduction to this book for a more thorough discussion of this topic.) Thus, most REBs depend on chronological age and not on cognitive capacity for decision-making in determining when parent consent is required for the participation of children and adolescents in research.

In practice, and in the absence of data, the default perspective of REBs appears to be that adolescents are not competent to provide informed consent. However, they are viewed as capable of providing informed *assent* or of dissenting to the project (Baylis, Downie & Kenny, 1999). Thus, while children and adolescents are included in the decision-making process in that informed assent must be obtained from them, parents appear to have the right of first refusal to their child's participation in research. This is particularly the case when schools and REBs require that information about the study be provided first to parents, and only then, after consent is obtained, to the adolescent. However, there are few guidelines (excepting the University of Toronto guidelines) relating to situations where, for whatever reason, parents refuse consent but adolescents assent. Thus, under current guidelines, adolescents' *dissent* is given the same moral authority as parents' *consent*, but the reverse is not true.

The irony of this situation is not lost on adolescents, particularly in cases where the age of consent considered by REBs is inconsistent with the statutory age of consent for medical treatment. For example, the

University of Waterloo's policy states that parent consent is required for anyone under eighteen, while the province of Ontario, under the Public Hospitals Act, has established the age of consent for medical treatment at sixteen. The reactions of adolescents to this disparity are illustrated by the response a sixteen-year-old made to my request for her parents' written consent to participate in the research I was conducting at her school. She approached me after my initial presentation to her class and said: 'I don't get it. I'm old enough to get an abortion without my mom's permission, but you want me to get her permission to participate in your study? That is *too* lame.'

Reliance on chronological age to determine competence may violate one of the fundamental principles of ethical research: respect for people's autonomy (King & Churchill, 2000; Kotch, 2000). This violation may be reflected in the response of adolescents to the consent procedures used in developmental research. Based on my own observations and on informal discussions with colleagues, students, and parents about these issues, many adolescents resent being told that their parents' permission is a necessary condition for their participation in social developmental research. This resentment may manifest itself as a lack of cooperation in the recruitment process. When letters are sent home to parents with adolescents, they may 'forget' either to deliver the forms home or to return them to the school. Or, as some authors have observed, older adolescents may forge their parents' signatures in order to participate in a study (Yuile, Pepler, Craig & Connelly, in this volume). Alternatively, when letters are mailed directly home, parents often tell me that they have consulted with their adolescent who, insulted by the researcher's apparent lack of respect for his/her autonomy, says that he/she is not interested in the project. Thus, parents' negative responses may not simply be due to a concern about the research protocol, but also the result of the adolescent's negative attitude towards the consent process.[3]

Although further research is required on the consent process (Runyan, 2000), several authors have argued that adolescents are capable of making informed decisions about their participation in research (Abramovitch, Freedman, Henry & Van Brunschot, 1995; Dorn, Susman & Fletcher, 1995; Scott, Reppucci & Woolard, 1995). Indeed, research suggests that adolescents and even younger children are capable of providing consent even in highly invasive and risky biomedical research (*Guidelines for Adolescent Health Research*, 1995, cited in King & Churchill, 2000; Susman, Dorn & Fletcher, 1992) and treatment procedures (Pearce, 1994; Weithorn & Campbell, 1982; Weithorn, 1983). Consistent with this perspective, developmental research suggests that by age fourteen, youth have developed reasoning abilities comparable to those of adults (Kuhn, Amsel, O'Loughlin, Schauble, Leadbeater & Yotive, 1988; Weithorn & Campbell, 1982). Thus, relying on chronological age to determine when parent consent is required for research is simplistic and may be particularly inadequate when evaluating developmental research involving a normative sample of adolescents.[4] Moreover, relying on chronological age in consent procedures may be especially damaging for research that has the potential to improve our understanding of emerging social problems among normative samples of adolescents. Given the increasing importance – not to mention the social and legal relevance – of this type of research, it seems justified to call for a re-examination of current ethical guidelines and standards regarding parent consent for adolescents in high school.

Some universities are considering waiving parent consent on the condition that each participant in the study has the cognitive capacity to understand the consent procedure (for example, Kabatoff, University of Saskatchewan, personal communication, 7 August 2003). However, it is left to the researchers to demonstrate to the REB that the procedures established for assessing competence are adequate. The criteria and procedures for determining competence to provide consent have yet to be clearly established and have aroused some controversy among researchers, ethicists, and funding agencies (see Baylis, Downie & Kenny, 1999; Hesson, Bakal & Dobson, 1993; and Runyan, 2000, for discussion of these issues). Consequently, just as there exists wide variation in the operational definition of competence, there may ultimately be wide variations in the procedures used to determine competence that are deemed acceptable by REBs. One of the implications of this situation is that research on socially sensitive issues among normal adolescents may be neglected in certain communities (for example, where the REBs are more stringent in their interpretations of the guidelines). This situation is potentially problematic because the results of research conducted in communities where REBs are more liberal in their interpretations of these guidelines may not be applicable to other communities in Canada (see Jansson, Mitic, Russell & Dhami, in this volume, for further discussion of definitions of competence and parental consent.)

ACTIVE VERSUS PASSIVE PARENTAL CONSENT

Assuming that parent consent remains a significant issue for REBs when they review research protocols on peer victimization, what procedures should be used to obtain it? Generally, particularly in research involving large numbers of participants, researchers send parents a letter outlining the purpose and procedures of the study, including the rights of parents and participants. Parents are asked to read the information about the study and to return the consent form either to the school or directly to the researcher. As outlined earlier, sometimes these letters are sent home with students and sometimes they are mailed directly to parents.

'Active' consent, as I use it in this chapter, refers to the requirement that parents of all participating students return these consent forms. When active consent is required, various strategies can be used to enhance the rate of return of parent consent forms. These include paying students to return the forms whether or not the parents provide consent; engaging students, teachers, and school administrators in a discussion about the project to enhance their interest and engagement in the project; speaking to parents' groups; and calling parents to remind them to return the letter. I have used all of these strategies in my own research, with very limited success. Even though I have invested large amounts of time and energy in the recruitment process, participation rates with active consent procedures continue to be, on average, fairly low – 50 to 70 per cent, which is consistent with most research involving adolescents.

Difficulty with obtaining written consent from parents of adolescents is not unique to the research enterprise. Indeed, several teachers with whom I have worked have noted their own difficulties in obtaining parents' written consent for their adolescents' participation in school activities such as school field trips. One superintendent of a school system in the United States observed that the rate of return of school forms is consistently low, even when adverse consequences (such as school transfers) for the child are associated with the failure to respond (Renger, Gotkin, Crago & Shisslak, 1998).

Consistent with other researchers (such as T. Biglan, personal communication published in Jason, Pokorny & Katz, 2001), I have found that parents who do not return written consent forms do not, for the most part, actively *dissent* to the research. That is, parents often do not return consent forms for reasons other than their unwillingness to allow their child's participation in my research (for example, the form was lost, they were too busy to sign it, or they didn't think it was important). In conversations with parents' groups and with individual parents in the schools where we are conducting our research, parents frequently do not grasp the importance of returning consent forms if they do not have any concerns about the research. For example, one parent told me over the telephone that she did not return the form because 'it just seemed silly for me to give my sixteen-year-old son permission to do a survey.' It is important to note that this response was received even after disclosure of the purpose of the study and the procedures to be used.

Some researchers have used passive consent procedures in research on peer victimization (for example, Espelage, Holt, & Henkel, 2003; Haynie, Nansel, Eitel, Crump, Saylor, Yu, & Simons-Morton, 2001; Stockdale, Hangaduambo, Duys, Larson & Sarvela, 2002). This procedure generally involves sending a letter home with the student or mailing a letter directly to the parents. The information provided in the letter is generally very similar to the information provided when active consent is sought. That is, the letter describes the goal of the study, the methods to be used, the risks and benefits associated with participation, and the rights of the participants. However, parents are then asked to return the form or contact the school only if they do *not* consent to their child's participation in the study.

It is clear from examining the research that participation rates are much higher when passive consent procedures are used rather than active ones. This may have important implications for research on peer victimization. Specifically, active consent procedures can lead to biases on significant dependent variables – biases that may negatively affect the generalizability of research results. For example, Anderman, Cheadle, Curry, and Diehr (1995) examined differences between Grade 9 and Grade 12 students with and without written parental consent to take part in a sensitive health survey. Students who received parental consent tended to be white, to live in two-parent households, to have a GPA of B or higher, and to be involved in extracurricular activities. The authors suggest that active consent procedures may actually prevent high-risk children from participating in research. (However, see Jansson and colleagues, in this volume, for the benefits associated with obtaining parental consent in these situations.) These observations are particularly relevant for research on peer victimization in schools.

The use of passive consent is controversial. For example, it may be difficult to confirm whether a parent has in fact consented through non-response. It is possible that parents did not actually see the letter or did not understand it. It is also possible that a parent replied negatively but the form did not reach the researcher for one reason or another; in this situation, the data may be collected from the adolescent against the parent's wishes. Clearly, procedures must be in place to address these potential situations. However, researchers and REBs must be aware of the implications of consent procedures for research on socially sensitive issues such as peer victimization in adolescence.

THIRD-PARTY CONSENT

One of the pivotal areas of disagreement between my community partners and the university REB concerned the legitimacy of the school administrators' third-party consent. The school administrators indicated that when research is conducted in the school for the purpose of informing educational practice, programs, or policy, parents are generally informed that a study is taking place in the school and are provided with the details of the study. However, active parent consent is not automatically obtained for children's participation. The position of the ethics committee was that the school administration could not provide third-party consent because it stood to benefit from the research and therefore was not objective. The school contended that administrators were ultimately responsible for the physical, social, and emotional well-being of their students during school hours. Thus, from their perspective, parents inherently authorize the school administrators to make daily decisions regarding their adolescents. The administrators believed that participation in a research project fell under this authorization. When I turned to the tri-council guidelines for assistance, I was disappointed by the vague description of third-party consent. I was unable to determine from Article 2.6 the conditions under which parent consent prevailed over school administration consent to participate in research. Article 2.6, section (a), states only that 'the authorized third party may not be the researcher or any other member of the research team.'

The difficulties associated with the issue of third-party consent provided by school administrators highlight the challenges confronting researchers who conduct community-based research. As noted by Fisher and Wallace (2000), community consultation is vital for conducting research on socially sensitive issues. One of the fundamental goals of my approach to community-based research is to engage the various stakeholders involved in the project as partners in the process. To this end, my research typically involves lengthy consultations with community partners. In identifying roles and responsibilities, I make an effort to ensure that the skills and knowledge of everyone at the table are recognized and respected. But after months of discussion with school administrators involved in the case presented here, their confidence in my belief in their status as equal partners in the research process was undermined by the REB's decision. My partners were upset that they had been evaluated as (from their perspective) incompetent to provide consent for their students' participation in the project by an anonymous group of academics with unknown experience working with adolescents. The trust that had developed over months of working with the group was threatened, and I had to spend many more hours discussing the project with them to regain that trust. Since this experience, several school administrators at various levels of governance have told me that they do not want to work with university academics because ethics committees do not adequately respect their responsibilities to the students attending their schools and to their parents. Indeed, they are beginning to view the entire university ethics protocol procedure as burdensome and overly restrictive. As a consequence, they are turning to research consultants who are not affiliated with any university and who are not supported by tri-council funding. These researchers are not bound by tri-council guidelines or by REB decisions regarding their research. Moreover, their work is not necessarily subject to standard peer review. If qualified researchers are excluded from the process because of the community's perception of unreasonable university REBs, one begins to wonder whether the tri-council guidelines are doing more harm than good (see Grayson, 2004, for further discussion on this issue).

Section II: Risk

Although some of the REBs surveyed for this chapter have started to address the issue of age of consent, decisions regarding the level of risk inherent in a study on peer victimization will likely influence REB decisions regarding consent procedures. For example, the University of Saskatchewan recently developed a policy for consent procedures involving older (that is, high school) adolescents. That university's REB guidelines have been revised so that the committee will consider waiving the requirements for parental consent if all of the following conditions are met (Kabatoff, personal communication, 7 August 2003):

1. The waiver is necessary for the conduct of the research.
2. The research presents no risk to the participants.
3. Adequate steps have been taken to inform the parents of the re-

search, and opportunity has been provided for them to withdraw their child's participation if they wish.
4. Each participant has the capacity to consent (that is, has the cognitive maturity required to understand the consent procedure and is emotionally mature enough to understand the implications of giving consent).

Researchers must demonstrate to the ethics committee that the above conditions have been met before any deviation from standard consent procedures will be considered. In the case of peer victimization research, three of the four conditions stipulated above could be reasonably satisfied. However, the stringent condition that the research present *no risk* to the participants may be difficult to achieve. As a result, questions arise regarding how the REB will calculate the risk/benefit ratio when reviewing consent procedures and what consultation will take place between the university REB and the community organization (here, the school) involved in the project.

Minimal risk is commonly defined as follows: if potential subjects can reasonably be expected to regard the probability and magnitude of possible harms implied by participation in the research to be no greater than those encountered by the subject in those aspects of his or her everyday life that relate to the research, then the research can be regarded as within the range of minimal risk. In research on victimization, the evaluation of risk must be examined in light of the methods that are frequently used. In much of this research, peer reports are often used to identify individuals who demonstrate the characteristics of victims and aggressors. For example, many researchers use a revised form of Masten, Morison, and Pelligrini's (1985) 'class play' protocol. Students are presented with a list of characteristics and asked to nominate peers who best fit each description. This method has been observed to be a valid and reliable measure of social behaviour in childhood. This method may provide better information regarding social behaviour compared to students' self-reports which may be influenced by social desirability or simply by a lack of awareness of their own behaviour. Moreover, observational studies such as those conducted in schoolyards with children are more difficult to conduct with adolescents, who are more likely to roam away from the prying eyes of adults during breaks in the school day.

At the same time, the use of peer nomination techniques with an adolescent population raises important ethical questions regarding the risks inherent in labelling and being labelled by one's peers. Indeed, the REB reviewing my ethics application expressed this type of concern. In suggesting revisions to my information letter to parents, it asked me to tell parents that there was the 'possibility that filling out this question- naire may serve as a catalyst to bullying behaviour.' The REB was also concerned that students would discuss their answers among them- selves and thereby create stress for students who had received nomina- tions for negative behaviours (for example, as someone who is 'bossy,' or someone who is often left out of activities). In response to these reviewers' concerns, I turned to the literature on sociometry to under- stand the potential consequences of these types of methods for study- ing peer victimization.

Bell-Dolan and her various colleagues (1989, 1992) conducted two studies to assess the potential negative impact on children of peer nomination techniques used for research purposes. Although she was specifically interested in examining the effects of friendship nomination procedures, the results of her research are relevant to the current discus- sion of peer evaluations of social behaviours such as aggression. In one study (Bell-Dolan, Foster & Sikora, 1989), fifth graders completed either a peer nomination sociometric task or a control task (i.e., nominating preferred and non-preferred school subjects). The authors conducted pre- and post-nomination assessments of the affective quality of partici- pants' peer interactions and self-reports of depressed mood and feel- ings of loneliness. The results indicated no differences between the peer and control nomination task groups on any of the outcome measures.

In another study, Bell-Dolan and her colleagues assessed the poten- tial negative reactions of children who participated in a study of peer relations, depression, and anxiety. In this study, girls in grades three and five, their parents, and their teachers completed questionnaires to assess reactions to the study, behaviour changes after participation, and information shared among participants about the sociometric mea- sures. The results indicated that participants did not report negative feelings about participation in the sociometric task and displayed no observable behaviour changes following the study.

The results of the research by Bell-Dolan and others (for example, Hayvren & Hymel, 1984; Iverson & Iverson, 1996) suggest that nomina- tion procedures involve minimal risk to participating students, particu- larly when strategies to minimize any potential negative interactions among students are set in place (see Underwood, Mayeux, Risser & Harper, in this volume, for a more detailed discussion on sociometric procedures). However, it is important to note that the research reviewed cannot be generalized to other age groups, particularly adolescence. Indeed, developmental tasks in adolescence may result in an increase in vulnerability to the potential negative effects of peer nomination procedures. In view of this, it is possible that the risk involved in the use of peer nomination techniques is greater when the population of interest includes adolescents. However, is it possible that the benefits to be derived from using these techniques outweigh the risks involved? If so, how do REBs assess this risk/benefit ratio?

Thompson (1990) suggests that most REBs are generally ill equipped to conduct adequate risk/benefit analyses of most research projects involving human subjects. He argues that while procedures for ensuring privacy, confidentiality, and informed consent are well established, procedures for assessing potential risks and benefits involved in research are inherently more difficult to establish. As a result, definitions regarding risk/benefit analysis are necessarily vague and open to wide interpretation. Contributing to this difficulty, according to Thompson, is the need for a developmental perspective in evaluating risk in research involving children or adolescents. Specifically, he suggests that it is necessary to consider how an individual's changing characteristics may influence vulnerability to research protocols. The example he provides to illustrate this necessity is particularly relevant for researchers who use peer nomination techniques:

> For example, a very young child cannot be easily embarrassed or humiliated before she has acquired the cognitive capacities necessary for self-referent thinking. Threats to the self-concept are limited until the child has developed a coherent system of self-referent beliefs and can incorporate others' evaluations and social-comparison information into that system. Worries about what will happen next in a research procedure depend, to a great extent, on an ability to think within a past-present-future temporal context and on an experiential background that leads one to anticipate threatening future events in a research setting ... Thus ... children are buffered against certain kinds of research risks because of limitations in their cognitive and experiential backgrounds ... and with increasing age (and corollary changes in self-understanding, inference processes, and other capabilities), vulnerability to [other types of] risks increases.' (1990, p. 6)

In adolescence a number of developmental changes occur at the level of the individual and at the level of the group, and these may increase vulnerability to the negative effects of peer nomination techniques in victimization research. Specifically, increased cognitive functioning allows adolescents to engage in more complex forms of thinking and to take multiple perspectives of self and other. Although these new skills are important for developing decision-making abilities, they are a double-edged sword. Associated with these cognitive changes – at least at the theoretical level – is a renewed form of egocentrism referred to as the 'imaginary audience' by Elkind (1967). This is when adolescents perceive themselves as if on 'centre stage' and believe that their every move is as important to and monitored by others as it is to themselves.

In addition to these intra-individual developmental changes, changes at the level of the peer group may have important implications for responses to peer nomination procedures during adolescence. Social networks potentially become unstable across the transition into adolescence; at the same time, the desire to be a part of a group increases. Negative evaluations of the self by others may potentially harm the adolescent's ego and self-esteem at a time when he/she is most sensitive to evaluations by others and when the importance of acceptance by one's peers is most strong.

As noted previously, Bell-Dolan's research on the impact of peer nomination techniques has generally examined these effects in samples of children. Although I was unable to find research that has examined these effects in adolescents, I would argue that it is extremely unlikely that participation in a survey on peer victimization would actually *cause* bullying, as the REB implies. In general, causes of bullying are generally not well understood, and bullying behaviours are by definition ongoing and frequently occur without any provocation by the victim. However, it is clear that we do not know the potential negative consequences of peer nomination procedures for adolescent participants' feelings of well-being. As a result, researchers interested in peer victimization must accept that there is the potential for risk in this method and ensure that adequate measures are taken to minimize these risks (see Underwood and colleagues, in this volume). Yet the question remains. Is the risk involved in participating in this research greater than the risk encountered by the adolescent in his or her everyday life, particularly for those individuals who have been victimized, who are being victimized, or who are at risk for being victimized as a part of their everyday experience with peers at school?

The risk inherent in the procedures used to assess victimization will likely prevent many REBs from waiving parent consent or approving passive consent procedures. Consequently, until adequate procedures for assessing the risks and benefits involved in this research are established, the difficulties associated with consent procedures outlined in the previous section of this chapter will likely continue to prevent a clear understanding of an important, sensitive issue for adolescents in school.

JUSTICE VERSUS CARE PERSPECTIVES

REBs have been criticized for relying heavily on abstract philosophical principles such as beneficence, non-malfeasance, autonomy, justice, and fidelity (Kitchener, 2000; Fisher, 2000). These critics have suggested that this emphasis overshadows the relationships between researchers and stakeholders (such as school administrators, parents, and participants), particularly when community-based research with youth at risk is being conducted. An ethic of 'care,' in contrast, emphasizes the importance of the researcher/participant relationship (Fisher, 1997). This emphasis demands more than simple adherence to abstract guidelines from an REB that is evaluating a research protocol and from researchers who are considering their responsibilities to the community involved in the research. An examination of the issue of risk in peer victimization research highlights the importance of assessing the nature of the relationship between the researcher and the community when the ethical standards of a research protocol are being evaluated.

As noted by Fisher and Wallace (2000), consultation with community members regarding research procedures is vital to adequately identify the potential harms and benefits of socially sensitive research. In my own research, I discuss the procedures to be used with students, parents, teachers, and school administrators. Teachers and school administrators are professionals who work daily with students who are occasionally participants in research projects. Consequently, I view them as 'professional experts' and rely on their advice and suggestions for conducting research in their schools. To this end, before a research project is conducted, we discuss potential costs and benefits of the research protocol to the school and to the students. In these discussions we pay particular attention to the risks and benefits associated with the use of peer nominations of social behaviours such as victimization. We discuss ways to deal with issues such as potential conflict or gossip between students following the administration of the survey. At the end of the survey, students are asked to indicate whether they wish to speak to an adult about any concerns they have with the survey or with any other issues they may be dealing with at their school. Students and parents are provided with my telephone number to call in case of any negative consequences resulting from the procedure or any concerns that they might have. In feedback sessions with teachers and school administrators, no negative incidents between students have been observed that can be specifically attributed to the research protocol used in the study we have been conducting for the past three years.

In view of the increasing demand for research accountability by the community, it is important for REBs to become better informed regarding practices involved in community-based research. Members of REBs evaluating this type of research must have the experience of conducting research in community organizations and must respect the nature of the relationship between the researcher and the community. Decisions about ethical practice must be based on evidence and on a clear understanding of the importance of the research for the community, and not simply on individual committee member's beliefs and concerns. In other words, REBs must find some way to ensure that researchers and the community partners involved in specific research projects are actively engaged in a process of consultation with the REB to assess the ethical standards of community-based research. Without this consultation, community partners are likely to continue to feel that the institution does not respect their professional training, values, and experience.

Policies that are perceived as 'ivory tower' ethics pose a considerable threat to the quality of social science research being conducted with children and adolescents. As noted earlier, researchers are beginning to notice that community organizations are becoming increasingly reluctant to engage in projects with university-based researchers (Grayson, 2004). Thus, relying primarily on legal opinions does not ensure that important ethical considerations, such as one's responsibility to the community, are met. Similarly, as noted earlier, decisions made by anonymous REB members may undermine the relationship between the researcher and the community organization – a relationship that is essential to socially sensitive research. It is possible that the individual preferences of REB members who are uninformed by disciplinary or professional expertise may influence REB decisions (see, for example, Grayson, 2004) and thereby undermine the entire review process by resorting to their individual beliefs or values, which may be inherently different from the community partners' beliefs and values. Furthermore, it may be necessary – though it will not be sufficient – to have a community representative on the REB as a solution to this type of challenge. Rather, an adequate consultation process between the REB, the researcher, and the members of the specific community organization involved in the project is needed. This process must recognize that ultimately, community members have equal voice in matters regarding research in their organizations. Consequently, if community members view the research protocol as meritorious (or not), the REB must respect this perspective in the decision-making process.

Section III. Ethical Responsibilities of Researchers Following Completion of Their Research

I was recently asked by a school principal from one of the school divisions with which I work to attend a presentation on bullying that he was hosting for parents of students in the community. The speaker was from a national not-for-profit organization that has made significant and meaningful contributions to society through its work. When we were introduced, the speaker informed me that she was working closely with a group of nationally recognized researchers in the area of bullying. Throughout her presentation, she referred to select research findings from these researchers as 'facts' without regard for basic scientific issues such as generalizability of results and the limitations of attributing causality from correlational studies. Her intention, clearly, was to alert teachers and parents to the dangers inherent in not addressing school bullying. Although the speaker was well intended, her presentation artificially inflated the problem of peer victimization by overlooking the unique differences between schools located in large urban centres (that is, where the research she was referring to was conducted) and schools in smaller urban or rural communities (that is, where she was presenting).

Undoubtedly, bullying and peer victimization are likely to be observed at any school, although some types of victimization (such as physical) are more likely to be observed than others (such as gossip and exclusion). What was particularly disturbing, however, was that the speaker seemed unaware of the limitations of the research she was presenting as broadly applicable 'facts,' or of the possible negative impact of applying those research findings to a very different community. Some of my community research partners have suggested that one of the negative effects of this type of misinformation is that it pressures school administrators with very limited financial resources to 'do something' about a problem that may not actually exist in their schools.

Surprisingly, the *Tri-council Guidelines* and policy statement have very little to say about researchers' responsibilities for disseminating results beyond our responsibility to subject our research to peer review:

> Researchers enjoy, and should continue to enjoy, important freedoms and privileges ... These freedoms include freedom of inquiry and the right to disseminate the results thereof, freedom to challenge conventional thought, freedom from institutional censorship ... However, researchers ... also recognize that with freedom comes responsibility to ensure that research involving human subjects meets high scientific and ethical standards. The researcher's commitment to the advancement of knowledge also implies duties of honest and thoughtful inquiry, rigorous analysis, and account-ability for the use of professional standards. *Thus, peer review of research proposals, the findings and their interpretation contribute to accountability, both to colleagues and to society.* (Interagency Advisory Panel on Research Ethics: *www.pre.ethics.gc.ca/english/policystatement/context.cfm*; accessed July 24, 2003)

Researchers working with community organizations on socially sensitive topics have a moral and ethical obligation to ensure that the results of their work are not misrepresented or used for misguided purposes (Kimball, 1993). Research on complex social issues is inher-ently limited in the extent to which it provides evidence for a particular conclusion. Thus, it is essential that researchers work closely with com-munity members to ensure that they understand the limitations of the research design and the inherent limitations to the conclusions that can be made based on the research.

For example, the initial goal of the project I am currently conducting was to identify the prevalence of peer victimization across the schools in a local school division. I was able to demonstrate that there were no statistically significant differences between schools in terms of the num-bers of students either self-reporting or peer-identified as victims. Fur-thermore, I was able to tell the school division that in general, the levels of peer victimization in its schools were quite low. School administra-tors were relieved that the evidence supported, to some extent, their impressions about the safety of their schools. However, I reminded them that the research was limited by the low participation rates in some schools and in some grades. Furthermore, more girls than boys participated across all grades, and some types of aggression among students were more prevalent than others. I also discussed the issue of individual differences and explained how, when one looked beyond simple numbers, some students did appear to suffer from the negative effects of peer victimization to a greater extent than others. Thus, the initial numbers supported their claim that peer victimization was not rampant in their schools; but at the same time, the observation that some students who *were* being victimized appeared to be suffering more than others alerted them to the need to continue to monitor the situation in their schools and to develop appropriate strategies for dealing with these cases. I continue to work with them as they develop strategies to respond to the results obtained from our survey. We also meet to determine what type of further research is needed. Clearly, we cannot expect community partners to be statisticians or methodologists. Thus it is the researcher's ethical responsibility to communicate the results of research in a manner that is both meaningful and realistic.

Summary and Conclusions

The *Tri-council Guidelines* were implemented in 2001 as an attempt to regulate ethical standards as they applied to diverse research problems, methods, and disciplines. However, the guidelines remain vague about many important issues and this has resulted in wide variability among university officials' interpretations of the guidelines. While vague guidelines allow for consideration of unique situations that are constantly emerging in research, questions arise concerning the dangers associated with the focus on legal opinions at the expense of ethical and methodological considerations in reviewing protocols. As noted by Lépine and Smolla (2000, p. 53):

> There is a danger of seeking solutions to ethical issues through a legal approach at the expense of an open debate involving all the societal stakeholders. The law only defines minimal protection criteria, the violation of which results in penalties. Solutions must come from those who design research and those who authorize it. Improving academic training for researchers on ethical matters relevant to their domain of research is mandatory. We also need to recognize that only a reflection initiated at the time of protocol design and based on knowledge of the research domain's methodology could ensure cogent answers to problems.'

Research on school-based peer victimization in adolescence is vital if we are to understand a problem that is garnering increasing attention in the media. Without well-designed, theoretically driven, empirical work in this area, we run the risk of leaving decisions about the social well-being of a large proportion of Canadian society in the hands of ill-informed school personnel and mental health professionals. Through no fault of their own, the interventions implemented may be inadequate to address the needs of their students. Thus, addressing the challenges to conducting this research that arise from questions regarding ethics is essential if we hope to ensure that some communities are not unnecessarily deprived of the information they need.

In conclusion, while the experience that stimulated this exploration of ethical procedures in research on peer victimization was difficult, I want to stress the valuable lessons it has provided me as a community-based researcher. We can attempt to teach graduate students the basics of ethical principles underlying social science research but it is difficult to predict the types of ethical challenges one may face when conducting research on socially sensitive issues with children and youth. The first step in this process involves exposing our research protocols to the close scrutiny of an institutional REB. Ultimately, it is the researcher's responsibility to communicate clearly to the REB and to anticipate potential difficulties before they occur. It is equally important, however, to have a mechanism in place that facilitates open and honest communication between REB members, researchers, and community partners.

NOTES

1 A summary of the results of this Web search can be obtained from the author.
2 There are cases in which individuals under eighteen are considered emancipated minors (for example, they are adolescents who are parents themselves or who do not live with parents or guardians). Research with this particular population raises another set of issues that are not addressed in this chapter. Thus, the issues discussed in this chapter are generally intended for researchers who study populations of adolescents who do not fall into this category.
3 This could be tested, empirically, by including an additional box on the consent form indicating that the adolescent is him/herself not interested in participating in the study.
4 By 'normative,' we are referring to a sample of adolescents who have not been targeted for study because of any unique characteristic other than the

fact that they are adolescents. In our research, these samples are drawn from public schools that are generally serving predominantly white, middle-class populations.

REFERENCES

Abramovitch, R., Freedman, J.L., Henry, K., & Van-Brunschot, M. (1995). Children's capacity to agree to psychological research: Knowledge of risks and benefits and voluntariness. *Ethics and Behaviour*, 5(1), 25–48.

Anderman, C., Cheadle, A., Curry, S., & Diehr, P. (1995). Selection bias related to parental consent in school-based survey research. *Evaluation Review*, 19(6), 663–74.

Baylis, F., Downie, J., & Kenny, N. (1999). Children and decision making in health research. *IRB: A Review of Human Subjects Research*, 21(4), 5–10.

Bell-Dolan, D.J., Foster, S.L., & Christopher, J.S. (1992). Children's reactions to participating in a peer relations study: An example of cost-effective assessment. *Child Study Journal*, 22(2), 137–56.

Bell-Dolan, D.J., Foster, S.L., & Sikora, D.M. (1989). Effects of sociometric testing on children's behavior and loneliness in school. *Developmental Psychology*, 25(2), 306–11.

Camodeca, M., Goossens, F.A., Meerum-Terwogt, M., & Schuengel, C. (2002). Bullying and victimization among school-age children: Stability and links to proactive and reactive aggression. *Social Development*, 11(3), 332–45.

Coleman, P.K., & Byrd, C.P. (2003). Interpersonal correlates of peer victimization among young adolescents. *Journal of Youth and Adolescence*, 32(4), 301–14.

Culbert, L., & Steffenhagen, J. (2000, 11 December). B.C. parents strike out against school bullies: Suits against school districts closely watched by Canada's educators. *Edmonton Journal*, A11.

Dimmock, G. (1999, 30 April). Accused Taber killer joked he had hit list: 'People picked on him and bullied him and called him a nerd, idiot and faggot,' said a student who faced the teen shooter. *Vancouver Sun*, A4.

Dorn, L.D., Susman, E.J., & Fletcher, J.C. (1995). Informed consent in children and adolescents: Age, maturation and psychological state. *Journal of Adolescent Health*, 16(3), 185–90.

Elkind, D. (1967). Egocentrism in adolescence. *Child Development*, 38(4), 1025–34.

Espelage, D.L., Holt, M.K., & Henkel, R.R. (2003). Examination of peer-group contextual effects on aggression during early adolescence. *Child Development*, 74(1), 205–20.

Fisher, C.B. (1997). A relational perspective on ethics-in-science decision making for research with vulnerable populations. *IRB: A Review of Human Subjects Research*, 19(5), pp. 1–4.

Fisher, C.B. (2000). Relational ethics in psychological research: One feminist's journey. In M. Brabeck (Ed.), *Practicing feminist ethics in psychology*. (pp. 125–42). Washington, DC: American Psychological Association.

Fisher, C.B., & Wallace, S.A. (2000). Through the community looking glass: Reevaluating the ethical and policy implications of research on adolescent risk and psychopathology. *Ethics & Behaviour*, 10(2), 99–118.

Grayson, J.P. (2004, January). How ethics committees are killing survey research on Canadian students. *University Affairs: Canada's Magazine on Higher Education and Academic Jobs*. Accessed on-line: 1/4/2004.

Haynie, D.L., Nansel, T., Eitel, P., Crump, A.D., Saylor, K., Yu, K., & Simons-Morton, B. (2001). Bullies, victims, and bully/victims: Distinct groups of at-risk youth. *Journal of Early Adolescence*, 21(1), 29–49.

Hayvren, M., & Hymel, S. (1984). Ethical issues in sociometric testing: The impact of sociometric measures on interaction behavior. *Developmental Psychology*, 20, 844–9.

Hesson, K., Bakal, D., & Dobson, K.S. (1993). Legal and ethical issues concerning children's rights of consent. *Canadian Psychology*, 34(3), 317–28.

Jason, L.A., Pokorny, S., & Katz, R. (2001). Passive versus active consent: A case study in school settings. *Journal of Community Psychology*, 29(1), 53–68.

Jiwa, S. (2000, 16 March). Tormented to death. *Vancouver Province*, A3.

King, N.M.P., & Churchill, L.R. (2000). Ethical principles guiding research on child and adolescent subjects. *Journal of Interpersonal Violence*, 15(7), 710–24.

Kimball, M. (1993, May). The misuses and uses of difference. Paper presented at the Canadian Psychological Association meeting, Montreal.

Kitchener, K.S. (2000). *Foundations of ethical practice, research, and teaching in psychology*. Mahwah, NJ: Lawrence Erlbaum Associates.

Kotch, J.B. (2000). Ethical issues in longitudinal child maltreatment research. *Journal of Interpersonal Violence*, 15(7), 696–709.

Kuhn, D., Amsel, E., O'Loughlin, M., Schauble, L., Leadbeater, B., & Yotive, W. (1988). *The development of scientific thinking skills*. San Diego, CA: Academic Press.

Lépine, S., & Smolla, N. (2000). Ethical issues concerning participants in community surveys of child and adolescent mental disorders. *Canadian Journal of Psychiatry*, 45(1), 48–54.

Masten, A.S., Morison, P., Pellegrini, D.S. (1985). A revised class play method of peer assessment. *Developmental Psychology*, 21(3), 523–33.

McMartin, P., Fong, P., & Skelton, C. (2000, 16 March). Surrey boy's suicide blamed on incessant teasing at school: He alluded to the teasing in a letter that he left on a chest of drawers in his bedroom. *Vancouver Sun*, A1.

Munro, H. (2000, 2 December). Dawn-Marie's tragic last days: She was 14 and hiding a terrible secret: She was being picked on by kids at school. She kept it to herself until the suicide note. *Vancouver Sun*, B1.

Nagy, S., Stewart, M., & Dudley, W. (1999, 29 April). Two teens gunned down. *Calgary Herald*, A1, A2.

Owens, A.M. (2000, 20 November). Charges recommended in suicide of girl, 14: Girls, 15, named as bullies in dead teen's letter to family. *National Post*, A4.

Pearce, J. (1994). Consent to treatment during childhood: The assessment of competence and avoidance of conflict. *British Journal of Psychiatry*, 165(6), 713–16.

Renger, R., Gotkin, V., Crago, M., & Shisslak, C. (1998). Research and legal perspectives on the implications of the family privacy protection act for research and evaluation involving minors. *American Journal of Evaluation*, 19(2), 191–202.

Rigby, K. (1998). The relationship between reported health and involvement in bully/victim problems among male and female secondary schoolchildren. *Journal of Health Psychology*, 3, 465–76.

Rigby, K. (1999). Peer victimization at school and the health of secondary school students. *British Journal of Educational Psychology*, 69, 95–104.

Rigby, K., Cox, I., & Black, G. (1997). Cooperativeness and bully/victim problems among Australian school children. *Journal of Social Psychology*, 137, 357–68.

Runyan, D.K. (2000). The ethical, legal, and methodological implications of directly asking children about abuse. *Journal of Interpersonal Violence*, 15(7), 675–81.

Scott, E.S., Reppucci, N.D., & Woolard, J.L. (1995). Evaluating adolescent decision making in legal contexts. *Law and Human Behaviour*, 19(3), 221–44.

Stockdale, M.S., Hangaduambo, S., Duys, D., Larson, K., & Sarvela, P.D. (2002). Rural elementary students,' parents,' and teachers' perceptions of bullying. *American Journal of Health Behaviour*, 26(4), 266–77.

Susman, E.J., Dorn, L.D. & Fletcher, J.C. (1992). Participation in biomedical research: The consent process as viewed by children, adolescents, young adults, and physicians. *Journal of Pediatrics*, 121, 547–52.

Thompson, R.A. (1990). Vulnerability in research: A developmental perspective on research risk. *Child Development*, 61(1), 1–16.

Tibbetts, J. (2002, 10 June). Students sue tormenters and teachers: Victims are finding justice in the courts. *Calgary Herald*, A3.

Tri-council policy statement: Ethical conduct for research involving humans (1998, with 2000, 2002 updates). Medical Research Council Canada, Natural Sciences and Engineering Research Council of Canada, and Social Sciences and Humanities Research Council of Canada. www.pre.ethics.gc.ca/english/policystatement/policystatement.cfm.

Weithorn, L.A. (1982). Developmental factors and competence to make informed treatment decisions. *Child and Youth Services*, 5(1), 85–100.

Weithorn, L.A., & Campbell, S.B. (1982). The competency of children and adolescents to make informed treatment decisions. *Child Development*, 53(6), 1589–98.

PART FOUR

The Special Case of Research with Groups

8 Youth on the Margins: Qualitative Research with Adolescent Groups

ANNE MARSHALL AND BLYTHE SHEPARD

Adolescents spend much of their time in groups – in classrooms, with their families, and among their peers. Connectedness with groups reinforces personal relationships and offers a context in which youth can learn about themselves as individuals (Connell, 1990; Harter, 1999). Peer groups are of particular importance in their lives, and very influential for most teens. Within this arena they may try out new styles, discover new selves, engage in new relationships, and encounter new ideas. The relational dynamics that unfold when conducting focus group research with young people are very similar to those encountered in other youth groups. The use of focus groups in research has been increasing steadily; this has been attributed to the method's practicality and production of rich data (Field, 2000; Morgan, 1997). There is tremendous potential for the generation of 'real-life' knowledge and understanding with this method; however, there is also potential for harm. Particular ethical issues and situations arise when focus group research is conducted, yet little has been published about ethics related to focus group or group interview methodology (Smith, 1995).

There is virtually no mention of group research in the documents guiding the ethical conduct of social science research in Canada and the United States. The *Tri-council Policy Statement on Ethical Conduct for Research Involving Humans* (2003), and the ethical codes of the American Psychological Association (2002), the Canadian Psychological Association (2000), the American Counseling Association (1995), and the Canadian Counselling Association (1999), provide guidelines and describe standards of practice on aspects of research such as informed consent, confidentiality, competence, and misrepresentation. As Wallwork (2002) observes, however, the culture of research ethics has been largely individualistic, and ethics documents and scholarship reflect this focus. Not one of the widely used guidelines specifically addresses the particular ethical issues, problems, and situations encountered in community-based focus group research contexts (Serrano-Garcia, 1994). Moreover, the guidelines were developed for researcher-directed studies and do not easily lend themselves to qualitative and community-based research designs, especially those involving groups (Goodey, 1999; Holstein & Gubrium, 2003; Welland & Pugsley, 2002).

Kellner's (2002) distinction between ethics and morality is relevant here. Ethics principles set norms or codify behaviour; such codification is necessarily situation-bound and therefore limited. In contrast, morality is an orientation to others that involves responsibility and caring; it is limitless in time and scope. Universal ethics criteria are different from moral criteria as well as difficult to apply in areas of human science such as community-based research. Weijer (2001) contends that research ethics boards (REBs) may be focusing too much attention on consent procedures and forms, and not enough time on analysing the actual risks and benefits related to the research. Moral concerns about mutual respect and the suspension of value judgments are as important in community contexts as the principles of informed consent and confidentiality. Qualitative focus group research studies pose complex moral dilemmas because of their evolving partnership designs.

In this chapter we discuss three ethics questions and problems that can arise when focus group interview research is conducted with youth: informed consent, confidentiality and anonymity, and group dynamics. We begin with some general considerations of ethical practices when collecting group data and a description of our Community Alliance for Health Research (CAHR) context. These sections provide a background for the ensuing discussion of the ethics issues, which will be illustrated with examples from our CAHR research with adolescent focus groups. The chapter ends with a discussion of the implications for research ethics as well as suggestions for future directions.

Ethics in Focus Group Research

The standard and widely accepted ethics codes and guidelines used by social science researchers in North America do not address the complex issues related to collecting group data. In documents such as the Ethical Guidelines for Group Counselors approved by the Association for Specialists in Group Work (Cottone & Tarvydas, 1998), the focus is on ethical practice in group therapy and facilitation settings, with only passing reference to research with groups. The British Sociological Association (2002) acknowledges that researchers enter into personal and moral relationships with those they study, be they individuals, household, social groups or corporate entities (2002, p. 2), and cautions that decisions may have effects on individuals as members of a group. Again, the emphasis is on ethical behaviour with already existing groups, in contrast to the typical focus group research situation, where individuals come together *for the purpose of the research itself.*

We could find no recommendations in Canada's *Tri-council Policy Statement* that specifically addressed the collection of group data. Section 6 of this statement acknowledges that research involving Aboriginal individuals may also involve the communities or groups to which they belong (2003, s. 6.1). However, the use of the term *group* in this context refers to ongoing membership or identification. The discussion focuses on the collective nature of such groups and on related issues such as contacting leaders, following protocols, ownership of the research data, and representation. These apply to conducting research with Aboriginal groups, other cultural or ethnic groups, and groups established for a particular purpose that have their own history and traditions. Focus group research, however, rarely involves participants who are members of a cultural or already established group. Some writers have suggested that focus group participants can form their own 'culture' during data collection (Field, 2000); however, the time they spend together is limited; similarly, the extent of their mutual relationships is limited to their participation in the research.

This absence of focus group research guidelines surprised us, especially given the method's popularity in the social sciences. As Wallwork (2002) notes, research ethics investigations and policies have focused almost exclusively on individuals, and new guidelines and policies specifically tailored to research with groups are needed.

A number of authors have addressed the ethics issues related to ethical practice in qualitative research investigations (van den Hoonaard, 2002; Welland & Pugsley, 2002; White, 2002). Research designs that involve greater engagement with participants present many opportunities for ethics dilemmas to arise. Because the direction and outcomes of the research are not always known at the outset, qualitative researchers may be unable to give detailed explanations about these to potential participants. In many qualitative studies, the participants themselves influence the data collection process. In participatory and action designs, participants are involved throughout the project, from conception to dissemination. Ethical dilemmas are an inescapable aspect of such collaborative relationships.

Our Research Context

Our research team's CAHR target project is titled 'Youth Coping with Social and Economic Restructuring: An On-going Dialogue Regarding Health.' The study investigates adolescents' experiences of physical and mental health risk and protective factors, within the current sociopolitical climate of globalization and restructuring. Because we wished to investigate the youths' own understandings of the relationship between health factors and their social and economic contexts, a qualitative and community-based research design was deemed appropriate. We focused on adolescents' perceptions of risk factors, health practices, and coping skills and on how they connect these to their own experiences of societal transition, personal and cultural belief systems, and social context. To enhance the authenticity of our data and their application to real-life situations, we conducted our interviews in two schools, a community youth program, and a youth employment agency. Our research team includes two university academic researchers (the present authors), ten graduate and undergraduate student research assistants (graduates have been replaced over the course of the project), and community partners from four community settings. Over two years, we have conducted group interviews with more than 160 youth between ages fifteen and twenty-three, with the majority being between sixteen and nineteen (Marshall, 2003; Marshall, Shepard, Rozeck-Allen & Saffrey, 2003).

Several ethics dilemmas emerged, related to consent, confidentiality, and group dynamics. We are experienced qualitative researchers and are familiar with REBs, research protocols, and ethics codes; even so, we did not fully anticipate some situations that we encountered when conducting these focus group interviews, particularly with economically disadvantaged participants.

The participatory research design was informed by Kemmis and McTaggart's (2000) ecological or contextual perspective, which acknowledges the complex interactions among ourselves as researchers, student assistants, community partners, agency and school personnel, and youth participants. Consequently, our study was influenced by multiple and sometimes conflicting viewpoints, values, and agendas. These features raised concerns about protection of individuals in the group, adequacy of informed consent, and respect for value diversity. We recognized that the differences in perspectives and experiences between the youth participants and ourselves as researchers constituted a cross-cultural encounter. Thus we needed to apply a cultural perspective to the evaluation of research risks and benefits (Fisher et al., 2002; Marshall & Batten, 2004).

Our community partners, as well as practitioners from schools and youth-serving community agencies, were instrumental is helping us address these ethics issues and potential problems. Regular meetings of researchers, student assistants, and partners were held as part of the project; these allowed us to develop the overall research design together, with the youth experience central to our decision process. Community partners contributed throughout the process, from initial ideas through design and data collection to dissemination. Each group interview guide was developed in consultation with community partners because they were the ones who knew the youth participants and who interacted with them regularly.

In keeping with Lincoln's principles (1998) of ethical social action inquiry, we deliberately built our research team activities to parallel how we would conduct our research with youth. Our ecological approach to understanding participants underscored the importance of contextual factors and their potential influence on the project. We critically examined our values and assumptions in research team meetings. We explored possible group scenarios that might trigger negative judgments and interfere with authentic data. Reactions to street language, clothing, body piercing, and communication styles (such as constant interrupting) were acknowledged and processed. The team established a continuous, reflective process that included research journals, team discussions, and group facilitator supervision before and after each research session. Although time-consuming, these practices created a positive team dynamic and acknowledged our commitment to working collaboratively within the team and with our community partners. We incorporated the skills of group communication to encourage an ethic of reciprocity and responsible caring. Team members also made a commitment to work collaboratively and cooperatively in order to model working in partnership in the field.

This careful attention to developing contextual familiarity and building relationships with our community partners contributed to mutually respectful and beneficial relationships with the youth at each community site. They were interested in our research and had many questions about what we were doing and why. In turn, we were able to obtain participants' candid and honest observations, opinions, and suggestions. Because of their largely adult-controlled lives, we wondered if the young people would be somewhat reluctant to share sensitive information about themselves with unknown adults. However, we found the youth to be open and eager to have their voices heard.

Informed Consent

One can argue that informed consent procedures form the basis of most research ethics codes and guidelines. Typically, they are a major focus of REB review procedures. Sieber (2001) underscores the importance of paying careful attention to both the protocol and the informed consent relationship. Pugsley (2002) observes that it is particularly difficult to explain consent and voluntary participation in a group. REBs typically require detailed consent forms for recruitment and consent. A checklist of items to be included can be almost two pages long, and the resulting consent form can be as much as three pages long if it includes thorough explanations of the procedures and limitations related to focus group research. The formality, language, and length of such documents can alienate some participants, particularly marginalized or disadvantaged youth. The time needed to read these consent forms is another factor. Faced with a lengthy letter, youth may not want to take the time needed to read it carefully. Also, if researchers have accessed participants through a teacher or community contact, participants may trust that this gatekeeper or sponsor has already determined that the research is OK. Formal agreements can be viewed as challenging such relationships or even undermining trust that has been established.

Our solution to these potential difficulties was to summarize the contents of the consent forms on a blackboard or flip chart before giving them to participants to read and sign. We explained that the reason for such detailed consent forms was to protect them as participants and to give them more power in the research relationship. This discussion and concrete display of the major consent form clauses also helped us address the problem of varied language and reading comprehension levels among the focus group participants. Some needed more time to read the forms, and we could accommodate this by extending the general discussion time until they had finished.

Obtaining authentic, informed consent also becomes more complicated if participants see signing a consent form as an expectation from authority figures. In school settings, for example, youth are used to acquiescing to adult requests and may not realize that they genuinely have the option not to participate in a research study. The possibility of peer pressure to participate (or not) is yet another topic for the consent process discussion. Focus group interviewers must to be sensitive to identifying participants' concerns and hesitancies, and provide alternatives for those in school class or other natural group settings who do not wish to participate. Options should be negotiated beforehand and include neutral activities such as reading or going to study hall. Some who choose not to participate may want to stay and listen. However, this can compromise confidentiality, so it was discouraged in our focus groups.

In qualitative studies using an evolving research design, researchers should adopt Munall's (1988) process consenting approach, or what Ramcharam and Cutcliffe (2001) term 'ethics as process.' Process consenting involves assessing consent throughout the research project to provide more protection and freedom of choice for participants. This means creating opportunities to receive feedback from participants and changing the research process in light of that feedback. Issues related to consent are discussed and addressed as they arise within a data collection session and in subsequent sessions, including during dissemination.

Confidentiality and Anonymity in Focus Group Research

Research participants have a fundamental right to privacy. The sensitivity of the information gathered (for example, about sexual health or substance abuse) and the plans for its dissemination (the general public versus only one person) add to the significance of privacy. Adhering to principles of confidentiality and anonymity is even more complex when collecting data in focus groups. Consent form templates and guidelines focus primarily on the data collection process and on safeguarding the identity of participants' raw data. In our research, questions relating to degree of disclosure, extent of participation, participant inclusion, and communication methods arose early in the planning stages and had to be addressed throughout the research process. Focus group researchers must also consider the implications of collecting data from multiple participants simultaneously. If one participant withdraws, what is the impact? How can information be shared if some members consent to its release while others do not?

The group's respect for confidentiality is a critical consideration. Personal information that is casually shared in a focus group (and which may or may not be true) can be spread as gossip, reported to parents or teachers, and used for subsequent retaliation or victimization. Researchers cannot control what participants choose to disclose after the research, but they can emphasize the importance of keeping group discussion materials confidential. During a session, one youth in our research referred to a situation at a party that could have resulted in physical injury. The youth prefaced the description of the scenario by stating: 'Well, we won't mention any names but ...' Though confidentiality had been established as a ground rule at the beginning of the session, it was evident that most of the youth in the focus group knew who the 'undisclosed' individuals were. This instance provided an opportunity for us to revisit the concept of confidentiality right in the focus group session and to discuss its implications with the participants.

Several characteristics of community-based research limit standard efforts to safeguard anonymity. The very act of engaging in extended research entails public visibility. The process of gaining access to natural settings involves negotiations with a number of people, such as principals, counsellors, teachers, and community agency coordinators, who know both where the research is taking place and whom the participants are. These gatekeepers could knowingly or accidentally reveal these identifying details to others. At the same time, anonymized accounts can take away the important contextualized understanding developed in the research. As Nespor (2000) says: 'Naming places and tracing their constitutive processes allows researchers to emphasize connections among people, places, and events and to highlight the systems of relationships and processes of articulation that produce boundaries and entities' (p. 556). Our solution to this challenge was to discuss the possible risks and benefits of naming the locations of the research with community partners and negotiate the extent of identification. We agreed, for example, to name a school, but not the individual teachers or youth participants.

A further point to consider when collecting focus group data is the possibility that participants will overdisclose. This point is especially salient if the research topic is sensitive (Smith, 1995). In a focus group taking place in a familiar setting with peers, participants can forget that the session is being recorded for later transcription and analysis. Preventive strategies can include ensuring that participants are advised of the topic to be discussed and made aware that the discussion could lead them to disclose information that they would not want shared. When outlining the limits to confidentiality in groups, it helps to use plain language. Interviewers can describe 'possible scenarios' to illustrate how a disclosure might be misused either by accident or by design. These scenarios can be based on previous focus group session experiences.

Fisher, Higgins-D'Alessandro, Rau, Kuther, and Belanger (1996) investigated confidentiality from the perspective of adolescents. They found that many youth think breaking confidentiality is acceptable when it comes to disclosing serious risks such as suicide ideation and maltreatment. Laws require the reporting of abuse of children and youth to child protection authorities (see Walsh and MacMillian, in this volume). In minimal-risk investigations, investigators can agree to protect the privacy of the individuals who participate if reportable behaviours are not elicited. Participants who disclose sensitive information may be hoping for intervention, and self-referral can be encouraged. Another option is to consult with an adult or professional with whom the participant interacts, such as a teacher or counsellor.

It is challenging to have youth agree on decisions to break confidentiality in the event of a disclosure that must be reported, such as one involving the current sexual abuse of a minor. Researchers also need to be sensitive to differing levels of comfort with the disclosure of personal information regarding cultural and ethnic minorities. Adolescents differ in their expectations regarding sharing information and valuing confidentiality about their peers, and these in turn differ from adult expectations.

When reporting or publishing focus group results, it may not be sufficient merely to use pseudonyms. The researcher may also need to conceal or change details that could identify the individuals. One way to address anonymity in published material is to give the report to the participants to read first, so that they can approve the researcher's approach to disguising revealing details, and perhaps change those details themselves.

Group Dynamics

For many focus group interviewers, the most challenging part of the data collection involves managing the group interviews. Experienced researchers have described the difficulties of balancing direction from the moderator or interviewer with the promotion of input from participants (Field, 2000; Koppleman & Bourjolly, 2001; Morgan, 1997). If participants agree to take part in a focus group and have understood that to involve everyone's input, how does the researcher ensure that equal participation takes place? Is this possible, or even desirable? Is there an ethical obligation to limit the discussion if someone indicates that she or he is feeling intimidated by another participant who is outspoken or who seems intent on sparking controversy in the group?

As Wallwork (2002) points out, there is no generally accepted formula for resolving conflicts that arise when the rights of an individual clash with those of a group. Adopting a process for decision-making in such situations is important. What courses of action are possible? And what are the risks and benefits of these actions? Most group interviewers would agree that a focus group session should be discontinued if there is major conflict; however, it is sometimes difficult to distinguish between controversy and conflict in the moment.

Group interview sessions require skilled group facilitators. All the interview facilitators in our study were counsellors or counsellors-in-training who were highly trained in communication and active listening. All were knowledgeable about and familiar with group dynamics and the process of making decisions about either limiting or expanding discussions. We designed specific training experiences for interviewers; these included reviewing procedures, discussing possible scenarios, practising skills, and brainstorming solutions. Even with extensive preparation, inexperienced interviewers can be somewhat overwhelmed at first by the pace and amount of content generated by participants in a thirty- to forty-minute group interview. Often, teens interrupt and talk over one another; occasionally they make negative comments when they disagree with one another. Maintaining reasonable order when the discussion becomes animated, while still encouraging meaningful participation, can be difficult. Although group interview question guides need to be and usually are carefully developed, interviewers also need to be responsive to content and process shifts that inevitably arise as part of an evolving and participatory research design (van den Hoonaard, 2002). Thus they must be able to mediate when conflicts arise and keep the session content within reasonable boundaries that are consistent with the research design and objectives.

Some focus group interviews are more structured than others. Some designs use a schedule of prepared questions and discourage divergent discussion. Qualitative and participatory designs usually encourage participants to expand their responses or add content they deem relevant. In the latter approach, particularly with youth, sessions can quickly develop into lively and sometimes heated discussions on sensitive and controversial topics, such as relationship violence or harassment from employers. Monitoring participation or intervening presents an ongoing challenge in such situations. Many adolescents present as outspoken and definite in their views; yet their autonomy can be compromised as a consequence of their susceptibility to peer influence and status hierarchies (in some instances) and of their relative inexperience. It takes highly skilled interviewers to allow research discussions to evolve without either too much interference or too much latitude.

The solution in our research was to have two interviewers per group, adapting the suggestion made by Krueger (1988) to have a lead moderator and an assistant. Because each session evolved differently to some degree, the interviewers worked out their own roles with respect to leader and supporter. The sessions were audiotaped so that the interviewers could devote most of their attention to facilitating the session. When new research interviewers joined the team, we paired an experienced interviewer with a more novice one. In addition, we met with community partners for planning before the sessions and for debriefing afterwards. These meetings helped remind us of our research goals, prepare for potential rough spots, make any last-minute adjustments, and (afterwards) recommend any changes for subsequent sessions.

One process we observed to be operating in some of our focus groups was what has been termed 'groupthink' in social psychology (Janis, 1982; Johnson & Johnson, 2002). The initial speaker or the first statement made at the beginning of a discussion tends to shape the subsequent course of the discussion. Dominant individuals often try to monopolize focus group sessions. It is simply not possible to ensure equitable and balanced participation without undue interference, particularly for quieter students or for those who speak English as a second language. In our research, one young Asian woman wrote us a note at the end of an interview in which she explained that she didn't speak much in group situations because she didn't think the other students really listened to her. It could be argued that she should have been 'protected' from participation until she felt more comfortable, or that the interviewer should have tried harder to include her in the session. Possibly, being part of the group was more important to her than contributing to the discussion. Nevertheless, the interviewer involved was able to offer this participant an individual interview.

These above situations underscore the importance of guidelines and strategies for inclusion and safe participation in focus group research. Agreed-upon guidelines are critical to the success of focus group research interviews. These can be generated by the group as part of the introduction and written on a flip chart or blackboard for reference during the interview. At all of our research sites, the adolescents were unanimous in their agreement about taking turns, respecting confidentiality, and no put-downs. We used examples that arose in the moment to illustrate and explore the positive and negative aspects of group interviews. Inevitably there were individuals who interrupted others or made judgmental comments about what others had said. Drawing on their training in counselling and communication, our interviewers were able to use active listening, open questions, and cognitive reframing skills to address undesirable group interview behaviours and to redirect the discussion. The use of humour was also extremely important, since it allowed the interviewers to challenge 'transgressors' without undue reprimands. These communication attributes were essential components in the research process and enabled us to build and maintain the positive atmosphere necessary for optimal data collection.

Implications for Ethical Research with Adolescent Groups

Several implications for research policy and practice have been identified throughout our research project. These relate to forming relationships, team building and training, the consent process, and confidentiality. Each of these will be discussed below, with suggestions for application to research with focus groups.

Ethical community-based research with youth must acknowledge the critical importance of building relationships. If we believe it is important to put youth at the centre of our research – to not only hear their voices but also recognize their key roles in our communities – we need to value and foster our personal and professional connections with them. Researchers who use their interview skills to obtain meaningful and intimate data and then leave soon after show little concern for the impact of the research interview process on the participants. Researchers can avoid this hit-and-run method by spending a little extra time with youth participants before and after the actual data collection. Choosing arrival and departure times to coincide with natural transition times can facilitate this. Researchers and assistants can volunteer to help school and community partners, provide refreshments, and generally make themselves available to answer questions that participants may be reluctant to raise within the group. Each research interview should also include a debriefing period. These strategies contribute to relationship building and are critical to the success of group research with adolescents.

Time is a key element affecting the ethical conduct of research with youth. Balancing adult researchers' need for sufficient detail while maintaining the interest of sometimes large groups of exuberant or even unruly youth is a major challenge. It takes time to establish respectful and authentic research relationships, although with typically full schedules, the temptation is to move the process along as quickly as possible. In an ideal situation, researchers will have been able to meet or at least observe the youth who will be participating in the groups. Planning time between such initial meetings and the actual data collection gives researchers an opportunity to prepare as fully as possible. Observations, impressions, reactions, potential problems, and procedural adjustments can then be discussed as part of the team's reflective research process; this in turn can strengthen the overall research design.

The consent process is critical to set the tone for how the research will proceed. The wording of consent forms is important, the explanation beforehand even more so. Researchers need to know in advance the reading comprehension levels of the adolescent participants and make sure the consent form or letter is understandable to all. Pilot testing consent forms and interview questions with a variety of youth is one important preliminary step. Also, consultation before data collection and enlisting the aid of adult sponsors can help identify individuals who may need more time to read the consent letter or understand its content.

A variety of factors can influence the confidentiality of participant information. In small communities, agencies, and even smaller adolescent peer groups, researchers must make a concerted effort to protect confidentiality, particularly when working with multiple groups of participants. Investigators should discuss their findings with community partners and service providers in order to identify and address instances that may compromise confidentiality (Socolar, Runyan & Amaya-Jackson, 1995).

Recommendations for a Research Ethics Agenda

Community-based focus group research holds promise for influencing young people's lives in a positive way. However, there are clearly ethics difficulties and challenges that need to be addressed if this approach is to realize its potential. We believe that researchers need guidelines and policies that are specifically tailored to research with groups. Once these have been developed, researchers will need to test out their utility in the lab and in the field. Reflective accounts and descriptions of researchers' experiences will be beneficial in helping extend understandings and practices related to group research ethics.

Our recent experiences highlight some areas for future investigation. First, how can we ethically achieve an authentic focus on and inclusion of youth in our research? How often does a conversation with adolescents end up being an adult-dominated experience? How much do we need to protect them from what we *might* perceive to be potentially harmful situations in research? Acknowledgment of the evolving and developmental nature of most interdisciplinary, community-based, and participatory research paradigms is extremely important. We need to further investigate and identify realistic procedures and measures for meaningful research with adolescent groups.

Second, training for focus group interviewers is absolutely essential. The accelerated pace of adolescent conversation, in concert with their normal developmental boundary testing tendencies, demands a high level of communication skills, knowledge of group dynamics, and experience with group interviewing. Without these skills, researchers run the risk of missing or misinterpreting data that are pertinent to the research objectives or important to the well-being of participants.

Third, more research must be conducted regarding the expectations of group participants when it comes to privacy and confidentiality. We need to systematically follow the process of the real-life risks and benefits involved in the discussion and disclosure of personal and sensitive information. Are we being overprotective of our young people when we try to manage the inevitable risks they often seem to go out of their way to embrace? Are we helping them act responsibly and make mature decisions when we keep limiting the scope of their decisions in an effort to avoid the possibility of harm? If we are overly cautious, we will miss opportunities for understanding and change that could help young people truly achieve the healthy and fulfilling lives we all wish for them.

In light of the continuing popularity of focus group research, it is imperative that we focus some attention on ethical conduct when using this method of collecting data. The need is particularly pressing for investigations involving sensitive topics with vulnerable youth populations, who are already in a relatively powerless situation. In our research we have found that an authentic exploration of youth perspectives requires an approach that promotes the reduction of the power dynamics between researchers and researched. This necessitates meeting youth in community settings, which has the benefit of levelling power differences and increasing access to rich data and natural observations. However, this approach results in less control in data collection and raises the need to closely monitor participation. Focus group research can provide an ethical method for including youth as contributors to knowledge and potential agents of change. We are more likely to reap its benefits when we are ready to acknowledge the difficulties and seek realistic solutions.

NOTE

The research described in this chapter was supported by a grant from the Canadian Institutes for Health Research. The authors would like to acknowledge contributions from Tamara Rozeck-Allen, Alan Churchill, Leah Wilson, Jenny Matthews, Rebecca Hudson Breen, Meghan Atherton, our community partners, and all the youth participants.

REFERENCES

American Counseling Association (1995). *ACA code of ethics.* Alexandria, VA: ACA.

American Counseling Association (1995). *ACA standards of practice.* Alexandria, VA: ACA.

American Psychological Association (2002). *Code of ethics for psychologists.* Alexandria, VA: APA.

British Sociological Association (2002). *Statement of ethical practice for the British Sociological Association.* Durham, UK: BSA.

Canadian Counselling Association (1999). *Code of ethics.* Ottawa: CCA.

Canadian Counselling Association (2001). *Standards of practice for counsellors.* Ottawa: CCA.

Canadian Psychological Association. (2002). *Canadian code of ethics for psychologists.* Ottawa: CPA.

Connell, J.P. (1990). Context, self, and action: A motivational analysis of self-system processes across the life span. In D. Cicchetti (Ed.), *The self in transition: From infancy to childhood* (pp. 61–97). Chicago: University of Chicago Press.

Cottone, R.R., & Tarvydas, V.M. (1998). *Ethical and professional issues in Counseling* (pp. 376–82). Columbus, OH: Merrill.

Field, J. (2000). Researching lifelong learning through focus groups. *Journal of Further and Higher Education*, 24(3), 323–35.

Fisher, C.B., Higgins-D'Alessandro, A., Rau, J.B., Kuther, T.L., & Belanger, S. (1996). Referring and reporting research participants at risk: Views from urban adolescents. *Child Development*, 67, 2086–100.

Fisher, C.B., Hoagwood, K., Boyce, C., Duster, T., Frank, D.A., Grisso, T., Levine, R., Macklin, R., Spencer, M., Takanishi, R., Trimble, J., & Zayas, L. (2002). Research ethics for mental health science involving ethnic minority children and youths. *American Psychologist*, 57(12), 1024–40.

Goodey, C. (1999). Learning disabilities: The researcher's voyage to planet Earth. In S. Hood, B. Mayall, & S. Oliver (eds.), *Critical issues in social research: Power and prejudice*. Philadelphia: Open University Press.

Harter, S. (1999). *The construction of the self: The developmental perspective*. New York: Guilford Press.

Holstein, J.A., & Gubrium, J.F. (Eds.). (2003). *Inside interviewing. New lenses, new concerns*. Thousand Oaks, CA: Sage.

Janis, I.L. (1982). *Groupthink* (2nd ed.). Boston: Houghton Mifflin.

Johnson, D., & Johnson, M. (2002). *Joining together: Group theory and group skills* (8th ed.). Boston: Allyn & Bacon.

Kellner, F. (2002). Yet another coming crisis? Coping with guidelines from the Tri-council. In W.C. van den Hoonaard (ed.), *Walking the tightrope: Ethical issues for qualitative researchers* (pp. 26–33). Toronto: University of Toronto Press.

Kemmis, S., & McTaggart, R. (2000). Participatory action research. In N.K. Denzin & Y.S. Lincoln (eds.), *Handbook of qualitative research* (2nd ed., pp. 567–605). Thousand Oaks, CA: Sage.

Koppelman, N.F., & Bourjolly, J.N. (2001). Conducting focus groups with women with severe psychiatric disabilities: A methodological overview. *Psychiatric Rehabilitation Journal*, 25(2), 142–51.

Krueger, R.A. (1988). *Focus groups: A practical guide for applied research*. Thousand Oaks, CA: Sage.

Lincoln, Y.S. (1998). From understanding to action: New imperatives, new criteria, and new methods for interpretative researchers. *Theory and Research in Social Education*, 26(1), 12–29.

Marshall, A. (2003). Self-described health behaviours among senior high school students. An investigation through the 'Healthy Youth' project. Unpublished manuscript, University of Victoria.

Marshall, A., & Batten, S. (2004). Researching across cultures: Issues of ethics and power. *Forum Qualitative Sozialforschung / Forum: Qualitative Social Research*, 5(3), art. 39. Retrieved 29 September 2004 from www.qualitative-research.net/fqs-texte/3-04/04-3-39-e.htm.

Marshall, A., Shepard, B., Rozeck-Allen, T., & Saffrey, C. (2003). At-risk students' decisions about health: 'Healthy Youth' group interview themes. Unpublished manuscript, University of Victoria.

Morgan, D.L. (1997). *Focus groups as qualitative research*. (2nd ed.). Thousand Oaks, CA: Sage.

Munall, P. (1988). Ethical considerations in qualitative research. *Western Journal of Nursing Research*, 10, 150–62.

Nespor, J. (2000). Anonymity and place in qualitative inquiry. *Qualitative Inquiry*, 6(4), 546–69.

Pugsley, L. (2002). Putting your oar in: Moulding, muddling or meddling? In T.Welland and L. Pugsley (Eds.), *Ethical dilemmas in qualitative research* (pp. 19–31). Aldershot, UK: Ashgate.

Ramcharam, P., & Cutcliffe, J.R. (2001). Judging the ethics of qualitative research: Considering the 'ethics as process' model. *Health and Social Care in the Community*, 9(6), 358–66.

Serrano-Garcia, I. (1994). The ethics of the powerful and the power of ethics. *American Journal of Community Psychology*, 22, 1–20.

Sieber, J.E. (2001). Privacy and confidentiality: As related to human research in social and behavioral science. Retrieved 15 August 2005 from www .georgetown.edu/research/nrcbl/nbac/pubs.html.

Smith, M. (1995). Ethics in focus groups: A few concerns. *Qualitative Health Research*, 5(4), 478–86.

Socolar, R.S., Runyan, D.K., & Amaya-Jackson, L. (1995). Methodological and ethical issues related to studying child maltreatment. *Journal of Family Issues*, 16(5), 565–86.

Tri-council policy statement on ethical conduct for research involving humans. (2003). Retrieved 16 August 2004 from www.pre.ethics.gc.ca/english/policystatement/policystatement.cfm.

Van den Hoonaard, W.C. (2002). Some concluding thoughts. In W.C. van den Hoonaard (Ed.), *Walking the tightrope: Ethical issues for qualitative researchers* (pp. 175–87). Toronto: University of Toronto Press.

Wallwork, E. (2002). Ethical analysis of group and community rights: Case study review of the 'Collaborative Initiative for Research Ethics in Environmental Health.' Retrieved 18 August from www.researchethcs.org/uploads/word/ethicalAnalysis3.doc.

Weijer, C. (2001). The ethical analysis of risks and potential benefits in human subjects research: History, theory, and implications for U.S. regulation. Retrieved 15 August 2004 from www.georgetown.edu/research/nrcbl/nbac/pubs.html.

Welland, T., & Pugsley, L. (Eds.). (2002). *Ethical dilemmas in qualitative research.* Aldershot, UK: Ashgate.

White, P. (2002). They told me I couldn't do that: Ethical issues of intervention in careers education and guidance research. In T. Welland and L. Pugsley (Eds.), *Ethical dilemmas in qualitative research* (pp. 32–41). Aldershot, UK: Ashgate.

9 Walking a Fine Line: Negotiating Dual Roles in a Study with Adolescent Girls

ELIZABETH BANISTER AND KIM DALY

Ethical issues can emerge at every stage of community-based research and intervention and can present significant challenges. Community-based research is often designed to contribute not only to science or knowledge but also to the participants and their community. Researchers must choose their methods with sensitivity, according to the culture, needs, and perspectives of the participant population. The community-based researcher also needs to take into account the participants' and gatekeepers' assessments of the risks and potential benefits of research, and furthermore, must take the lead in apprising all involved and the community of these issues (Sieber, 2000).

Researchers using qualitative research methodologies may face additional challenges. Qualitative approaches, with their methodological features of (for example) small sample size and a close researcher–participant relationship, can compromise participants' confidentiality and privacy. Moreover, ethics and methodological features are 'inextricably related' (Sieber & Sorensen, 1992, 46). Attention to the protection of confidentiality facilitates the gathering of high-quality data. When participants believe that researchers and other participants are working to protect their confidentiality, they can develop trust in the research environment. Under such conditions participants are more likely to provide researchers with rich, contextualized descriptions of their social worlds.

In the following sections we consider two ethical issues that arose while we were managing a qualitative study that examined healthy dating relationships of adolescent girls in a community-based context. First, we faced dual roles as research–practitioners, and second, we needed to protect the confidentiality of participants in a focus group setting in which personal concerns about dating relationships would be discussed. To illustrate the intricacies of these issues and the ways we discovered and addressed them, we draw extensively on our fieldwork experiences. We end with a discussion of the implications with regard to conducting community-based research with adolescents. First, however, we provide a brief overview of the study.

Need for and Description of the Project

Research has shown that the health status of adolescent girls has not improved in recent years (Azzarato, 1997; King, Boyce & King, 1999). The major causes of morbidity are related to health-risk behaviours such as unprotected sexual activity and substance use (McCreary Centre Society, 1999). These health-compromising behaviours often occur in the context of dating relationships. Accordingly, we designed our study to explore adolescent girls' perceptions of their health within their intimate relationships (Phase I) and to prepare for the development of a mentoring program to enhance healthy relationships (Phase II). The study involved a partnership between the University of Victoria's CAHR research team and four community partners. We collected and analysed ethnographic data between September 2001 and May 2002.

We recruited forty adolescent girls, ages fifteen to sixteen, through three local secondary schools (including one designated as an alternative school for youth facing social, emotional, and/or educational challenges); a youth health clinic; and a rural First Nations secondary school. We accessed participants through site contacts, who included school counsellors, teachers, and a clinic nurse. To be included in the study, girls had to have been in a dating relationship for at least one month and had to be willing to participate in focus groups. We had little difficulty accessing volunteers for the study. Both staff and the girls placed a high level of importance on dating relationship concerns. Staff agreed that the study could offer value for the girls. A high school counsellor speaks to this in the following interview excerpt:

We're so short of resources in schools now that any kind of professional organization that comes in that's doing work with our students that I think is valued – I'm always supportive of those sorts of things. I used to run groups but it's something I can't even get to now. It's really missed in schools. Our ratio is three counsellors to fifteen hundred students, so we can't get to this kind of work – to pick up issues.

During Phase I of the study, we conducted four focus group conversations, each at five sites lasting about one hour. Each group comprised around eight girls and was facilitated by one of five female graduate students. Each group also had an adult female mentor whose presence was intended to offer positive role modelling and support. Staff at three sites recruited three mentors, and members of the research team knew two. We tape-recorded the group sessions and transcribed them for analysis (see Banister, Jakubec & Stein, 2003). During Phase II we adapted a mentoring program that had focused on education, skill building, and social action (Wolfe, Wekerle & Scott, 1997) to help participants identify and end relationship violence. We delivered the program weekly over a sixteen–week period, in ninety-minute group sessions. Elsewhere we have described strategies we used to educate participants about dating health issues (Banister & Begoray, 2004). About twelve weeks into Phase II, the girls reported their perceptions of the interviews in individual interviews. After the end of Phase II, also in individual interviews, the gatekeepers and mentors gave their impressions of the part of the study that had taken place at their respective sites.

Key Ethical Issues That Emerged

In qualitative research, ethical decisions can emerge throughout the research process, from conceptualizing the problem, to gathering and analysing data, to writing the final report (Edwards & Mauthner, 2002). Researchers must attempt to maximize the benefits of any research for science, society, and the participants while respecting those who participate in the study as well as the culture in which the research takes place (Sieber, 2000). These principles are implemented through valid research designs, competent researchers, risk/benefit assessments, and voluntary informed consent (Sieber & Sorensen, 1992). In our study we needed to consider these principles as we balanced decisions about the ethical implications of our use of research-practitioner relationships, with our need to protect the confidentiality of participants.

The benefits of research to participants should outweigh the risks (Canadian Psychological Association, 2000). In conducting a risk/benefit assessment of our research, our aim was to respect the youth who participated, with the full realization that all those involved in the study, whatever their capacity, would be sharing in the process of knowledge creation. We also attempted to take into account that research processes are imbued with power relations; this is especially so with adult–youth relationships, where youth occupy the more vulnerable position (Leyshon, 2002; Nespor, 1998). This relationship is inherently unequal, even when attempts are made to share power, such as through participatory research methods.

For research-practitioners, ethical dilemmas can also accompany divided loyalties between research and professional employment (Bell & Nutt, 2002, 70). Research-practitioners function in two professional roles vis-à-vis the participants. For example, in this study, Ms Daly, the second author, served as a research assistant and also as a nurse and counsellor at one of the study sites (a local youth health clinic). As research assistant, she was responsible for facilitating the focus group and for delivering interventions. Under such conditions, close relationships involving mutual trust will inevitably develop between participants and the researcher; these are necessary for gathering high-quality data. However, when the duties of the two roles conflict or when boundaries become blurred, the risk that privacy or confidentiality could be breached increases (Ensign, 2002).

When we made the decision that Ms Daly would take on both roles, we were bound ethically to consider the risks and benefits carefully. We believed that we would be able to minimize risks sufficiently and that including her in the study would allow us to build on the expertise she brought to both her roles. Furthermore, her 'insider' position with the youth culture and clinic staff provided access to high-risk participants and an understanding of the clinic context that could facilitate program implementation.

To understand one of the potential problems, one must consider the nature of the nurse–patient relationship and the nature of the researcher–participant relationship (Edwards & Chalmers, 2002). The nurse's primary loyalty is to those who are under her care, and her primary interest is in their well-being (ibid.). The researcher's primary loyalty is to the research, and primary interest is in obtaining valid knowledge that can contribute to best practices. The 'self-regulation' that is required of the research-practitioner calls on that person to balance these roles when carrying out the research (Bell & Nutt, 2002).

Research-practitioner roles carry clear ethics implications. For example, they directly affect what is meant by informed consent. Participants needed to understand fully the risks and benefits of participating in the research (Canadian Psychological Association, 2000). It we are to obtain rich and thickly contextualized descriptions from participants, we must ensure that they are comfortable sharing this personal information. In our situation, obtaining focus group data from participants who also were clients at the clinic raised potential issues about confidentiality. For example, participants shared information about their mental health and family situations that affected their dating relationships, and some had outside relationships with other participants in the group. As a research-practitioner, Ms Daly also had to ensure she did not inadvertently reveal, in the focus group, information that participants had shared with her in confidence within the clinic setting. In one example, a participant in the clinic setting revealed to Ms Daly information about alleged sexual infidelities implicating one of the focus group participants. Revealing this confidence in the group setting would clearly breach the trust of all involved and would threaten the credibility of the study.

Participants in the focus groups often requested health information. Adults working with youth place an emphasis on confidentiality and the protection of privacy. However, the girls in the study appeared to have little concern about sharing highly personal information in the focus group setting. For example, some participants freely admitted that they had had unprotected sex and that they were afraid of being pregnant. They announced their intention to get pregnancy testing right after the group was over. As another example, some girls freely discussed the unhealthy relationships they were engaged in, and talked about people who had stalked them or the physical and emotional abuse they had experienced. Ms Daly knew that the girls perceived the environment as safe and as sympathetic to their experiences, but she attempted to limit such disclosures. In these situations, she chose not to use counselling skills such as empathy, which might have encouraged them to disclose more than they wished (Bell & Nutt, 2002).

It became increasingly apparent that the girls likely had little experience in making decisions about what is safe to talk about in a focus group context. Petersen and Leffert (1995) contend that even though adolescents at this stage of development are capable of making decisions as adults, unfamiliar situations could 'tax their decision making ability' (1995, p. 299). In this view, Brody and Waldron (2000) note that youth may have difficulty understanding research concepts and suggest that they need to be reminded of the difference between the research goals and therapeutic ones. In research interviews that they experience as therapeutic or as places to share their stories and have someone listen, participants may mistakenly assume that the researcher is a therapist or friend (Moyle, 2002; Ortiz, 2001). So the research-practitioner must have good facilitation skills and must set clear bound-aries to prevent a focus group from shifting into more therapeutic interactions. Regardless of the counselling qualifications of the researcher, therapy is not a goal of qualitative research. The principle of 'respect for free and informed consent' can be violated if the participant misunder-stands the researcher's role (Banister, 2002).

In our experience, while the girls were aware that 'research' was the primary reason for the groups' existence, this not their primary motiva-tion for attending meetings. For them, the groups provided a regular and safe haven that met their strong need to discuss issues that were arising in their peer and family relationships. We were aware of differ-ences between their agenda and our own, so we were able to discuss these with the girls and to respond to *their* views of the benefits of participation.

We did not regard it as problematic that the girls might be motivated to participate in the group for reasons different from our own for conducting the research. Nevertheless, Miller and Bell (2002) encourage us to consider the degree to which participants are indeed 'informed' when they consent to participate in a study. When we assume that adolescents' consent to participate is fully 'voluntary,' we risk ignoring the complex power dynamics and values that can effect consent (ibid.). To counteract any misconceptions the prospective participants might have of our research, we informed them as clearly as possible about the nature of our research and about what we would expect of them as participants. We also told them about the referral procedures we had built into the research process to ensure their safety if unforeseen difficul-ties were to arise. One entire group session was devoted to setting group rules and discussing issues of informed consent and confidentiality.

We were also aware that the dynamic nature of social research im-plies that the research that participants were consenting to participate in could change over time (ibid.). We reviewed the confidentiality and anonymity issues on an ongoing basis for three reasons: to provide a means for addressing issues of confidentiality as they arose; to include the participants as much as possible in the design of the research; and to stress the importance of maintaining confidentiality, in the interests of participant comfort and safety as well as collection of rich and valid data.

With these considerations in mind, at the initial meeting Ms Daly began by asking the participants for their interpretations of the terms outlined in the consent forms. Once it seemed that each girl understood the meaning and legal limitations of confidentiality, she initiated a discussion to develop group guidelines and assign those guidelines a name, such as 'ways to be with each other':

Ms Daly: How about confidentiality? What agreements do we have with that?
Participant 1: Keep it in this room, or in this building.
Ms Daly: Are there any ways that you girls figure we could set up an agreement about what thing should happen so that we at least have some agreement to that?
Participant 3: Well, what are you supposed to do after people know outside of this room what you said? What are you going to do after that?
Participant 4: Yeah, you took that risk by saying stuff, so ...
Participant 2: I think they should leave.
Participant 1: Yeah, I don't think they should come back.
Participant 5: Because there's always another chance that they could go back out and talk.
Ms Daly: Okay, say somebody blabs, and you girls say they should be kicked out. How is that decision going to be made?

The conversation reveals the girls' limited appreciation of, or experience with, the subtleties required in effective conflict resolution and ethical reasoning. The suggestion that the offending person should just leave the group was not carefully considered with regard to the process by which it would be conducted or the long-term consequences to the group or individuals involved. The fact that an adult would develop a complex plan for problem solving in such a situation, in contrast with the adolescent participants' more concrete solutions, illustrates – as noted above – the differences in culture, experiences, and decision-making capacity between the adolescents and adults. However, in terms of power dynamics, the exercise fostered in the girls a sense of having more 'control' over the group interaction. This in itself conveyed the researchers' respect for their input.

Despite the differences in emphasis on group rules between the adult researcher assistant and the adolescent participants, the conversation also illustrates the importance of the position held by both groups – that personal information divulged in the group needed to be kept confidential. But this task was problematic from the start. To establish clarity, group 'rules' were created through consensus by all members present in the early sessions, and a written 'working' document was provided to everyone. These rules addressed expectations for behaviour and attendance in the group, and outlined processes for managing both conflict and breaches of confidentiality.

The girls disliked the process and did not readily appreciate the issues involved. Ms Daly presented them with specific problems and used the formality of signing to prompt them to participate actively in establishing the guidelines. For example, she asked: 'What would you do if two people in the group were having a fight? How would we like to manage that?' This process of developing guidelines was uncomfortable for all involved, given that the need for written group rules was a priority only for Ms Daly with her adult concerns about ethics and group processes, and not for the participants.

The above examples point to the challenges researchers face as they weigh the risks of research against its benefits for participants (Canadian Psychological Association, 2000). This task was further complicated in our case by our need for Ms Daly to fulfil the role of research-practitioner. We needed to be cognizant not only of participants' needs but also of the need to maintain professional behaviour. As representative of the clinic, Ms Daly was responsible not only for meeting the participants' needs for protection and care, but also for upholding the community standards for practice (Bell & Nutt, 2002). We also had to acknowledge – and help our participants understand – that in qualitative research, confidentiality can be difficult to ensure. Some researchers assert, quite correctly, that 'watertight confidentiality has proven to be impossible' (Christians, 2000, p. 139). Even though we spent considerable time stressing the importance of maintaining confidentiality within the group, we did not have control over whatever information participants disclosed outside the group (Krueger, 1994).

Emergent Ethical Concerns

Researchers must 'manage' any predictable ethical issues during the planning stages, before the actual research even starts, by assessing the likely occurrence of both harmful and beneficial outcomes of various aspects of the research and by making decisions accordingly (Corbin & Morse, 2003). But in community-based research, not all concerns will be apparent until the research is underway, and ongoing processes for revealing and dealing with these are needed. Under such circumstances, admitting to an incapacity to 'manage' issues may be the most ethical move the researcher can make. Researchers need to develop strategies for addressing ethical issues as they emerge. To ensure the integrity of the research, they also need to be flexible in their research approach and seek practical solutions when problems arise (Allen, 2002). In this section we discuss our management of the ethical issues noted above.

Our first consideration of ethical issues occurred during the initial planning stages of the research. We were careful to establish open communication with each prospective participant about the purpose of the research and the nature of the researcher–participant relationship. We discussed with participants, for example, the possibility that they might feel uncomfortable seeing Ms Daly in both of her roles – as researcher and nurse – and that it might be appropriate to share information in one context but inappropriate to share the same information in the other context. We explained that Ms Daly would keep confidential information private, but that if the participant would prefer to meet with her in only one of her roles, that decision would not affect the care the participant received. We articulated this in conversations about informed consent for group participation. Within this context the researcher could learn of the participant's concerns, explain measures in place to protect confidentiality, and help her make an appropriate decision about whether to consent to participate. The emergent nature of qualitative research may generate inherently unpredictable ethical dilemmas as it progresses (Bell & Nutt, 2002), and we hoped that these concerns could be revisited throughout the data collection phase.

In planning Phase I of this research, we decided that to work effectively with the participants, we would need to include them in the process of developing guidelines for group functioning. This would help ensure 'buy in' regarding the guidelines; furthermore, it would help develop group trust and rapport and create a means for auditing any ethical concerns as they emerged through the course of the group sessions. Given the participants' minimal interest in this process, however, the facilitator's original plans for holding regular discussions about these guidelines seemed counterproductive. We decided to drop this activity from the research plan. We considered this decision with care, to assure ourselves that it would meet our own criteria for maintaining the integrity of the research. We were aware of the participants' more pressing needs to discuss their shared health-related concerns. By allowing participants to explore their own agendas, we hoped to increase the benefits they gained from the focus groups. This illustrates how much improvisation and flexibility are needed in research design, as well as the need for regular reflection on ethical considerations (Miller & Bell, 2002). We treated the girls' agenda as an opportunity to foster group cohesion and as something that would help them achieve some control over the research. This renegotiation of the research agenda also helped equalize power within the group, which in turn contributed to the participants' sense of safety.

To address the risk that in posing questions about personal issues, the girls might inadvertently share information about their personal lives that could compromise their wish for confidentiality, we framed our responses in a general way, as useful to all participants. For example, when we received requests for information about pregnancy testing or the emergency contraceptive pill, we presented the information as if it were required by all young women. Given the high level of participation during these teaching moments, it was clear that all of the girls were interested in accessing the same information concerning their sexual health. The strategy of framing individual questions as general group concerns promoted respect for the girls' boundaries. If sensitive personal topics arose in the course of these group health discussions, we tried to ensure confidentiality by directly asking participants if they preferred to withhold personal information or to arrange a private consultation with the facilitator.

A more demanding ethical decision-making task for the facilitator involved moment-to-moment negotiations of levels of personal relationship with client-participants. The facilitator had to be vigilant to notice when either she or the participants was sharing personal information in the group. For example, Ms Daly would often choose to reveal aspects of her personal experience, as was necessary to establish and maintain an appropriately personal relationship. However, she was careful to avoid material that was highly reactive for her. This might include admitting to a personal struggle in a relationship with a particular family member, while declining to provide a detailed account of the particular issues involved. In this way, the focus could appropriately remain on the research and on the girls' experiences. Decision-making by the researcher about the content and amount of information to reveal required both research and clinical experience and a high level of skill in working with this population. Furthermore, it brings to the forefront that 'all researchers have to be self-regulating in their standards of ethical behaviour' (Bell & Nutt, 2002, p. 81).

The facilitator had to be aware of the ethical difficulties that could arise if she shifted to doing therapy in the research setting, since using therapeutic approaches could encourage participants to reveal more than they wished (Bell & Nutt, 2002). Even though researchers are motivated by benevolent regard for the participants, 'research is not therapy' (King & Churchill, 2000, p. 714). In practical terms, this means that the researcher should recognize 'decision points' in the conversations and remain focused on 'problem-solving' instead of moving into therapeutic intervention, such as emotional and body-centred work that could encourage painful disclosures. The girls viewed the group experience as therapeutic; even so, the researcher maintained a focus on searching for common themes among their experiences. With proper management, we all benefited from including an experienced practitioner as a member of our research team.

Implications for Conducting Community-Based Research with Adolescents

In any research, role conflicts and the protection of confidential information are ethical concerns. Role conflicts can be a component of community-based research, which by definition is embedded in a community and invites members of that community to contribute to the research process. Given that qualitative, community-based research can generate unforeseen situations, standard research guidelines may not adequately address the ethical questions raised by this research. In this section we highlight some implications for community-based research with adolescents.

First, researchers 'need to encourage ethical research and to maintain the necessary vigilance to safeguard the rights and welfare of the subjects' (Levine, 1995, p. 29). We have found that the potential for harm inherent in research-practitioner relationships and risk of breach of confidentiality can be reduced or eliminated if handled properly through diligent planning, commitment to the spirit of ethical practice, and highly skilled management of group dynamics, communication, and negotiation. In particular, when assessing the risks and benefits of their research, community-based researchers need to consider that the community's definitions of risk and benefit may differ from those of the researcher. This requires ongoing collaborative and creative decision-making that acknowledges the intricacies of each ethically sensitive situation. It also requires researchers to regularly reflect on such intricacies so that methodological and ethical considerations are continually reassessed (Banister, 2002; Miller & Bell, 2002).

Second, there are a number of benefits to involving a practitioner as an active member of a community-based research team. In our study the research-practitioner role provided access to the culture of the adolescent participants (Bonner & Tolhurst, 2002) and directed the focus groups towards productive discussion of health issues. We did not anticipate the extent of the benefits of this to both the participants and the research. We were able to break down barriers to accessing care – barriers that are quite considerable in the adolescent population. An adolescent girl who experiences one successful encounter with the health care system may develop increased confidence in the system, as well as an understanding of what is expected of her as a patient, and thus become more comfortable in seeking care in other settings. The girls who participated in the research group had the experience of a positive interaction with a health care worker – who happened to also be a researcher.

Another benefit of the research-practitioner's role in the research was that it increased opportunities to offer the participants information about relationships and sexual health. This information-sharing aspect of the research had not been anticipated, and led the researcher into unexpected territories. It also had proactive benefits relating to the practitioner's work. Furthermore, it furthered group cohesion: participants felt comfortable asking questions in the supportive presence of their peers. Possibly, this contributed to the validity of the study by providing an environment in which the girls could set the agenda and voice their health concerns.

During the study, all the participants availed themselves of the opportunity for individual sessions with the practitioner. This met the young women's needs for reliable information about their health problems in their dating relationships; it also provided us with another source of information for our research. In this instance, the frequency of 'pregnancy scares' and the girls' high levels of anxiety became apparent. This speaks to another ethical advantage: the nurse and researcher were able to provide referrals to other professionals at the clinic site when a participant needed support beyond the group context.

Third, research-practitioners need to coordinate their double roles with great care, to reduce risks to the participants and to the research process. In our study, the research-practitioner accomplished this coordination by applying her knowledge of ethical principles and her skills and experience as a researcher and health care professional to her task of facilitating the focus group. She also engaged in professional consultations as she deemed necessary, in accordance with, for example, her professional ethical guidelines. To the extent that the researcher is alone with the participants, he or she is solely responsible for protecting their rights (Corbin & Morse, 2003). A person in such a position of power must possess impeccable integrity for the sake not only of the participants but also of the research. In this case, the research-practitioner was also a research assistant in the study, so she depended on the principal investigator – who was also her research supervisor – to possess the integrity to support her, particularly as she faced the challenges generated by the interaction between her two roles (Banister, 2002). In this way, the research-practitioner was able to raise her concerns about potential ethical compromises during supervision. Regular check-ins with the principal investigator were established, and regular collection dates for field notes provided structure for the processes of reflection as well as a way to engage in ongoing reassessment of ethical and methodological considerations related to the research.

Fourth, ethical concerns can inform the use of qualitative methodology in community-based research. In our study, the use of a research-practitioner model provided benefits such as sustained engagement between researcher and participant, flexible research design, and psychological closeness of the researcher to the participants. We addressed ethical issues appropriately as they arose, according to the particular needs of the situation (Christensen & Prout, 2002).

The subjective nature of qualitative research and role of researchers as research instruments obligate researchers to reflect constantly on their subjective responses, on intersubjective dynamics, and on the research process itself (Banister, 2002; Findlay, 2002). This reflexive work is propelled by researchers' acknowledgment and exploration of the ambiguous and ambivalent reactions experienced during fieldwork (Findlay, 2002; Janesick, 2000). Researchers' ongoing reflexive processes while engaged in fieldwork can help them understand and solve the ethical difficulties that emerge.

Our research on adolescent girls' health behaviour provided a means to illuminate and address the intricacies of ethical research design and decision-making in the context of a qualitative, community-based study. By its nature, the study required us to walk a fine line. We came to understand that the ethical tensions involving research-practitioner and participant relationships are not absolute and that the effective management of such relationships can foster unique benefits to both the research and the participants and their communities. As we continue to address and solve our ethical challenges, we expect to discover new intricacies in ethical practice that can inform our ethical principles and guidelines.

Concluding Comments

Whether engaging a research-practitioner in community-based research with adolescent girls meet ethics standards is a complex issue. We found that in our research, the protection of participants in a focus group context translated into having a research-practitioner/facilitator with a high skill level in facilitation and a strong code of professional ethics. With skill and ethics, research-practitioners can offer adolescent participants a window of opportunity to share their health concerns, contributing to greater understanding of their worlds.

REFERENCES

Allen, D. (2002). Research involving vulnerable young people: A discussion of ethical and methodological concerns. *Drugs: Education, Prevention and Policy*, 9(3).

Azzarto, J. (1997). A young women's support group: Prevention of a different kind. *Health & Social Work*, 22(4), 299–304.

Banister, E. (2002). Considerations for research ethics boards in evaluating qualitative studies: Lessons from the field with adolescent females. *Annals of the Royal College of Physicians and Surgeons of Canada*, 35(8), supplement, 567–70.

Banister, E.M., & Begoray, D.L. (2004). Beyond talking groups: Strategies for improving adolescent health education. *Health Care for Women International*, 25(5), 481–8.

Banister, E., Jakubec, S., & Stein, J. (2003). 'Like, what am I supposed to do?' Power, politics and public health concerns in adolescent women's dating relationships. *Canadian Journal of Nursing Research*, 35(2), 16–33.

Bell, L., & Nutt, L. (2002). Divided loyalties, divided expectations: Research ethics, professional and occupational responsibilities. In M. Mauthner, M. Birch, J. Jessop & T. Miller (Eds.), *Ethics in qualitative research* (pp. 70–90). Thousand Oaks, CA: Sage.

Bonner, A., & Tolhurst, G. (2002). Insider-outsider perspectives of participant observation. *Nurse Researcher*, 9(4), 7–19.

Brody, J.L., & Waldron, H.B. (2000). Ethical issues in research on the treatment of adolescent substance abuse disorders. *Addictive Behaviours*, 25(2), 217–28.

Canadian Psychological Association (2000). *Canadian code of ethics for psychologists* (3rd ed.). Ottawa: Canadian Psychological Association.

Christensen, P., & Prout, A. (2002). Working with ethical symmetry in social research with children. *Childhood*, 9(4), 477–97.

Christians, C.G. (2000). Ethics and politics in qualitative research. In N.K. Denzin & Y.S. Lincoln (Eds.), *Handbook of qualitative research* (2nd ed., pp. 133–55). Thousand Oaks, CA: Sage.

Corbin, J., & Morse, J.A. (2003). The unstructured interactive interview: Issues of reciprocity and risks when dealing with sensitive topics. *Qualitative Inquiry*, 9(3), 335–54.

Edwards, M., & Chalmers, K. (2002). Double agency in clinical research. *Canadian Journal of Nursing Research*, 34(10), 131–42.

Edwards, R., & Mauthner, M. (2002). Ethics and feminist research: Theory and practice. In M. Mauthner, M. Birch, J. Jessop & T. Miller (Eds.), *Ethics in qualitative research* (pp. 14–31). Thousand Oaks, CA: Sage.

Ensign, J. (2002). Ethical issues in qualitative health research with homeless youths. *Journal of Advanced Nursing*, 43(1), 43–50.

Findlay, L. (2002). 'Outing' the researcher: The provenance, process, and practice of reflexivity. *Qualitative Health Research*, 12(4), 531–45.

Janesick, V.J. (2000). The choreography of qualitative research design. In N.K. Denzin & Y.S. Lincoln (Eds.), *Handbook of qualitative research* (2nd ed.) (pp. 379–99). Thousand Oaks, CA: Sage.

King, A.J.C., Boyce, W.F., & King, M.A. (1999). *Trends in the health of Canadian youth*. Ottawa: Health Canada.

King, N.M., & Churchill, L.R. (2000). Ethical principles guiding research on child and adolescent subjects. *Journal of Interpersonal Violence*, 15(7), 710–24.

Krueger, R.A. (1994). *Focus groups: A practical guide for applied research* (2nd ed.). Thousand Oaks, CA: Sage.

Levine, R.J. (1995). Adolescents are research subjects without permission of their parents or guardians: Ethical considerations. *Journal of Adolescent Health*, 17, 287–97.

Leyshon, M. (2002). On being 'in the field': Practice, progress and problems in research with young people in rural areas. *Journal of Rural Studies*, 18, 179–91.

McCreary Centre Society (1999). *Healthy connections: Listening to BC youth*. Burnaby, BC: McCreary Centre Society.

Miller, T., & Bell, L. (2002). Consenting to what? Issues of access, gate keeping and 'informed' consent. In M. Mauthner, M. Birch, J. Jessop & T. Miller (eds.), *Ethics in qualitative research* (pp. 53–69). Thousand Oaks, CA: Sage.

Moyle, W. (2002). Unstructured interviews: Challenges when participants have a major depressive illness. *Journal of Advanced Nursing*, 39(2), 266–73.

Nespor, J. (1998). The meaning of research: Kids as subjects and kids as inquirers. *Qualitative Inquiry*, 4(3), 369–88.

Ortiz, S.M. (2001). How interviewing became therapy for wives of professional athletes: Learning from a serendipitous experience. *Qualitative Inquiry*, 7(2), 192–220.

Petersen, A.C., & Leffert, N. (1995). Developmental issues influencing guidelines for adolescent health research. *Journal of Adolescent Health*, 17(5), 286–96.

Sieber, J.E. (2000). Planning research: Basic ethical decision-making. In B.D. Sales & S. Folkman (Eds.), *Ethics in research with human participants* (pp. 13–26). Washington, DC: American Psychological Association.

Sieber, J.E., & Sorensen, J.L. (1992). Ethical issues in community-based research and intervention. In F.B. Bryant, J. Edwards, R.S. Tindale, E.J. Posavac, L. Heath, E. Henderson & Y. Suarez-Balcazar (Eds.), *Methodological Issues in Applied Social Psychology* (pp. 43–63). New York: Plenum Press.

Wolfe, D.A., Wekerle, C., & Scott, K. (1997). *Alternative to violence: Empowering youth to develop healthy relationships*. Thousand Oaks, CA: Sage.

PART FIVE

Child Protection Issues in Research with Vulnerable Children and Youth

10 Respect and Protect? Conducting Community–Academic Research with Street-Involved Youth

MIKAEL JANSSON AND CECILIA BENOIT

This chapter discusses two difficult ethical challenges we faced in conducting a community–academic research collaboration: 'Risky Business? Experiences of Youth Involved in the Sex Trade.' This University of Victoria CAHR project followed a sample of street-involved youth over time, examining their risk behaviours (including incidental or entrenched involvement in trading sex) and the impact of those behaviours on their health and well-being.

Methodologically, it is difficult to reach these youth because they are marginalized both socially and economically and because much of their behaviour – including interactions with the drug or sex trades – is highly stigmatized. Street-involved youth also have, on average, a low level of attachment to their parents or guardians, to the educational system, and to the formal labour market.

Individuals involved in selling sexual services belong to what academics differently call sensitive (Lee, 1993), underresearched (Berg, 1999; Standing, 1998), and hard-to-reach or hidden populations (Sudman and Kalton, 1986; Watters and Biernacki, 1989; Spreen and Zwaagstra, 1994). These populations share three main characteristics: (1) there are no lists of the members of the group, the size of the membership is unknown, and the group boundary is difficult to define and verify; (2) acknowledging that you belong to the group is threatening because membership is stigmatized and can evoke being the object of hate or scorn, as well as fears of prosecution; (3) members are distrustful of non-members, do whatever they can to avoid revealing their identities, and are likely either to refuse to cooperate with outsiders or to give unreliable answers to questions about themselves and their networks (Hagan and McCarthy, 1997; Heckathorn, 1997). For instance, intravenous drug users and males who have sex with other males share hidden population characteristics, and members of both groups are doubly stigmatized if they also trade sex for money. In the case of our own research participants – street-involved youth – multiple stigmas are likely to be present, due not only to sex trade activity but also to poverty, homelessness, illicit drug use, and sometimes homosexuality and involvement in an assortment of illegal activities.

A number of ethical hurdles confronted us in this research project. We focus on two of the dilemmas we faced. First, how were we to balance mandatory reporting of designated individuals to the provincial authorities while obtaining informed consent, with overcoming sample bias? And second, how were we to maximize youth participants' anonymity and confidentiality while following them in the multiyear panel study? We begin this chapter with an overview of our research project and then outline the main features of our longitudinal research design and the chosen methodology. This will be followed by a description of the major ethical dilemmas and our tentative solutions for resolving them. The paper discusses these ethical challenges as they relate to the academic literature on youth health and injury prevention, and then concludes with some suggestions for future research on the ethics of research with hard-to-reach, marginalized youth populations that are involved in risky behaviours that threaten their health and well-being.

Overview of the 'Risky Business?' Research Project

'Risky Business?' is part of a broader research initiative titled 'Healthy Youth in a Health Society,' a community alliance for the prevention of injury in children and youth. The 'Risky Business?' subproject aims to contribute knowledge about the concerns of marginalized youth at risk for involvement in, or already involved in, trading sex. The project built on a prior community–academic collaboration project, 'Dispelling Myths and Understanding Realities,' which focused on adult sex workers in the Capital Metropolitan Area of British Columbia (Benoit & Millar, 2001). Cecilia Benoit conducted the study in collaboration with the Prostitutes Empowerment, Education and Resource Society (PEERS). It involved interviews with 201 female and male sex workers about their working conditions and health and safety. This methodologically challenging project helped set the stage for the 'Risky Business?' project, which focused specifically on street-involved youth (Benoit, Jansson, Millar & Phillips, 2005).

Prior to initiating 'Risky Business?' we contacted with a number of provincial government agencies and other affiliated community organizations that serve youth in the metropolitan area. We diversified our community research partnerships and at the same time continued to work closely with PEERS. We also aligned our research goals to reflect the circumstances of local street-involved youth. Our goal was to develop a methodology that was academically sound but also practical for the research site, and to devise innovative strategies to recruit potential youth participants, who are normally wary of academics.

Four community partners participated: PEERS, the Victoria Youth Empowerment Society (VYES), the Victoria Native Friendship Centre (VNFC), and the Greater Victoria Child and Family Counselling Association (CAFCA). All have long histories of involvement with vulnerable youth, including those who sell sex services for money, drugs, a place to stay, or other compensation. The study offered an opportunity for community partners to learn more about the root causes of the problems of their respective youth client populations, and to discover innovative ways to improve outreach services to reduce youth injury and promote their health and well-being. An advisory committee that included representatives from these four community partners facilitated connections with marginalized youth. Many youth had been or were currently connected with the Ministry of Children and Family Development (MCFD), the agency responsible for child protection services in British Columbia. The overall research design and research instrument were also developed through biweekly meetings of the advisory group.

Research Rationale

Research literature and crime statistics suggest that sex trade involvement among youth leads to increased accidents, injury, and death (Badgley, 1984). This body of research maintains, in particular, that young female sex workers face inordinate risks for injury and death as a consequence of their work and their exposure to drugs and violence (Federal/Provincial/Territorial Working Group on Prostitution, 1998). The data show that between 1991 and 1995, 7 of the 63 known sex workers who were murdered in Canada were youth between fifteen and seventeen (Canadian Centre for Justice Statistics, 1997). The seven youth were all female; in fact, 60 of 63 murdered were female.

Other research indicates, however, there are large differences within the sex trade community in the levels of risk behaviour of engaged youth and that a singular focus on the sexual exploitation of youth shifts the focus from other fundamental problems faced by these young people, including social and economic marginalization (Brock, 1998). Homelessness, for example, is strongly associated with high-risk sex trade behaviour among youth (Hagan and McCarthy, 1997). Studies also point to heterogeneity within the sex trade in most Canadian cities, with adult sex workers varying widely in socio-economic background (Shaver, 1993). Benoit and Miller (2001), using interviews with 201 adult sex workers located both on and off the street, showed that sex workers' health and well-being varied significantly with their social and economic situation, early family dynamics, history of abuse and neglect, age of entry into the sex trade, situations faced while involved in the industry, risk behaviours, and general health status.

The goal of the 'Risky Business?' project was to learn what motivated youth to enter the sex trade, their length of involvement in high-risk sex trade behaviour, and the trade's effects on their health and well-being. Despite evidence that a significant number of street-involved male youth are active in the sex trade locally (Sexually Exploited Youth Committee, 1997), little research has addressed their involvement. The research team wondered whether male youth were better off than female youth involved in the local sex trade and whether the former found themselves doubly stigmatized owing to their sex trade involvement and their association with a largely male (that is, same sex) clientele.

The initial purpose of the 'Risky Business?' research project, then, was to better understand the causes and consequences of youth marginalization in our society. In particular, we aimed to investigate the relationship between health and injury and marginalization among youth. We know that marginalized youth have relatively poor health; less clear is the direction of the causal relationship. Is poor health the cause or the consequence of their marginalization?

Methodology: A Longitudinal Design

To shed light on our research question about how sex trade involvement affects the health and well-being of marginalized youth, we needed to control for health status before entry into the sex trade. In other words, we needed to disentangle the temporal links between health status and sex trade involvement. We adopted a longitudinal research design of the sort that gathers data at several points in time to assess variation with a group of street-involved youth with regard to the following: (1) social determinants of becoming street-involved; (2) the extent and severity of health-compromising risk behaviours; (3) involvement in the sex trade and, if applicable, factors determining entry and length of involvement; and (4) 'injuries' resulting from involvement in various risk behaviours, including involvement in the sex trade.

We decided that youth participants in the study would be interviewed twice in the first month and approximately every two months for as long as they were willing to participate in the study (maximum four years). A $20 honorarium would be provided after the first interview, and participants would receive a $25 honorarium after subsequent interviews. Owing to the particular characteristics of this hidden population, we used an assortment of sampling strategies to recruit participants. These were based in part on contacts made during the earlier 'Dispelling Myths' project and were further developed in discussions with staff at the four partner organizations, who helped us establish strategies for contacting respondents. Thanks to the knowledge of the community partners and their proximity to the respondent population, these sampling techniques provided access to the various subgroups of marginalized youth who were at risk of entering or had already entered the local sex trade (for example, those working out of parks or malls, or on the street, or indoors). This enhanced our sample's representativeness. We also worked through contacts with the provincial Ministry of Health Services and other outreach services in the metropolitan area, and advertised the study at various locations where youth were concentrated, to develop a list of research participants.

We also used respondent-driven sampling to reach potential respondents who might otherwise not have heard about the study. This technique is especially appropriate for studying hard-to-reach or hidden populations who are stigmatized; for such populations, no sampling frames exist and acknowledgment of belonging to the group can be threatening (Heckathorn, 1997; Heckathorn, Broadbead & Sergeyev, 2001). Research participants served as 'seeds' and were each given three recruitment coupons to hand to other youth they believed might come forward for an interview. This was based on the rationale that reclusive youth are more likely to respond to the appeals of their similar-age peers who have had experience with a project, than to more privileged adults from university or community agencies. The 'seeds' were paid a nominal fee of $10 for each peer who came forward for interview. The 'seeds' were paid at their own next interviews. Youth were asked to call a dedicated cell phone number and were selected into the study based on their answers to a series of screening questions that assessed their age and their levels of involvement with the parent or guardian, the school system, the formal labour market, and the street economy (for example, with panhandling, sex trade, and/or petty crime).

A small number of older marginalized youth whom community partners identified as candidates for the position of 'indigenous research assistant' applied for and were considered for interviewing positions. We selected two of them – one female, one male – and our academic and community partners trained them. Other research assistants, university and non-university based, were added as the project progressed. The research assistants administered closed-ended and open-ended questions in individual interviews, which ranged from forty-five minutes to almost two hours. The length of interviews depended primarily on the willingness of the youth to give thorough answers to the open-ended questions and on the relevance of particular questions. For example, youth who had never worked for a salary or wage are not asked lengthy sets of questions about paid employment.

Major Ethical Concerns

Before we could start the research interviews, we needed to address two major ethical dilemmas, which were exacerbated by the marginalized status of the youth respondents. First, we hoped to balance adherence to provincial child protection laws with minimizing the impact of these laws on the sample. Participants needed to be aware of these laws in order to provide informed consent; however, we worried that youth would perceive the risk of intervention by authorities as threatening and thus choose not to participate. Second, we had to provide as much anonymity and confidentiality to the respondents as possible while at the same time maintaining their participation in future interviews by holding their contact information. We discuss each dilemma in turn below.

Consultation with the university's Human Research Ethics Committee (HREC) and with a lawyer revealed that no prior studies at our institution had involved either ethical concern. An electronic request by our HREC chair to other Canadian academic institutions also failed to reveal any similar research projects that had been through the ethical review process.

Respecting Youth through Informed Consent While Protecting Them from Harm

As in most jurisdictions in Canada and the United States, B.C. residents face a legal requirement to report a child or youth younger than twenty to the appropriate provincial authorities if they believe the child or youth is in need of protection. In our local area, this requirement is found in section 14 of the B.C. Child, Family and Community Service Act (1996). Reports concerning the need to protect a child or youth must be made to MCFD. There are at least three defining characteristics of this legislation that are important here. First, it imposes a positive duty to report; this is the norm in Canada. Second, the positive duty to report is imposed on all B.C. residents; in other provincial jurisdictions, including Nova Scotia, Ontario, and Newfoundland, this positive duty is imposed only on those who carry out professional or official duties with a child or youth. Third, the B.C. legislation encompasses past abuse. In some other provincial jurisdictions, this is not the case – for example, in Saskatchewan and Quebec, only current abuse must be reported (Bessner, 1999).

Obviously, the aim of section 14 is to protect young people in the community by obligating all B.C. residents to report past or present instances of abuse or neglect. After consulting with lawyers, MCFD representatives, service providers, ethicists, and other researchers, it became clear to us that this legislation has never actually been applied and was not well understood. For example, lawyers told us they had difficulty interpreting the law because it had not been interpreted in the courts as part of legal proceedings – for example, against someone who had failed to make a report. Moreover, we found no longitudinal studies on street-involved youth in the province or nationally to consult for ethical guidance on this matter. For two reasons, we needed to establish criteria for distinguishing which youth should be reported to MCFO in the context of a research project focusing on street-involved youth. First, we required clarity to guide the interview staff, who would be interacting directly with youth participants. Second, these criteria would have to be explained clearly to potential participants so that they could provide *informed* consent.

Because the legislation covers such a broad range of youth behaviours and experiences (see Appendix A), ranging from 'being absent from the home in circumstances that endanger the child's safety or well-being' (section 13(1)(i)), to sexual abuse by a parent (section 13(1)(b)), we surmised that the B.C. law would require us to make a formal report to the MCFD of each and every youth whom we deemed eligible for the

'Risky Business?' project (that is, who indicated multiple characteristics of street involvement). Thus we would also be obligated to inform all prospective participants that we would likely have to report them to MDFD, as part of the information they needed to consider before giving consent. We saw this scenario as highly problematic: few youth would agree to participate in the study once they knew they would almost automatically be reported to provincial authorities. This led to a further concern: only youth who already had frequent contact with the MCFD would agree to participate, whereas youth who had no MCFD contact or who were not on good terms with the MCFD would be unwilling to take part in our study. The impact of this would be hard to estimate; however, we predicted that street-involved youth not in contact with MCFD or local service networks would be underrepresented. This was the group we knew the least about and who were arguably in the greatest need of help. This group – the most marginalized and least powerful youth – were also most likely to benefit from the knowledge gained through research on the health and well-being of street-involved youth! We surmised that the more our research explained their situation, the more likely societal resources would be allocated towards preventing and/or alleviating their structural marginalization. At the same time, once we had gained their trust, these disenfranchised youth might be more willing to approach our partner agencies and avail themselves of community services.

In the end, the most instructive guidance we received came from conversations with a lawyer from the MCFD. The interpretation we received was that their priority was to intervene when there was a young person currently living in a dangerous situation, particularly if the young person was living with an abusive adult (in the vast majority of cases a parent, step-parent, or guardian). 'Dangerous situation' was also interpreted in relation to a child's or youth's age; for example, sleeping in a downtown park for several nights in a row would be seen as dangerous for a pre-teen but not necessarily for a mid-teen. A scenario was outlined to us that would always warrant reporting: if a youth participant who was living on the street mentioned being abused by a parent or guardian or other relative in a household that currently had a young person living in it. In this particular instance, the MCFD would intervene swiftly on behalf of the younger person (likely a sibling,) but not on behalf of the youth participant if the latter had already left the abusive situation.

Another important priority for the MCFD was to enhance its limited knowledge of the situation of marginalized youth with whom they had no ongoing contact. To this end, an MCFD representative wrote a letter of support for the research project and arranged for an experienced child protection worker to be our contact for any situations where we needed specific assistance with making a report to the MCFD.

Perhaps most important was our own change in attitude following these discussions. In the beginning we had worried that we would be forced by the letter of the law to routinely report on our confidants. Our face-to-face discussions with the MCFD lawyer helped us realize that we could help highly vulnerable youth access crucial services. We would be able to tell them that no one would intervene directly in their lives unless they (or a vulnerable sibling) were in real danger of being harmed. We developed a strong obligation to assist street-involved youth in need of help. To this end, we drew up a list of local service agencies that helped youth in need. The interviewers provided these referrals to all youth who expressed an interest and also to those whom they recognized would likely be helped by the available services.

The data collection instrument we ultimately worked out – with MCFD guidance and in consultation with our four community partners – also helped us give our vulnerable street youth population the information they needed to consent to participate. The letter of consent offered our participants two distinct options for answering potentially sensitive questions of the sort that raised protection concerns: they could privately mark down the answers themselves, or they could give their answers verbally, for the interviewer to record. The interviewer would describe each option to the participant in the context of both the act that obligated us to report to the MCFD and our goal of helping youth access locally available services. If the youth chose to mark down his or her own answers to those questions that could elicit protection concerns, the interviewer was left unaware of those concerns. Similarly, the data entry person who opened the sealed data envelope would not know the identity of the youth disclosing protection concerns because it was filed separately. We interviewed fifty-five youth during Wave I; about two-thirds of them were interviewed again for Wave II and a smaller portion for Wave III. About half these participants chose to fill out part of the questionnaire themselves. We expect a similar breakdown as the study progresses.

Maximize Anonymity and Confidentiality While Maintaining Participation over Time

A second ethical problem we considered before beginning our research interviews involved ensuring anonymity and confidentiality for the participants, while at the same time maximizing our chances of following them over time. During the first interview, we wanted to gather contact information so that we would be able to (1) link the data collected at different points in time in order to understand life changes and to (2) to recontact and reinterview our highly mobile street-involved participants. Gathering identifying information meant that anonymity was impossible and also made it harder for us to maintain confidentiality.[1] The most effective way to increase the validity of sensitive data is to maximize anonymity and confidentiality (Bradburn, 1983). Given that we were asking participants about illegal activities and highly stigmatizing experiences, we wanted to pay particular attention to protecting anonymity and confidentiality as possible.

Our approach to this problem had two defining characteristics. First, we maintained two databases that were not linked to each other. Second, the link or 'key' connecting the different waves of interview data could only be supplied by the respondent at each interview. These two characteristics allowed us to promise the participant a high degree of anonymity.

During the initial interviews, research assistants administered a relatively short questionnaire that asked participants for basic demographic data, family situation, educational experiences and the characteristics and behaviour of their friends. The answers given were used to confirm that the respondent qualified for the research project. Qualified respondents were then asked to provide an information key that could be used to link their responses to the current interview wave to their responses on subsequent waves. The key consisted of three facts that would not normally be known to anyone but themselves, such as the respondents' favourite teacher, favourite colour, and favourite music group. At each subsequent interview, questions were asked to elicit these three facts, and the answers were used to link the various interviews. At the first interview, the youth were also asked to provide as much contact information as possible and as they were willing to share, including e-mail addresses. These contact data were entered into a separate database that only contained the contact information and the approximate date of the next interview. All of this helped ensure that there would be no direct link between the project database containing answers to the questions laid out in the research instruments and the database containing respondent contact information.

This strategy allowed us to promise a high degree of anonymity to our respondents while still allowing us to contact the respondents for subsequent interviews. There were nevertheless lingering ethical concerns with the strategy we adopted. First of all, the level of anonymity that we could guarantee was limited by the detailed information we collected on the youths' background and their social and cultural location on the margins of our society. Given the relatively small number of youth participating in our research project, there was a chance that somebody cognizant of a youth's participation in the project and who had intimate knowledge of their background could identify particular cases in the data base. Second, following the first interview, the questionnaire data and the contact information were in the same envelope while in transit between the interview location and the research coordinators' office. This meant that the recently collected data were not anonymous during this short time. Third, we did not know whether we would be able to link the data over time through the three personal facts collected, although we were hopeful that this would be the case.

Discussion and Conclusion

Ethics concerns in our ongoing community–academic collaboration with a hard-to-reach/hidden population – that is, marginalized youth who are involved in a number of high-risk activities, including incidental or entrenched sex trade – continue to be discussed. In this chapter we have argued that 'Risky Business?' could not have proceeded without the ongoing involvement and commitment of representatives of the local community and the reporting authority. Our community partner organizations were cognizant of the social worlds of the potential research participants and had effective strategies for reaching them (Lee, 1993; Heckathorn, 1997; Heckathorn, Broadbead & Sergeyev, 2001; Benoit, Jansson, Millar & Phillips, 2005).

This project demanded that we pay close attention to ethical concerns that had hitherto received little attention. While we did not find black-and-white answers to the thorny ethical questions, and while our search for the right path forward took a great deal of time and effort, our overall experience was positive. On reflection, this is largely because of the strong commitment we received from representatives of the provincial MDFD as well as our university's REB. For both parties, the focus was on the vulnerable youth who hitherto had not been reached through longitudinal research processes and who might benefit from increasing knowledge of their risk states and health.

Other researchers undertaking similar endeavours would do well to pay close attention to the existing guidelines and laws governing a positive duty to report, and should also seek assistance from those who are responsible for enforcing those guidelines and laws. Workable solutions to ethical dilemmas can be found in these collaborations, and we continue to seek and receive support from them as we face new ethical problems in executing this long-term project.

Appendix A

Sections 13 and 14 of B.C.'s Child, Family and Community Service Act (1996)

Protection is needed when,

13 (1) A child needs protection in the following circumstances:

(a) if the child has been, or is likely to be, physically harmed by the child's parent;

(b) if the child has been, or is likely to be, sexually abused or exploited by the child's parent;

(c) if the child has been, or is likely to be, physically harmed, sexually abused or sexually exploited by another person and if the child's parent is unwilling or unable to protect the child;

(d) if the child has been, or is likely to be, physically harmed because of neglect by the child's parent;

(e) if the child is emotionally harmed by the parent's conduct;

(f) if the child is deprived of necessary health care;

(g) if the child's development is likely to be seriously impaired by a treatable condition and the child's parent refuses to provide or consent to treatment;

(h) if the child's parent is unable or unwilling to care for the child and has not made adequate provision for the child's care;

(i) if the child is or has been absent from home in circumstances that endanger the child's safety or well-being;

(j) if the child's parent is dead and adequate provision has not been made for the child's care;

(k) if the child has been abandoned and adequate provision has not been made for the child's care;

(l) if the child is in the care of a director or another person by agreement and the child's parent is unwilling or unable to resume care when the agreement is no longer in force.

(1.1) For the purpose of subsection (1) (b) and (c) and section 14 (1) (a) but without limiting the meaning of 'sexually abused' or 'sexually exploited,' a child has been or is likely to be sexually abused or sexually exploited if the child has been, or is likely to be,

(a) encouraged or helped to engage in prostitution, or

(b) coerced or inveigled into engaging in prostitution.

(2) For the purpose of subsection (1) (e), a child is emotionally harmed if the child demonstrates severe

(a) anxiety,

(b) depression,

(c) withdrawal, or

(d) self-destructive or aggressive behaviour.

Duty to report need for protection

14 (1) person who has reason to believe that a child needs protection under section 13 must promptly report the matter to a director or a person designated by a director.

(2) subsection (1) applies even if the information on which the belief is based

(a) is privileged, except as a result of a solicitor-client relationship, or

(b) is confidential and its disclosure is prohibited under another Act.

(3) person who contravenes subsection (1) commits an offence.

(4) person who knowingly reports to a director, or a person designated by a director, false information that a child needs protection commits an offence.

(5) No action for damages may be brought against a person for reporting information under this section unless the person knowingly reported false information.

(6) A person who commits an offence under this section is liable to a fine of up to $10 000 or to imprisonment for up to 6 months, or to both.

(7) The limitation period governing the commencement of a proceeding under the Offence Act does not apply to a proceeding relating to an offence under this section.

NOTE

1 For a discussion of the relationship between confidentiality and anonymity, see Medical Research Council Canada, Natural Sciences and Engineering Research Council of Canada, and Social Sciences and Humanities Research Council of Canada, 1998.

REFERENCES

Badgley, R. (1984). *Sexual offences against children: Report of the Committee on Sexual Offences against Children and Youths*. Ottawa: Canadian Government Publishing.

Benoit, C., & Millar, A. (2001). *Dispelling myths and understanding realities: Working conditions, health status, and exiting experiences of sex workers*. Sponsored by Prostitutes Empowerment, Education and Resource Society (PEERS). Funded by the B.C. Health Research Foundation, Capital Health District, and the B.C. Centre of Excellence on Women's Health.

Benoit, C., Jansson, M., Millar, A., and Phillips, R. (2005). Community-academic research on hard-to-reach populations: Benefits and challenges. *Qualitative Health Research*, 15(2), 263–82.

Berg, J. (1999). Gaining access to under-researched populations in women's health care research. *Health Care for Women International*, 20, 237–43.

Bessner, Ronda (1999, September). 'The duty to report child abuse.' Paper presented at Department of Justice Canada Conference on Working Together for Children: Protection and Prevention, Ottawa. Retrieved 2 October 2003 from http://canada.justice.gc.ca/en/ps/yj/rp/doc/Paper106.pdf.

Bradburn, Norman M. (1983). Response effects. In P.H. Rossi, J.D. Wright and A.B. Anderson (Eds.), *Handbook of survey research*. New York: Academic Press.

Brock, D. (1998). *Making work, making trouble: Prostitution as a social problem*. Toronto: University of Toronto Press.

Canadian Centre for Justice Statistics. (1997). *Juristat*, 17. Canadian Centre for Justice Statistics, Statistics Canada.

Federal/Provincial/Territorial Working Group on Prostitution (1998). *Report and recommendations in respect of legislation, policy and practices concerning prostitution-related activities*. Ottawa: Department of Justice.

Hagan, J., & McCarthy, B. (1997). *Mean streets: Youth crime and homelessness*. Cambridge: Cambridge University Press.

Heckathorn, D. (1997). Respondent-driven sampling: A new approach to the study of hidden populations. *Social Problems*, 44, 174–99.

Heckathorn, D., Broadhead, R., & Sergeyev, B. (2001). A methodology for reducing respondent duplication and impersonation in samples of hidden populations. *Journal of Drug Issues*, 31, 543–64.

Jackson, L., Highcrest, A., & Coates, R. (1992). Varied potential risks of HIV among prostitutes. *Social Science and Medicine*, 35(3), 281–6.

Lee, R. (1993). *Doing research on sensitive topics*. London: Sage.

Sexually Exploited Youth Committee (1997). *Wanted: Vulnerable youth and children*. Report of the Sexually Exploited Youth Committee of the Capital Regional District, Victoria, British Columbia.

Shaver, F. (1993). Prostitution: A female crime? In E. Adelberg & C. Currie (Eds.). *In conflict with the law: Women and the Canadian justice system*. Vancouver: Press Gang Publishers.

Spreen, M., & Zwaagstra, R. (1994). Personal network sampling, outdegree analysis and multilevel analysis: Introducing the network concept in studies of hidden populations. *International Sociology, 9*, 475–91.

Standing, K. (1998). Writing the voices of the less powerful: Research on lone mothers. In R. Edwards & J. Ribbens (Eds.), *Feminist dilemmas in qualitative research*. London: Sage.

Sudman, S., & Kalton, G. (1986). New developments in the sampling of special populations. *Annual Review of Sociology, 12*, 401–29.

Watters, J., & Biernacki, P. (1989). Targetted sampling: Options for the study of hidden populations. *Social Problems, 36*(4), 416–30.

11 Conducting Research in Child Maltreatment: Problems and Prospects

CHRISTINE WALSH AND HARRIET MACMILLAN

Child maltreatment is an important public health problem that requires a commitment to scientifically rigorous research if we are to understand its prevalence, risk and protective factors, and sequelae. This information is critical to inform the development of effective approaches to prevention and treatment. Researchers must carry out scientifically sound inquiries while protecting the subjects of research from harm. This dilemma is no more pronounced than when children and adolescents are participants and child abuse and neglect is the focus of the research. The clear articulation of the ethical and methodological problems faced by child maltreatment researchers is crucial in advancing knowledge, improving future research designs (Putnam, Liss & Landsverk, 1996), and minimizing any potential harm to children and families.

Child maltreatment is generally recognized as having four main subtypes: physical abuse, sexual abuse, emotional abuse, and neglect. Although child maltreatment is one of the 'biggest public health challenges,' research in this area is 'dwarfed' by research on other aspects of child health (Editorial, 2003). According to Sieber and Stanley: 'Sensitive research addresses some of society's most pressing social issues and policy questions. Although ignoring the ethical issues in sensitive research is not a responsible approach to science, shying away from controversial topics, simply because they are controversial, is also the avoidance of responsibility' (1988: 55).

Most child maltreatment data in Canada arise from cases reported to official sources (child welfare authorities, police, or hospitals). The effect of this is to drastically underestimate the true extent of the problem (MacMillan, Jamieson & Walsh, 2003). This has had an adverse impact on the development of sound policies for prevention and treatment. The lack of commitment to research in the field of child maltreatment is noteworthy. Despite the long-standing avoidance of research in the area of child maltreatment, researchers and policy makers are increasingly appreciating that to gather essential information about how to reduce the burden of suffering associated with child maltreatment, they will have to tackle the complex ethical issues inherent in this field of study. To this end, they will have to examine the research process with the goal of reviewing, critiquing, and improving their moral and ethical decisions in their future research (Gallager, Creighton & Gibbons, 1995; King & Churchill, 2000). Our goal in this chapter is to explore some of the complex ethical issues inherent in conducting research in the field of child maltreatment when it involves children and adolescents as participants. In particular, we are interested in reviewing this material in a Canadian context, since much of the available literature is based on American policies and practices. There are few definitive solutions to the ethical dilemmas posed by this area of investigation. It is our hope that by identifying some of the critical issues, we will be contributing our experiences to the emerging dialogue about how best to address these problems. Whenever possible, we will be highlighting case examples from our own research. We hope these will be useful to other investigators who are interested in understanding the social, physical, and emotional life of children and adolescents.

What Are the Benefits and Harms for Youth Involved in Maltreatment Research?

In the field of child maltreatment, according to Runyan (2000, 679), 'we know startlingly little about the impact of research procedures and the relative benefits and potential harms to subjects.' Two sources of inherent risks have been identified: children may experience distress or discomfort; and children and families may be, or may perceive themselves to be, adversely affected by a report of abuse to child protection authorities that arises as a result of participation in the research (Knight, Runyan, Dubowitz, Brandford, Kotch, Littowik & Hunter, 2000). Unfortunately, there has been no study evaluating the impact of asking children about experiences of maltreatment. Recent studies of adults with victimization histories suggest that the impact is minimal (Martin, Perrott, Morris & Romans, 1999; Newman, Walker & Gefland, 1999; Riddle & Alponte, 1999). One cannot necessarily conclude from this that children answering such questions will have similar responses, but it does suggest that the potential impact may be less than assumed by those resistant to such research. In the Youth Mood Project, our research team has been following a cohort of female adolescents referred from child protection with a documented history of maltreatment, with the goal of identifying risk markers for the development of depression. Data are collected on the degree of difficulty, discomfort, and trauma experienced by the adolescent participants in completing question-naires about their maltreatment exposure. It is anticipated that the data from this study will provide information in the near future regarding the impact of this type of questioning on youth.

The second potential harm to children and families results from a disclosure of abuse. Disclosures of abuse can occur in study popula-tions without known abuse histories, or new or previously unreported disclosures of abuse can be made in cohorts with known abuse histo-ries. In each case the possible consequences for a child disclosing abuse include the risk of further emotional harm, the risk of further harm as a punishment for disclosing abuse, and the potential for involvement in an investigation by police and child protection agencies. Virtually noth-ing is known about the immediate or longer-term consequences of disclosure on children or families, particularly in the context of research (Putnam, Liss & Landsverk, 1996). The inadvertent disclosure of abuse raises the issue of how to balance the legal mandate requiring reporting of abuse with the commitment to protect the confidentiality of indi-vidual participants. The dilemmas created by these competing demands are discussed in the following section.

Researchers must also be aware of the potential for indirect harms. Epidemiological research has the potential to gather information that can be used to 'paint an adverse picture of an entire population [that] may eventuate in harm to that group, either directly or as a result of the adoption of laws or policies that have a negative impact on the welfare of group members' (Capron, 1991, p. 185). Attention to the potential for indirect harms is vital when conducting research with disadvantaged, marginalized, or oppressed populations. In our research with the Ontario First Nations Regional Health Survey (OFNRHS), a community-based survey gathered information on the health and well-being of First Na-tions people, including youth residing on reserves in Ontario (MacMillan et al., 1998), the possibility for indirect harms was of concern. The survey was conducted under a code of ethics, which stipulated that 'care will be taken to ensure that information which might be detrimental or diminishing to any of the communities surveyed will not be published.' Members of the First Nations Technical Advisory Committee reviewed manuscripts for publication, and no individual communities were identified (MacMillan et al., 2004a).

The majority of studies in the field of child maltreatment involving child participants do not afford direct benefits to the participants; they are designed to contribute to the advancement of knowledge and the betterment of society. It is important to acknowledge that disclosure can lead to potential harm as outlined above; however, there is also the possibility that individuals will benefit through the identification of child maltreatment that was previously unrecognized. If abuse or neglect is disclosed and this leads to a report to the child protection agency and to actions that prevent any further maltreatment, this is a potential benefit. At this point in time, largely because of a lack of research, the risks and benefits associated with a disclosure arising in the context of a research study are unknown. In the absence of direct benefits to young people, researchers must be careful to minimize the risks to participants, including both direct and indirect harms. Studies must be designed to avoid any potential trauma associated with collecting sensitive information and the inadvertent disclosure of abuse.

Are Researchers Mandated Reporters of Suspected Child Abuse?

Although arguments have been raised that researchers are morally and legally bound to report suspected child abuse (Hoagwood, 1994; Kinard, 1985; Mearig, 1982; Melton, 1989), there is no state law in the United States that specifically designates researchers as among those required to report suspected child abuse (Steinberg et al., 1999). The situation is different in Canada. In every Canadian jurisdiction except Yukon, a person who in the course of conducting research becomes aware of a situation in which he or she should reasonably suspect child abuse is legally mandated to report this suspicion (Loo, Bala, Clarke & Hornick, 1999). The obligation to report overrides any issues of confidentiality. The one exception to the law is through the federal Statistics Act (110), section 17, which provides that researchers who have been sworn to secrecy under the act and who are carrying out studies for Statistics Canada cannot disclose any identifying information learned in the course of their research.

Fisher (1994) outlines some of the ethical difficulties concerning the requirement for reporting when studying at-risk or socially disenfranchised children. One concern relates to the validity of the investigators' perception of risk, in that many of the instruments used in research are designed to detect group differences, which means that their individual diagnostic utility is questionable. Furthermore, instruments may not have been standardized for the population under study. She contends that investigators using diagnostically valid assessment instruments must establish informed consent procedures that outline what information will be shared and with whom. According to Putnam and colleagues (1996), many research studies include a simple statement that any guarantees of confidentiality will be superseded by the necessity of reporting information as required by law. They contend that this cryptic reference makes it unlikely that parents will understand the nature or consequences of mandated reporting. There is no clear standard as to what information should be provided to study participants regarding the possible risks or harms should a disclosure of abuse be made in the course of a research study.

Ontario's Child and Family Services Act includes a requirement to report suspected child abuse or neglect for children under sixteen. In the Youth Mood Project, the limits to confidentiality are provided to the participants verbally and on the consent form, as follows: 'I have been told that if I am under the age of 16 at the time of completing the interview, and if the research team becomes aware of any abuse or neglect that is happening or has happened to me in the past that has not been reported to the child protection agency, they are required to report it. If this information has already been reported, no additional reporting is required. I understand this law is the same as for any health care professional.' Interviewers are advised of their reporting responsibilities during training sessions. What is not made explicit to participants in this research project are the potential consequences (investigation by child protection agency and/or police involvement, apprehension, and so on) of reporting suspected abuse.

In the therapeutic context, considerable differences exist as to the practice and extent of forewarning; here, the limits of confidentiality are explained at the outset (Crenshaw & Lichtenber, 1993; Thompson-Cooper, Fugére & Bruno, 1993). Forewarning may deprive children of the benefits of mandatory reporting laws (Budai, 1996). There is a lack of scientific information about the processes by which, and the extent to which, research participants are informed about the limits to confidentiality and the effects of forewarning on research. In the absence of information, we suggest that in conducting studies with children or families where disclosure might realistically be expected, participants should be advised about the limits of confidentiality and the potential consequences arising from a disclosure of suspected child abuse. In addition, children who are completing anonymous questionnaires about victimization should be informed that their responses to items on a questionnaire do not indicate a disclosure. Additional information should be provided to all participants should they wish to make a disclosure or seek assistance.

Scott-Jones (1994) advised researchers to exercise caution in making informal or formal reports of child abuse because of the problems that arise in reporting and verifying child abuse. Potential problems include the following: the possible harm for children and families in cases of erroneous reports; low rates of substantiation; reporting biases due to ethnic and socio-economic status; and the fact that reporting does not always lead to appropriate intervention for children and families.

In Canada, with few exceptions, researchers are mandatory reporters of suspected child abuse. Research participants should be informed of the investigators' duty to report. Studies should be designed to minimize inadvertent disclosures of abuse while protecting children from harm and providing them with means to seek assistance. The Family Connections Study is a randomized controlled trial of public health nurse (PHN) intervention in preventing the recurrence of physical abuse or neglect in families that were referred by the child protection agency (MacMillan et al., 2004b). Since interviewers and PHNs were accessing families in their home, direct and indirect disclosures of maltreatment occurred. For example, on one occasion during the initial study interview, the interviewer observed the inappropriate physical discipline of a young child. The parent was informed of the interviewer's concerns, and the child protection agency was contacted. The family continued participating in the study, and the child protection agency continued to be involved.

How Can the Confidentiality of Respondents Be Protected within the Research Context?

Researchers have an ethical responsibility to maintain the confidentiality of participants. Bussell (1994), as reported in Haggerty and Hawkins (2000), described that in discussions with lawyers and bioethicists, three predominant views arose regarding how to handle confidentiality issues in the context of research: (a) no disclosure on possible limitations of confidentiality, with the premise that a breach would be an un-anticipated emergency; (b) a discussion with participants of the potential need for breach of confidentiality, without a full explanation of the reasons for breaching confidentiality unless requested; and (c) complete disclosure of the circumstances necessitating limited confidentiality.

In our research we reassure youths that information they provide in the research context will not be disclosed to others (parents/guardian, or educational, health, social, justice, or child welfare agencies). Youths are also advised that the assurance of confidentiality is overridden by the legal requirement to report suspected child abuse or mental health concerns (risk of self-harm or harm to others). The maintenance of confidentiality can be problematic for investigators who learn about youths' involvement in high-risk activities that are not covered under these provisions. For example, the Youth Mood Project involves a clinical interview assessing youths' emotional health; interviewers often become aware of youths' involvement in high-risk activities (drug or alcohol misuse, high-risk sexual activity). Interviewers advise youth about the possible consequences of these activities and offer referral.

Depending on the nature of the research project, we have used different approaches to balance the protection of confidentiality with the individual's and the researcher's responsibilities to report. For example, in the Ontario Mental Health Supplement, a large household survey that contained a subsample of youth reporting on maltreatment (MacMillan et al., 1997), data were collected anonymously and there was no mechanism for linking self-reports of exposure to maltreatment with specific individuals. Thus, it was unlikely that inadvertent disclosure would occur. In the Childhood Experiences of Violence instrument development and validation study (Walsh et al., 2002), protecting the confidentiality of youths was more problematic. Youths were informed verbally and on the consent form about the limitations of confidentiality. To prevent the research team from becoming aware of suspected abuse, they only had access to anonymous data. Subject rosters linking names with identification numbers were maintained by the referring agency (for example, the school). At the other end of the continuum, the research team knew the participants in the Youth Mood Project, and the youths participated in clinical interviews. So it was not uncommon for previously undisclosed abuse to be identified during the research process. Before the study was launched, a process for handling new disclosures was established in collaboration with the local child protection agencies; this involved notifying an agency worker, who in consultation with the supervisor appointed specifically to the study would determine what steps if any should be taken.

The OFNRHS presented unique challenges to the ethical mandate to maintain the confidentiality of the adolescent participants. Difficulties arose from the sensitivity of the questions (which touched on child abuse, substance use, and high-risk sexual behaviours) and the nature of the setting, as many reserves were sparsely populated and geographically isolated. The following procedures were instituted to protect the youths' confidentiality: (a) participants were selected randomly by band list membership, and no identifying information was placed on the questionnaire; (b) no identifying information was removed from the community; (c) the mode of administration was changed from interviewer-administered to a self-complete format to ensure that the local interviewer did not have access to sensitive data about the youths; (d) a practice questionnaire with non-sensitive, similarly formatted items was developed; (e) the practice questionnaire was administered in the presence of the interviewer to reduce problems with literacy; (f) youths completed self-administered questionnaires in private and sealed them in envelopes; (g) interviewers mailed the unopened questionnaires out of the community for data entry; and (h) although the raw data were owned and controlled by the participating communities, all completed questionnaires, and the raw, unaggregated data were stored in a central repository.

Maintaining the confidentiality of youths engaged in research while protecting them from harm requires that researchers seek creative solutions to meet these challenges.

How Are Youths' Needs for Clinical Services Met within a Research Study?

The need for clinical intervention for minors may arise in the context of their participation in research. The investigator must inform participants verbally and through written information on the consent form what will happen should this become the case. When the need for clinical services arises, a potential dilemma exists between the youths' needs for privacy and parental rights to information. Brooks-Gunn and Rotheram-Borus (1994) have outlined principles to assist researchers in making decisions in these situations. The guiding principle is to provide clinical care for a youth; the authors suggest that this need supersedes parents' rights to know what is happening to their children, now that society is taking on more responsibility for guarding the well-being of youth than for informing parents. Scott-Jones (1994) identified the potential for 'devastating effects' – particularly for low-income and minority individuals, families, and communities – arising from the failure to report children and refer them for treatment within intervention trials.

A direct need for intervention may arise from a youth's request or through an interviewer becoming aware of such a need during the research process. For example, in the Youth Mood Project during the clinical interviews assessing youths' emotional health, a direct need for clinical services was often identified. Interviewers were trained to provide referrals for youth who are engaging in high-risk activities or who are manifesting behavioural or emotional symptoms. Permission was sought from the youth to inform a parent or guardian of these concerns and/or to make an appropriate referral for clinical services. If the youth agreed, a referral was made. If the youth declined an offer of assistance, including referral to other services, this was respected and no further action was taken. An indirect need may arise when a study participant requires clinical services but the need is not identified during the research. However, all participants involved in research were provided with information about how to seek services should the need arise.

What Are the Requirements for Obtaining Informed Consent for Research Involving Children and Adolescents?

Article (2.1) of the *Tri-council Policy Statement* identifies that an individual must be legally competent in order to consent to participate in research. However, practice varies and there are no clear guidelines regarding children's abilities to consent to, or refuse, participation in research (Pearce, 2002). There is considerable debate about the age at which children may be able to consent to research on their own behalf (Tan & Jones, 2001). One study concluded that children under nine cannot be expected to consent or assent to clinical research in a meaningful way (Ondrusek, Abramovitch, Pencharz & Koren, 1998), while another suggested that children younger than eleven have limited understanding of their role as research participants (Tait, Voepel-Lewis, & Malviya, 2003). The developmental capacities of twelve- to eighteen-year-old adolescents are substantially greater than those of children and are often not easily distinguished from those of adults (Feldman & Elliot, 1990). In the absence of clear guidelines about children's abilities to consent, the law recognizes that consent is valid when made by a fully autonomous person – that is, by one who has attained the legal age and who is able to make decisions for him/herself (Meaux & Bell, 2001). Assent is a child's informed agreement to the conditions of participation when the legal age of consent has not been attained (Conrad & Horner, 1997). A child's assent should be sought whenever that individual has sufficient competence to make a decision about participating in the research. Factors to consider in determining a child's competence include the child's cognitive and emotional development to make independent, considered, and reliable decisions on his/her own behalf without being unduly influenced by the desires of others and to understand the seriousness and impact of that decision in the short and long term.

Meaux and Bell suggest that to maintain a balance between recruiting children as research subjects and protecting this vulnerable population from undue risk, researchers need to attend to three levels of safeguards. The first level, the institutional level, comprises those laws, regulations, and guidelines that outline procedures for conducting research with children. The family provides the second level of safeguards for children though the provision for informed consent by a parent or guardian before the child is approached for assent, and the third level is the uncoerced voluntary assent of the minor.

The Youth Mood Project involved participants aged between twelve and sixteen, who were followed over two years. First, written consent was obtained from the parents or guardians; then assent was obtained from the youths. A substantial minority of youth recruited for the study were in the care of child protection agencies; in such circumstances, consent for participation was sought from the appropriate child protection worker. As the study progressed and modifications to its protocol were made with REB approval, subjects and their parents or guardians were informed about the changes, and consent was sought for these. As youth became legally competent to consent, or as the legal guardianship changed, the appropriate consent was sought.

The above discussion relates to active consent procedures. There are, however, several ways to obtain the permission of a parent or guardian for a minor to participate in research. Passive consent procedures typically consist of a letter sent to a child's parent or guardian describing the study and providing the parent or guardian with a mechanism for withdrawing permission (Jason, Pokorny & Katz, 2001). Hoagwood, Jensen, and Fisher (1996) contend that active consent should be obtained in most studies of youth but that for some studies, use of active consent may place adolescents at psychosocial and physical risks. The requirement for active consent does not always protect the welfare of minors; for example, the solicitation of parental consent for children from abusing or neglecting families may violate a child's privacy or jeopardize his/her welfare (Beauchamp & Childress, 1994).

In studies involving adolescent samples where sensitive issues such as child maltreatment are addressed, passive and active consent procedures compete with each other. Passive consent procedures increase the likelihood of acquiring a random sample that is most representative of a target population. However, this approach is often at odds with the REB's requirement for active parental consent (Risjord & Greenberg, 2002). The requirement for active parental consent results in higher rates of sampling bias owing to the underrepresentation of certain populations. Furthermore, underrepresentation typically occurs for those populations that researchers are most interested in, and this jeopardizes the generalizability of the samples (Baker, Yardley & McCaul, 2001). Studies of non-responders to passive consent procedures indicate that they are similar to parents who consent rather than refuse (ibid.), and this suggests that REBs should be more willing to allow passive consent procedures than is currently the case in research with children. Santelli and Rogers (2002) suggest that if the requirement for parental permission makes obtaining a representative sample unlikely, investigators should obtain waivers of that requirement and devise sound protections for adolescent participants. Passive consent procedures should be considered when researching sensitive topics or vulnerable populations, and procedures should be put in place to protect participants.

What Is the Appropriate Setting for Maltreatment Research?

Maltreatment research can be and is conducted across multiple settings, each of which has its own inherent advantages and disadvantages. The setting may involve layers of gatekeepers, who exercise power over the research activity and the consent process. This in turn dictates, in part, the amount of self-determination and autonomy accorded to children in the consent process and in the research itself. The school setting may be appropriate for the study of sensitive issues such as child abuse, although the ethics of conducting research in a school setting may create special challenges (David, Edwards & Alldred, 2001). The potential for coercion exists, in that the research procedures may be seen as just another form of schoolwork. That is, use of the educational setting may imply to the child that he/she is expected to participate; this may in turn have the effect of limiting the rights of children to make free choices. Also of concern is the stigma that could be associated with either participation or refusal (ibid.). Finally, children with maltreatment histories or other disadvantages may not be adequately represented in the school setting (McGloin & Widom, 2001).

More often, the home setting is used in studies involving children. However, this setting is problematic for child maltreatment research. The privacy and confidentiality of the children may be difficult to maintain in the home setting, and the child may be placed at further risk if he/she is living in an abusive home. Children assessed in the home setting may be less willing to answer sensitive questions in response to their estimation of the risk.

Children residing in clinical, justice, or child welfare settings may not feel free to consent to or dissent from research. Researchers and others responsible for children must ensure that their rights are adequately protected and that any participation in research involves an informed choice – one that is free of coercion. Researchers should affirm that a child's participation or refusal to participate in research will have no impact on his/her need for services.

To increase the acceptability of the research and to reduce the potential for harms, investigators for the Youth Mood Project collaborated extensively with local child protection personnel. Procedures for recruiting participants included the following: (a) case workers familiar with youth identified those individuals who were not to be approached for the study because of issues related to their emotional health; (b) a letter was sent to eligible youth and their families informing them about the study, and these people were provided with a phone number to call if they were not interested in participating in the study; (c) if no call was received, study personnel contacted youth and their parents or guardians to provide information about the study and to seek permission to visit the home to obtain consent; and (d) consent was obtained from parents and guardians and youth provided assent.

In any research setting, procedures must be established to ensure that children have the opportunity to provide meaningful consent/assent or dissent, that their privacy and confidentiality are maintained, and that the risk of harm is minimal. When youth are unable to provide consent because of age, authorized third parties such as parents or legal guardians should provide free and informed consent on behalf of the child.

Summary

Ethical dilemmas, including the need to strike an appropriate balance between benefits and harms, present formidable challenges to child maltreatment researchers, who must also contend with reporting obligations and the requirements for confidentiality, the demands of the research, and youths' need for clinical services. Investigators are urged to seek creative ways to overcome these ethical challenges in conducting research with children. The methods used must contribute to our knowledge of this significant public health problem while protecting young people from harm. The ethical dilemmas encountered in research, and their resolutions, need to be identified and reported so as to inform the field and improve research on sensitive issues with vulnerable populations.

Overall recommendations are:

1. Studies of vulnerable children that explore their perspectives regarding involvement in research are necessary to inform our decision-making about their participation in research.
2. Studies concerning the social, physical, and emotional life of children should include measures of victimization.
3. Research that evaluates exposure to child maltreatment should include approaches that ask children directly about their experiences, based on age and developmental state. Such investigation is ethically responsible and will contribute to our understanding of this issue.
4. Ethical and methodological issues raised by child maltreatment research require continued exploration but should not be considered barriers to conducting research in this important field.
5. Children should be fully informed about the risks and benefits of participating in research, including the researcher's responsibility to report in some circumstances.
6. Depending on age, assent or consent should be obtained directly from the child participants.
7. Investigators should be aware of and anticipate the need for clinical services for youth involved in research. In general, their needs for intervention and protection from harm override a parent's right to information about their youth or the needs of the study.

8. Youths' rights for confidentiality should be respected should they refuse clinical services.
9. Children should receive fair compensation for participating in research, taking their age and developmental stage into account.
10. To add to the emerging debate, researchers should be encouraged to disseminate information about the reasoning behind the ethical and methodological choices they make.

NOTE

This chapter was supported by the Wyeth Canada Inc. Canadian Institutes of Health Research (CIHR) Clinical Research Chair in Women's Mental Health and by the CIHR Institutes of Gender and Health; Aging; Human Development, Child, and Youth Health; Neurosciences, Mental Health, and Addiction; and Population and Public Health.

REFERENCES

Baker, J.R., Yardley, J.K., & McCaul, K. (2001). Characteristics of responding, non-responding and refusing parents in an adolescent lifestyle choice study. *Evaluation Review*, 25(6), 605–18.

Beauchamp, T.L., & Childress, J.F. (1994). *Principles of biomedical ethics*. New York: Oxford University Press.

Brooks-Gunn, J., & Rotheram-Borus, M.J. (1994). Rights to privacy in research: Adolescents versus parents. *Ethics & Behavior*, 4(2), 109–21.

Budai, P. (1996). Mandatory reporting of child abuse: Is it in the best interest of the child? *Australian and New Zealand Journal of Psychiatry*, 30(6), 794–804.

Capron, A.M. (1991). Protection of research subjects: Do special rules apply in epidemiology? *Law, Medicine & Health Care*, 19(3–4), 184–90.

Conrad, B., & Horner, S. (1997). Issues in pediatric research: Safeguarding the children. *Journal of the Society of Pediatric Nurses*, 2(4), 163–71.

Crenshaw, W.B., & Lichtenberg, J.W. (1993). Child abuse and the limits of confidentiality: Forewarning practices. *Behavioral Sciences & the Law*, 11(2), 181–92.

David, M., Edwards, R., & Alldred, P. (2001). Children and school-based research: 'Informed consent' or 'educated consent'? *British Educational Research Journal*, 27(3), 347–65.

Editorial. (2003). The neglect of child neglect. *The Lancet*, 361(9356), 443.

Feldman, S.S., & Elliot, G.R. (1990). At the threshold: The developing adolescent. Cambridge: Harvard University Press.

Fisher, C.B. (1994). Reporting and referring research participants: Ethical challenges for investigators studying children and youth. *Ethics & Behaviour*, 4(2), 87–95.

Gallagher, B., Creighton, S., & Gibbons, J. (1995). Ethical dilemmas in social research: No easy solutions. *British Journal of Social Work*, 25(3), 295–311.

Haggerty, L.A., & Hawkins, J. (2000). Informed consent and the limits of confidentiality. *Western Journal of Nursing Research*, 22(4), 508–14.

Hoagwood, K. (1994). The certificate of confidentiality at the National Institute of Mental Health: Discretionary considerations in its applicability in research on child and adolescent mental disorders. *Ethics & Behavior*, 4(2), 123–31.

Hoagwood, K., Jensen, P.S., & Fisher, C.B. (Eds.). (1996). Ethical issues in mental health research with children and adolescents. Mahwah, NJ: Lawrence Erlbaum Associates.

Jason, L.A., Pokorny, S., & Katz, R. (2001). Passive versus active consent: A case study in school settings. *Journal of Community Psychology*, 29(1), 53–68.

Kinard, E.M. (1985). Ethical issues in research with abused children. *Child Abuse & Neglect*, 9, 301–11.

King, N.M.P., & Churchill, L.R. (2000). Ethical principles guiding research on child and adolescent subjects. *Journal of Interpersonal Violence*, 15(7), 710–24.

Knight, E.D., Runyan, D.K., Dubowitz, H., Brandford, C., Kotch, J., Litrownik, A., & Hunter, W. (2000). Methodological and ethical challenges associated with child self-report of maltreatment: Solutions implemented by the LongSCAN Consortium. *Journal of Interpersonal Violence*, 15(7), 760–75.

Loo, S.K., Bala, N.M.C., Clarke, M.E., & Hornick, J.P. (1999). Child abuse: Reporting and classification in health care settings. Minister of Public Works and Government Services Canada. Cat. No. H49-123/1999E.

MacMillan, H.L., Fleming, J.E., Trocmé, N., Boyle, M.H., Wong, M., Racine, Y.A., Beardslee, W.R., & Offord, D.R. (1997). Prevalence of child physical and sexual abuse in the community: Results from the Ontario Health Supplement. *Journal of the American Medical Association*, 278(2), 131–5.

MacMillan H.L., Jamieson, E., & Walsh, C.A. (2003). Reported contact with child protection services among those reporting child physical and sexual abuse: Results from a community survey. *Child Abuse and Neglect*, 27, 1397–1408.

MacMillan, H.L., Walsh, C.A., Faries, E., MacMillan, A., McCue, H., Wong, M.,

Offord, D., & the Technical Advisory Committee of the Chiefs of Ontario. (1998). Ontario First Nations Regional Health Survey Final Report.

MacMillan, H.L., Walsh, C.A., Jamieson, E., Wong, M., Faries, E.J., McCue, H., MacMillan, A.B., & Offord, D.R, with the Health Coordination Unit of the Chiefs of Ontario. (2004a). Partnerships in Research: The Ontario First Nations Regional Health Survey. (Part 1) Manuscript submitted for publication.

MacMillan, H.L., Thomas, B.H., Jamieson, E, Walsh, C.A., Boyle, M.H., Shannon, H., and Gafni, A. (2004b). Effectiveness of public health nurse home visitation in preventing the recurrence of child physical abuse and neglect: A randomized, controlled trial. Manuscript in preparation.

Martin, J.L., Perrott, K., Morris, E.M., & Romans, S.E. (1999). Participation in retrospective child sexual abuse research: Beneficial or harmful? What women think six years later. In L.M. Williams & V.L. Banyard (Eds.), *Trauma and memory* (pp. 149–159). Thousand Oaks, CA: Sage.

McGloin, J.M., & Widom, C.S. (2001). Resilience among abused and neglected children grown up. *Development and Psychopathology*, 13(4), 1021–38.

Mearig, J.S. (1982). Ethical implications of the children's rights movement for professionals. *American Journal of Orthopsychiatry*, 52(3), 518–29.

Meaux, J.B., & Bell, P.L. (2001). Balancing recruitment and protection: Children as research subject. *Issues in Comprehensive Pediatric Nursing*, 24(4), 241–51.

Melton, G.B. (1989). Children's rights: Where are the children? *American Journal of Orthopsychiatry*, 52(3), 530–38.

Newman, E., Walker, E.A., & Gefland, A. (1999). Assessing the ethical costs and benefits of trauma-focused research. *General Hospital Psychiatry*, 21(3), 187–96.

Ondrusek, N., Abramovitch, R., Pencharz, P., & Koren, G. (1998). Empirical examination of the ability of children to consent to clinical research. *Journal of Medical Ethics*, 24(3), 158–65.

Pearce, M. (2002). Children as subjects in nontherapeutic research. *Grimes v. Kennedy Krieger Institute, Inc. Journal of Legal Medicine*, 23(3), 421–36.

Putnam, F.W., Liss, M.B., & Landsverk, J. (1996). Ethical issues in maltreatment research with children and adolescents. In K. Hoagwood, P.S. Jensen & C.B. Fisher (Eds.), *Ethical issues in mental health research with children and adolescents* (pp. 113–32). Hillsdale, NJ: Lawrence Erlbaum Associates.

Riddle, K.P., & Aponte, J.F. (1999). The Comprehensive Childhood Maltreatment Inventory: Early development and reliability analyses. *Child Abuse & Neglect*, 23(11), 1103–15.

Risjord, M., & Greenberg, J. (2002). When IRBs disagree: Waiving parental consent for sexual health research on adolescents. *IRB*, 24(2), 8–14.

Runyan, D.K. (2000). The ethical, legal, and methodological implications of directly asking children about abuse. *Journal of Interpersonal Violence*, 15(7), 675–81.

Santelli, J., & Rogers, A.S. (2002). Parental permission, passive consent, and 'children' in research. *Journal of Adolescent Health*, 31(4), 303–4.

Scott-Jones, D. (1994). Ethical issues in reporting and referring in research with low-income minority children. *Ethics & Behavior*, 4(2), 97–108.

Sieber, J.E., & Stanley, B. (1988). Ethical and professional dimensions of socially sensitive research. *American Psychologist*, 43(1), 49–55.

Steinberg, A.M., Pynoos, R.S., Goenjian, A.K., Sossanabadi, H., & Sherr, L. (1999). Are researchers bound by child abuse reporting laws? *Child Abuse & Neglect*, 23(8), 771–7.

Tait, A.R., Voepel-Lewis, T., & Malviya, S. (2003). Do they understand? (part II): Assent of children participating in clinical anesthesia and surgery research. *Anesthesiology*, 98(3), 609–14.

Tan, J.O.A., & Jones, D.P.H. (2001). Children's consent. *Current Opinion in Psychiatry*, 14, 303–7.

Thompson-Cooper, I., Fugére, R., & Cormier, B.M. (1993). The child abuse reporting laws: An ethical dilemma for professionals. *Canadian Journal of Psychiatry*, 38(8), 557–62.

Tri-council policy statement: Ethical conduct for research involving humans (1998, with 2002, 2002 updates). Medical Research Council Canada, Natural Sciences and Engineering Research Council of Canada, and Social Sciences and Humanities Research Council of Canada. www.pre.ethics.gc.ca/english/policystatement/policystatement.cfm.

Walsh, C.A., MacMillan, H.L., Trocmé, N., Boyle, M., Jamieson, E., Daciuk, J., & Racine, Y. (2002). The Childhood Experiences of Violence Questionnaire: A Brief Self-Report Measure of Child Maltreatment for Youth. Internal Document, Statistics Canada and Federal Department of Justice.

12 The Study of Suicidality among Children and Youth: Preliminary Recommendations and Best Practices

TRACY VAILLANCOURT AND VIOLETTA IGNESKI

In recent years, increased research attention on the mental health of children and youth has exposed disconcerting findings regarding the prevalence of suicidality, which includes suicidal ideations, plans, attempts, and completions. Suicide is the second-leading cause of death among Canadian youth between 10 and 19 (Health Canada, 1999) and the third-leading cause of death among American youth between 15 and 24 (Anderson, 2002; Centers for Disease Control and Prevention, 2004; National Institute for Mental Health, 2003). Data from the Youth Risk Behavior Study (see Grunbaum, Kann, Kinchen, Williams, Ross, Lowry & Kolbe, 2002), a national survey of students in Grades 9 to 12 conducted by the Centers for Disease Control and Prevention in the United States, also provide alarming statistics. Specifically, 19 per cent of high school students indicated that in the past year they had 'seriously considered attempting suicide' (ideation), and 14.8 per cent had a specific suicide plan. Suicide attempts were made by 8.8 per cent of the students surveyed, and 2.6 per cent of the youth studied had made suicide attempts that required medical involvement.

Researchers from a variety of backgrounds, including anthropology, sociology, education, social work, nursing, psychology, and psychiatry, have responded to these disturbing statistics by paying more attention in their research to understanding the causes of youth suicide (O'Carroll, Crosby, Mercy, Lee & Simon, 2001). Although a broad range of disciplinary perspectives is important for the advancement of knowledge, this diversity in academic approaches and professional training also raises ethical and legal concerns for researchers. For example, current ethical guidelines are formulated to help researchers pursue knowledge in ways that do not harm participants, but it is not clear how these

general guidelines apply to very specific issues that confront researchers who are working with suicidal children and youth. Given this
paucity of specific direction, the purpose of this chapter is twofold: (1)
to highlight important areas of ethical concern that require further
thought and discussion by the broader academic community who study
child and youth suicidal ideology and behaviour; and (2) to provide
preliminary best-practice recommendations that can guide researchers.

Duty to Report

The duty to report has been debated extensively as it relates to child
maltreatment, and this debate has implications for how researchers
respond to evidence of suicidality. In 1993, Celia Fisher noted in a *Child
Development* social policy report on the integration of science and ethics
as it relates to high-risk children and youth that it was unclear whether
researchers have the same obligations as clinicians to report child abuse
and thereby break confidentiality. Since the seminal paper, the issue has
been clarified. In the case of child maltreatment, it is the legal responsibility of professionals to report their suspicions; furthermore in *all*
Canadian provinces and American states it is the responsibility of *all*
citizens to report their concerns or observations about child maltreatment (see Department of Justice Canada, 2003, for Canada, and federal
law 42 C.F.R., Part 2, 1993, for the Unites States) (see also Walsh &
MacMillian, and Jansson & Benoit, in this volume). It is interesting to
note that while the legal responsibility of all citizens to report child
abuse is clearly stated in Canadian and American law, it is not formally
stated in ethical guidelines governing researchers, such as the *Tri-council Policy Statement for Ethical Conduct in Research Involving Humans* (put
forth by the Medical Research Council Canada, the Natural Sciences
and Engineering Research Council of Canada, and the Social Sciences
and Humanities Research Council of Canada in 1998), the American
Psychological Association (APA, 1999), and the Canadian Psychological
Association (CPA, 1999), to name but a few. What this means is that
researchers cannot rely solely on their research ethics boards (REBs) for
guidance about best practices when conducting research. They must
also familiarize themselves with their own state, provincial, or territo-
rial laws to establish what their individual responsibilities are concerning the reporting of child abuse (Fisher, 1993).

The need to break confidentiality and report child abuse has been a
long-standing professional obligation applying to child care profession-

als (such as psychologists, nurses, social workers, teachers, and physicians). Recently, this legal obligation has been extended to all citizens. However, there are circumstances that legally obligate mental health professionals but not researchers specifically. For example, the professional guidelines for mental health workers set out by most state and provincial/territorial regulatory and licensing bodies require that confidentiality be broken when a client poses a physical threat to another individual (for example, threatens homicide) or poses a threat to self (for example, threatens suicide) (see Sattler, 2001; Taylor & Adelman, 1999).

Breaking Confidentiality When a Client Poses a Physical Threat to Others

The legal requirement faced by mental health professionals to break confidentiality when a client poses a physical threat to others is based on the California Supreme Court's 1976 decision *Tarasoff v. Regents of the University of California*, in which it was stated that such professionals have an obligation to warn third parties of their clients' intentions to physically harm them. Specifically, the Supreme Court of California stated that 'the public policy favoring protection of the confidential character of patient-psychotherapist communications must yield to the extent to which disclosure is essential to avert danger to others. The privilege ends where the public peril begins' (p. 24).

In other words, the court ruled that communications between client and clinician are no longer privileged when the client poses a physical risk to another person. In this situation, it is the responsibility of the clinician to warn either the intended victim or his/her parents or guardians (see Everstine et al., 1999). However, the 'duty to protect' law was written in reference to clinical settings, which means there is no clear legal requirement for non-clinically trained professionals, including researchers, to report these concerns (see Appelbaum & Rosenbaum, 1999). In fact, Applebaum and Rosenbaum have argued that professionals without clinical training 'should fall outside the requirements of the duty to protect, as should relatively untrained research assistants who collect data' (1999, 177). They base this argument on the fact that violent behaviour is difficult to predict, especially when not observed in a face-to-face interview by a trained clinician (Douglas & Webster, 1999). These authors consider the validity and reliability of the data obtained (which are less than ideal) and the potential harm that can befall the client through inaccurate reporting, and conclude that the fundamental ethical right to confidentiality in research settings should be maintained, even though the risk in a given circumstance may seem great.

The Case of Self-Threatening Harm

The arguments advanced by Appelbaum and Rosenbaum (1999) regarding threats to others can also be made in reference to the study of suicidal behaviour. That is, while mental health professionals are legally required to intervene on behalf of a client when he/she poses a threat to self, and thus break confidentiality, this requirement does not legally extend to researchers studying suicide. Furthermore, despite important advances in the development of suicidality assessment measures, there are currently no instruments available with high predictive validity for imminent risk for suicide attempts (Glowinski et al., 2001). In fact, while many youth will have suicidal ideas, few will attempt and even fewer will complete (Carlson & Cantwell, 1982; Grunbaum, et al., 2002). To further complicate matters, it has been suggested that a better predictor for suicidal behaviour and completion is not ideation but rather hopelessness (e.g., Beck, Steer, Kovacs & Garrison, 1985). Given the limited predictive validity of these types of data, does it follow that researchers who study suicidal behaviour should also 'fall outside' the obligation to break confidentiality when someone poses a threat to self (see Appelbaum & Rosenbaum, 1999)? We argue in more detail below that the threat is severe enough to warrant the requirement that all researchers studying suicidal behaviour in children and youth follow up on suspicious cases. We recommend ways to do this that can help minimize potential harms and improve the accuracy of reports.

Confidentiality and the Prevention of Harm

Among the ethical principles guiding researchers is the obligation to respect participants' privacy and confidentiality (see APA, 1999; CPA, 1999; Tri-council Working Group, 2003). Confidentiality is essential to the development and maintenance of a relationship of trust between the parties involved. Indeed, without such trust, the respondents may hesitate to disclose personal information, especially information as sensitive as suicidal ideas or behaviour (Nowell & Spruill, 1999; Marcenko, Fishman & Friedman, 1999).

Confidentiality is clearly important for the appropriate respecting of persons and for the advancement of knowledge, yet there are situations where reserachers may need to break it. The threat of suicide poses a particular challenge to researchers, who though not legally required to break confidentiality, are ethically obligated both to respect confidentiality and to minimize harm to participants. In the case of threats of suicide, the obligation to minimize harm to participants can require the breach of confidentiality. That is, even though questionnaire data may not have strong predictive value, there will be cases when a child or youth will be spared great harm if the risk of suicide is reported – for example, when a suicide attempt can be prevented by putting the child or youth in contact with the appropriate professionals.

When researchers decide to limit a person's right to privacy in cases where there is a significant amount of risk for harm (that is, suicide attempt or completion), they can undertake some strategies to minimize the impact of breaking confidentiality. To highlight the potential ethical challenges associated with the study of suicidality among children and youth and to recommend strategies to deal with these issues, we present a research vignette. While this vignette certainly does not represent frequent or *typical* situations that arise when conducting research in this area, it is useful for highlighting areas that require careful consideration.

Sara (age fourteen) gave assent to participate in a study that investigated the link between depression and youth involvement with dating. One of the questionnaires she completed was a depression inventory. She indicated on this survey that she was suicidal. Another questionnaire asked her about her involvement with dating. On this questionnaire, she indicated that she was sexually active. Sara is contacted by one of the researchers. The researcher tells her that because she indicated that she was suicidal, confidentiality must be broken and her parents will have to be notified so that a proper assessment can be made. Sara is deeply disturbed by this phone call. She is worried that her parents will also be told about her sexual activities. She is also very angry because she feels that the researchers who told her that her answers were private misinformed her.

As this vignette demonstrates, breaking confidentiality is not uncontroversial and is not without risk of harm to research participants (King & Churchill, 2000). There are both positive and negative implications to consider and assess. It is unclear whether and how existing legal and ethical guidelines for breaching confidentiality apply to researchers. This lack of clarity may lead to decisions with significant consequences for children's well-being and that of their families. For example, a researcher who is also trained as a clinician may be legally bound to break confidentiality for the purpose of intervening when a child or youth is suicidal, even when a non-clinically trained researcher would not be legally required to do so. Obviously, the lack of clarity in current guidelines generates confusion and perhaps at times a contradiction in what is required. Furthermore, while all researchers are ethically obligated to minimize harm, breaking confidentiality may not always represent the best approach (from the perspective of a participant like Sara). So what are researchers to do?

Sara has placed a high value on privacy and also clearly (and reasonably) expects that her disclosures will be kept confidential. She has trusted the researchers. It is quite possible that if she had understood that her parents might be informed about the results of her questionnaire, she would not have made the disclosures. Her worries that her parents will be told about her sexual activities will turn out to be unfounded if disclosure is limited to concerns about her harming herself. Some of these negative consequences can be addressed by the requirement to clearly inform participants about the limits to confidentiality and to assess their understanding of the scope and consequences of these limits. Indeed, participants have a right to know, when making their decision to participate, that there may be times when their data will not remain private.

Nevertheless, explicitly addressing the limits to confidentiality with research participants is also not uncontroversial. When it comes to threats of self-harm, some youth will choose not to disclose and not get the help they need (see Nowell & Spruill, 1999). This also has consequences for the accuracy and efficacy of the research being conducted – consequences that can limit the benefits of the research. In terms of ethics, however, helping children and youth who are at risk for self-harm must be the overriding consideration. This cannot be compromised even for the sake of obtaining valid data.

In addition to all this, participants must be informed about how a breach of confidentiality will be handled. If there is a need to break confidentiality, researchers must be sensitive in how they actually do so (Fisher, 1993). For example, instead of contacting the parents or guardians directly, the case could be passed on to a clinician who is trained in these matters and who is in a better position to explain the significance of the test results and to recommend the appropriate follow-up procedure (for example, further assessment, psychological support, and so on) (see Marcenko, Fishman & Friedman, 1999). Researchers should have in place arrangements for obtaining support from a clinician who is not part of the research project (and thus is less invested in protecting the data) and who can follow up on assessments and contact parents or guardians if necessary. Alerting parents or guardians (that is, notifying them by phone) may in some situations worsen the individual's life circumstances, especially if he/she does not have a good relationship with them. For example, it is possible that a parent/guardian may be angered by this information and feel that the child is simply seeking attention. Notifying parents or guardians prematurely can also result in inappropriate follow-through or no follow-through on their part.

Another alternative – one that allows for follow-up while minimizing the drawbacks to infringing privacy – is to encourage children and youth to refer *themselves* to an appropriate health care service or practitioner. Researchers can provide all participants with information about counsellors who are available to help, or they can give participants the opportunity to check off a box if they want help with problems they are facing. However, there are limitations to self-referral. For instance, higher suicidal ideation is related to lower levels of help-seeking (Carlton & Deane, 2000; Deane, Wilson & Ciarrochi, 2001; Saunders, Resnick, Hoberman & Blum, 1994). Thus, the children and youth who are most likely in need of help may be least likely to ask for help. Accordingly, then, the self-referral option in the case of suicidality has its limits and may not be the best way to protect children and youth from self-harm.

An additional consideration for researchers who study suicidal thoughts and behaviour among children and youth is the need to identify at-risk participants promptly so that they can receive support or further assessment. The research questionnaires may contain very important information that, if attended to quickly and effectively, could prevent a great deal of pain and even save a life. In other words, given the time sensitivity of the disclosures, it is essential that the data be examined promptly, thus allowing for any appropriate follow-up to be pursued in a timely manner. The worst-case scenario is one in which a child or youth does not disclose (so there is no means of identifying that individual), or does disclose, and then follows through on his/her suicidal thoughts and attempts (or completes) suicide. However, in the absence of guidelines, there is often no procedure in place to ensure that the test will be scored promptly, or that those identified will receive support or further assessment. In the absence of professional support or assessment, the child or youth is no better off disclosing than not disclosing. Answering 'yes' to the suicide questionnaire is of no significance if the questionnaire stays buried under a stack of papers on a researcher's desk.

Finally, in balancing the need to respect privacy and confidentiality with the need to minimize harm, it is important to consider the age of the participants being studied. Ethical principles for the prevention of harm hold for all people, but, in the case of children and youth there is an additional obligation to ensure that the procedures and implications of this type of research are explained in a way that the child or youth can comprehend (see Abramovitch, Freedman, Thoden & Nikolich, 1991; Broome & Stieglitz, 1992; Fisher, 1993; Hoagwood, Jensen & Fisher, 1996; Thompson, 1990). Specifically, the confidentiality agreement and its limits must be made clear when informed consent is obtained. While one should always be concerned about the extent of paternalism being imposed by either researchers or clinicians, in the case of children the acceptable threshold is higher. This is widely recognized in many social contexts as necessary for making the well-being of the child a priority.

Conclusion

Researchers in all disciplines share the commitment to respect the dignity of individuals. This fundamental principle justifies a commitment to both respect people's privacy and to override this obligation when risks for significant harm or potential harm are evident. At the present time there are no specific guidelines for researchers that govern the appropriate procedures for conducting and following up on research involving suicidal ideation among children and youth. The lack of guidelines is particularly worrisome considering that researchers with no clinical experience or special training in ethics may administer questionnaires designed to assess suicidality. In an effort to fill this void and begin the necessary discussion around these important issues, we offer some preliminary ethical guidelines specifically aimed at researchers who study suicidality in children and youth. These guidelines are briefly summarized as follows:

1. When obtaining informed consent, clearly state the limits to confidentiality and the procedures that will be followed in the event that a person says he or she is suicidal (see guideline 4).

2. When stating the limits to confidentiality, be clear that the only information to be shared is that which concerns the 'intent to harm.'
3. Score assessments of suicidality immediately.
4. Assess and follow up on suspicious cases with assessments by trained clinicians, and contact parents/guardians for appropriate intervention when appropriate.
5. Encourage children and youth to self-refer, keeping in mind that those most at risk may not seek help.
6. At the end of each testing session, provide all children and youth with information concerning where and how to access help if needed.

We intend these guidelines to be taken as a starting point for a fruitful discussion in this important area of research. Ethical guidelines are important, not only for clinicians but also for researchers working with children and youth, especially when the issues facing them are complex and potentially harmful. Only by carefully considering the ethical issues involved can we begin to weigh the various considerations and decide how to best carry out our research. In this chapter we have highlighted the need to balance the respect we have for the privacy of individuals against our commitment to minimize harm. Working out these difficult ethical conflicts is necessary so that our research can be carried out in a fashion that advances knowledge, and does so in a manner that is respectful of the individuals necessary for this pursuit.

NOTE

The authors wish to thank Mitchell J. Prinstein, Bonnie Leadbeater, and Elizabeth Banister for their helpful comments regarding this chapter. The authors also wish to thank Shannon Servos and Amanda Krygsman for their help with the compilation of materials for this chapter.

REFERENCES

Abramovitch, R., Freedman, J.L., Thoden, K., & Nikolich, C. (1991). Children's capacity to consent to participation in psychological research: Empirical findings. *Child Development, 62,* 1100–09.
American Psychological Association. (1999). Ethical principles of psycholo-

gists and code of conduct. In D.N. Bersoff (Ed.), *Ethical conflicts in psychology* (2nd ed., 7–25). Washington, DC: American Psychological Association.

Anderson, R.N. (2002). Deaths: leading causes for 2000. National Vital Statistics Reports 50(16). Hyattsville, MD: National Center for Health Statistics.

Appelbaum, P.S., & Rosenbaum, A. (1999). Tarasoff and the researcher: Does the duty to protect apply in research settings? In D.N. Bersoff (Ed.), *Ethical conflicts in psychology* (2nd ed., pp. 176–81). Washington, DC: American Psychological Association.

Broome, M.E., & Stieglitz, K.A. (1992). The consent process and children. *Research in Nursing and Health*, 15, 147–52.

Beck, A.T., Steer, R.A., Kovacs, M., & Garrison, B. (1985). Hopelessness and eventual suicide: A 10–year prospective study of patients hospitalized with suicidal ideation. *American Journal of Psychiatry*, 142, 559–63.

Carlson, G., & Cantwell, D. (1982). Suicidal behavior and depression in children and adolescents. *American Academy of Child Psychiatry*, 21, 361–8.

Carlton, P., & Deane, F. (2000). Impact of attitudes and suicidal ideation on adolescents' intentions to seek professional psychological help. *Journal of Adolescence*, 23, 35–45.

Canadian Psychological Association. (1999). Canadian code of ethics for psychologists. In D.N. Bersoff (ed.), *Ethical conflicts in psychology* (2nd ed., 26–39). Washington, DC: American Psychological Association.

Centers for Disease Control and Prevention. (2004). *Suicide in the United States*. Retrieved 25 March 2004 from www.cdc.gov/ncipc/factsheets/suifacts.htm.

Deane, F., Wilson, C., & Ciarrochi, J. (2001). Suicidal ideation and help-negation: Not just hopelessness or prior help. *Journal of Clinical Psychology*, 57, 901–14.

Department of Justice Canada. (2003). The duty to report child abuse. Retrieved 25 March 2004 from www.justice.gc.ca/en/ps/yj/rp/doc/Paper106.rtf.

Douglas, K.S., & Webster, C.D. (1999). Predicting violence in mentally and personality disordered individuals. In R. Roesch, S.D. Hart & J.R.P. Ogloff (eds.), *Psychology and law: The state of the discipline* (pp. 175–239). New York: Kluwer Academic/Plenum Publishers.

Everstine, L., Sullivan Everstine, D., Heyman, G.M., True, R.H., Frey, D.H., Johnson, H.G., & Seiden, R.H. (1999). Privacy and confidentiality in psychotherapy. In D.N. Bersoff (ed.), *Ethical conflicts in psychology* (2nd ed., 162–4). Washington, DC: American Psychological Association.

Fisher, C. (1993). Integrating science and ethics in research with high-risk children and youth. *Social Policy Report: Society for Research in Child Development*, 4, 1–27.

Glowinski, A., Bucholz, K., Nelson, E., Fu, Q., Madden, P., Reich, W., & Heath, A. (2001). Suicide attempts in an adolescent twin sample. *Journal of the American Academy of Child and Adolescent Psychiatry*, 40, 1300–7.

Grunbaum, J.A., Kann, L., Kinchen, S.A., Williams, B., Ross, J., Lowry, R., & Kolbe, L. (2002). Youth risk behavior surveillance – United States, 2001. Retrieved 25 March 2004 from www.cdc.gov/mmwr/preview/mmwrhtml/ss5104a1.htm.

Health Canada. (1999). Measuring up: A health surveillance update on Canadian children and youth. Retrieved 25 March 2004 from www.hc-sc.gc.ca/pphb-dgspsp/publicat/meas-haut/mu_y_e.html.

Hoagwood, K., Jensen, P.S., & Fisher, C. (1996). Toward a science of scientific ethics in research on child and adolescent mental disorders. In K. Hoagwood, P.S. Jensen & C. Fisher (Eds.), *Ethical issues in mental health research with children and adolescents* (pp. 3–14). (Mahwah, NJ: Lawrence Erlbaum Associates.

King, N.M.P., & Churchill, L.R. (2000). Ethical principles guiding research on child and adolescent subjects. *Journal of Interpersonal Violence*, 15, 710–24.

Marcenko, M., Fishman, G., & Friedman, J. (1999). Reexamining adolescent suicidal ideation: A developmental perspective applied to a diverse population. *Journal of Youth and Adolescence*, 28, 121–38.

National Institute of Mental Health. (2003). Suicide facts. Retrieved 25 March 2004 from www.nimh.nih.gov/research/suifact.cfm.

Nowell, D., & Spruill, J. (1999). If it's not absolutely confidential, will information be disclosed? In D.N. Bersoff (Ed.), *Ethical conflicts in psychology* (2nd ed., pp. 196–9). Washington, DC: American Psychological Association.

O'Carroll, P., Crosby, A., Mercy, J., Lee, R., & Simon, T. (2001). Interviewing suicide 'decedents': A fourth strategy for risk factor assessment. *Suicide and Life-Threatening Behavior*, 32, 3–6.

Sattler, J.M. (2001). *Assessment of children: Cognitive applications* (4th ed.). San Diego, CA: Jerome M. Sattler.

Saunders, S., Resnick, M., Hoberman, H., & Blum, R. (1994). Formal help-seeking behavior of adolescents identifying themselves as having mental health problems. *Journal of the American Academy of Child and Adolescent Psychiatry*, 33, 718–28.

Supreme Court of California. (1976). *Tarasoff v. Regents of the University of California* (Tarasoff II), 551 P.2d 334.

Taylor, L., & Adelman, H.S. (1999). Reframing the confidentiality dilemma to work in children's best interests. In D.N. Bersoff (Ed.), *Ethical conflicts in psychology* (2nd ed. pp. 205–8). Washington, DC: American Psychological Association.

Thompson, R. (1990). Vulnerability in research: A developmental perspective on research risk. *Child Development*, 61, 1–16.

Tri-council Working Group. (1998). *Tri-council policy statement: Ethical conduct for research involving humans* (with 2000, 2002 updates). Retrieved 11 March 2004 from www.pre.ethics.gc.ca/english/policystatement/policystatement.cfm.

PART SIX

Summary and Recommendations for Ethical Guidelines, Research, and Training

13 Unique Roles, Unique Challenges: Graduate Students' Involvement in Community–Academic Research

JOSH SLATKOFF, RACHEL PHILLIPS, SARAH CORRIN,
TAMARA ROZECK-ALLEN, AND TERESA STRONG-WILSON

Academics, policy makers, and practitioners are forming collaborative research partnerships to increase the evidence base for policy and practice, and graduate students are central to research that is being conducted. The Healthy Youth in a Healthy Society Community Alliance for Health Research (CAHR) project at the University of Victoria aims to train graduate students to forge, maintain, and advance community–academic research partnerships in the course of their target projects and throughout their careers.[1] One aspect of this training involves helping them develop an understanding of the ethical dilemmas that can arise in the context of community–academic partnerships, and of how to respond to these challenges. In this chapter we discuss ethical dilemmas that graduate students may well face when they collaborate in research projects with community partners. We begin by describing the CAHR's approach to training graduate students. We then examine how relationships that graduate students form with their supervisors and community partners can lead to role conflicts during the research. Using examples from our experience, we identify ways to approach and resolve such conflicts.

The graduate students in the CAHR project are admitted to their respective department-based graduate programs; there, they are supervised by a CAHR faculty member and work directly on one of the target projects. Students also participate in a monthly, not-for-credit colloquium. During the project's first year, this colloquium was initiated and led by a senior faculty member, who also acted as a consultant to the project. His primary role was to facilitate students' interdisciplinary training. In the second and subsequent years of the seminar, graduate students have taken the lead in facilitating the colloquiums, in consultation with faculty advisers. The seminars are intended to provide an interdisciplinary forum for students to interact with one another, to enhance students' interdisciplinary research training, and to provide students with opportunities to work collaboratively across the CAHR target projects.

To facilitate interdisciplinary perspectives, the students spend time in these colloquiums discussing their backgrounds, positions, and responsibilities in the target projects, as well as their methodological orientations, academic interests, and past research experiences. They are provided with opportunities to discuss the particular challenges they are encountering in individual target projects, including ethical challenges related to project methodology and design, working with vulnerable populations, and obtaining informed consent. Also, CAHR faculty lead workshops on a variety of topics such as conducting research with focus groups, developing conceptual models, qualitative methodologies, ethics, and writing for academic publications. The seminars support students as they generate ideas and develop their own research initiatives. Past student initiatives included facilitating a workshop and roundtable discussion on translating prevention research into policy and practice; presenting research findings at national conferences; documenting interdisciplinary processes within the CAHR project; and collaborating on the writing of this chapter.

Participation in the colloquium strengthens graduate students' ability to critically examine issues as they emerge from work on the target projects and to generate solutions to these challenges. While ethics questions in research generally focus on the participants, in this chapter we explore those concerns which relate to the little-considered role of graduate students. Drawing on our experience as graduate trainees and paid research assistants, we describe three types of ethical dilemmas that graduate students may well experience with respect to managing multiple roles, faculty–student relationships, data interpretation, and authorship. We share strategies that have been followed in the CAHR project to mitigate potential harms and enhance benefits for graduate students.

Ethical Dilemma I: Managing Dual Relationships between Graduate Students and Faculty Members

In community-based research, students may occupy dual roles as both trainees and paid research assistants. As graduate trainees, they are mentored by their faculty supervisors and gain research experience by participating in research projects. However, as paid research assistants, they enter contracts for employment, and such employment can be distinct from the trainee role. In practice, similar types of activities can be undertaken in the context of each of these roles. Thus, the distinction between a student's role as a trainee and his/her role as a paid research assistant can blur.

Being a graduate trainee and at the same time a paid research assistant in community-based research can have both advantages and disadvantages. An advantage to working with faculty members who have already formed relationships with community partners is that when conducting thesis or dissertation work, students may be able to access participants in the community who would otherwise be unavailable. However, the complexities of data collection and research ethics board (REB) approval in community-based research projects often result in a protracted research process. Agreeing on topics than can be supported within an adviser's projects and partnerships with communities may increase the likelihood that the thesis will be completed. Students may be able to use the extra time required in community-based research projects to develop other professional skills such as writing for publication, organizing workshops, preparing conference presentations, and writing grant proposals. Graduate students can benefit from participation in interdisciplinary, community-based research when they are treated as important members of the partnership rather than hired hands who are paid by the hour.

In the CAHR project, faculty members try to provide a working environment that accommodates the demands of students' academic lives – for example, by allowing flexible work schedules and by encouraging students to work on portions of research projects for course credit. Furthermore, the CAHR project attempts to create an intellectual climate in which students are integral to the research process. In practical terms, this means that faculty members solicit and use students' feedback about research design, encourage them to play an active role in research meetings with community partners, and coauthor academic research presentations and papers.

But elevating the role of the research assistant above that of a hired hand or hourly wage earner requires ongoing open discussions about the changing roles of students. Students advance a collegial climate when they show initiative and commitment to faculty-led projects by generating hypotheses, exploring data sets, and approaching faculty with ideas for publications. Several processes for resolving concerns have been put in place. Students and faculty can discuss the evolving roles of the student, from a junior role as a data manager to a more senior role as an author of scholarly publications. In the CAHR training model, students who are experiencing friction with their supervisors also benefit from the opportunity to consult confidentially with a senior, respected faculty member. This person serves as an adviser to the CAHR project but is not directly involved in its operations and thus falls outside the supervisory hierarchy. This senior adviser is well positioned to provide objective guidance to students. Concerns can also be addressed at regular project meetings, in CAHR colloquiums with other graduate students, and in a course specifically developed by a CAHR faculty member to explore issues in interdisciplinary research (Marshall, in progress).

Discussions about role conflicts can be productive sources of knowledge for CAHR funders, target projects, and individual project members. However, such discussions could be constrained by the power hierarchies that an academic environment enforces on faculty and graduate students.

As Gottlieb (1993) argues, dual roles can become problematic when a power difference exists between members of the relationship, when the relationship is of long duration, or when the point of termination is uncertain. A power difference is inherent in faculty–student relationships, and this can lead to a complicated situation for graduate students who occupy dual roles as both graduate trainees and paid research assistants. Students may feel that as academic advisers and employers, faculty members hold leverage over their future careers because they evaluate students' work and recommend students to potential employers or for scholarships. Faculty–student relationships can also vary in the degree to which they are supportive, collaborative, hierarchical, and supervisory. Students may anticipate harsher consequences for terminating the relationship than faculty members, especially if no replacement research supervisor or employer is available (Blevins-Knabe, 1992). Thus, they may feel considerable pressure to maintain positive relations with faculty members and are reluctant to refuse requests related to a research project.

Student–faculty relationships can be more productive when faculty members are supported by graduate research assistants who are committed to the project's goals, when faculty offer significant opportunities for professional development, and when faculty and graduate students are willing to discuss their concerns.

Ethical Dilemma II: Negotiating the Interpretation of Findings

Interdisciplinary graduate student training can enhance the integration of multiple forms of knowledge; however, epistemological differences that exist within academic institutions (that is, among and within academic departments) need to be acknowledged. Discussions about the nature of knowledge (for example, with regard to objectivity versus social construction) can lead to different views about research strategies and methods and their validity. Differences in academic and non-academic approaches to data interpretation can also arise when some forms of knowledge are prioritized over others (Hartstock, 1997). For instance, community and academic partners may weigh anecdotal or practical and empirical sources of knowledge differently. Through their close contact with academic and community partners, graduate students can be challenged to reconcile and integrate these various sources of knowledge and to apply them to both theory and action.

Graduate students may experience differences with their community partner or faculty supervisor as tensions that are hard to resolve. The community partner hopes to use the findings to lobby for a particular policy or program, whereas for the academic partner, the findings must meet standards of scientific rigour. Also, the research findings may conflict with the experiential knowledge of community partners or be controversial. Community partners may be less concerned than academic partners about generalization, reliability, and validity – that is, about the kind of evidence debated and valued in academic circles. In addition, community partners may hold the ideal of advocating first and foremost for the interests of the individuals and organizations they serve. In sum, the priorities of community partners may differ from those embodied by the university, the principal investigators, or the graduate students. For instance, in research designed to evaluate program effects, community partners may have a vested interest in demonstrating positive program effects; in contrast, academic-based evaluators generally strive to support community partners, but also to provide unbiased evidence of program efficacy.

Graduate students who work within academic–community collaborations may find themselves caught between loyalties vis-à-vis faculty and community partners. When graduate students are members of the target population (for example, when they come from Aboriginal communities) or have a history of employment with a community partner, they may feel conflicting allegiances as academics-in-training who at the same time identify with the perspective of the community partner. This sort of dual role can give rise to ethics dilemmas for any researcher, but particularly for a graduate student, who must somehow navigate the multiple context while also being cognizant of his/her place as a trainee.

CAHR graduate students have identified several strategies for soothing the tensions that can arise from discrepant forms of knowledge and approaches to data interpretation. Students may find that their epistemological views already fundamentally agree with those of faculty members. Alternatively, their values may undergo a shift as they participate in the research project. For instance, students may gain knowledge of how qualitative and quantitative data complement each other through course work; they can then apply this knowledge in their research project. However, when epistemologies conflict, graduate students may need to temporarily set aside questions emerging from their background so as not to interfere unduly with the research process. Sometimes doing so can be immensely beneficial, as graduate students learn from watching a research process unfold. This experience can expand students' own professional development. However, the tensions emanating from the overall research design cannot always be alleviated, particularly when graduate students occupy positions of assistance rather than responsibility within the research partnership. When loyalties appear to conflict, these need to be discussed with both faculty and community partners.

In applied, community-based, collaborative research, graduate students can play an active role in ensuring that the community partners' concerns about the research process are heard and addressed. In interactions with community partners, graduate students *must* understand and articulate the rationales for academic positions on project issues. In some cases, graduate students may be able to respond to community partners' concerns simply by listening to and validating the challenges that community partners are experiencing with the research process. For instance, graduate students can explain to teachers the need for, and benefits of, surveys in school-based research, and also acknowledge that such surveys can be time-consuming and therefore disruptive of school routines. Usually, graduate students can convey the concerns to the faculty member, who can then address the questions directly with the community partner. As front-line workers in a research project, graduate students may be in an ideal position to inform faculty members about the community partners' concerns and to help address these concerns. Because graduate students play a junior role in the research partnership, their actions are circumscribed by their need to maintain collegial relations with both academic and community partners.

Graduate students in community-based research may be exposed to community partners' perspectives and to dilemmas arising from interpretations of the research findings. In an interdisciplinary, academic–community research environment such as CAHR, the existence of multiple perspectives is inevitable and generally benefits the research process. Tensions arising from differing perspectives can prompt those involved to reflect on their assumptions and to negotiate new or more developed explanations of research phenomena. Differing perspectives of this sort may be perceived as complementary rather than conflicting if they represent multiple experiences or positions in relation to the subject of study and if they are integrated to provide a richer description of the findings. Graduate students can engage in discussions about ways that non-academic partners can apply findings to their communities and respond to feedback about the degree of 'fit' between findings and local knowledge. Issues arising from differing data interpretations can be minimized when community and academic partners are clear from the start about roles and expectations in the research process. Academic partners are often responsible for interpreting and documenting research findings because they possess skills and expertise in these activities. However, in an interdisciplinary community–academic context, academic partners must consider and incorporate community partners' interpretations when analysing data and disseminating findings. Graduate students can play key roles as mediators when they work closely with community partners as research assistants and when they are also members of the community under study.

Other courses of action exist for graduate students if they become aware of differing data interpretations between community and academic partners. Graduate students can take an active, collaborative role in discussing findings with the principal investigator and the community partner. Students' roles in the research process can bring them in close contact with the target population and community partners. When they convey the views of community partners to academic partners and encourage community partners to raise their concerns with academic partners, they are strengthening the research process overall.

Ethical Dilemma III: Negotiating Authorship

Credit for authorship of academic reports, papers, and other research dissemination materials has often been a point of contention for faculty and students. In community–academic research settings, there are multiple partners who can be invited into the writing process, as well as multiple audiences to whom the findings can be presented.[2] The dilemmas and potential solutions outlined below represent, from the perspective of graduate students, a few of the challenges that arise when negotiating authorship in interdisciplinary, community–academic research projects.

Negotiating access to and ownership of the research ideas and data that give rise to opportunities for publication can be complicated. As employees, graduate students may be integrally involved in collecting and analysing data, but their paid work as research assistants typically does not, in and of itself, justify access to the data for their own projects; nor does it grant them authorship.

Faculty and graduate students in multipartnership research environments must have clear processes for negotiating who is involved in authorship, how authorship responsibilities and credit are to be divided among collaborators, and how to incorporate multiple perspectives and writing styles in interdisciplinary writing. For example, during the writing of this collaborative chapter, students from several disciplines were invited to participate because of their involvement in the graduate students' colloquiums. Besides negotiating roles and timelines in writing the chapter, the group also had to find ways to continue to collaborate as their involvement in the CAHR project and in the university shifted over time (that is, as some graduated and moved into new positions).

Strategies for mitigating potential authorship problems have been the topic of substantial discussion, and guidelines have been established in the context of the CAHR project. Typically, students have been able to merge their roles as research assistants and trainees by preparing literature reviews and program evaluation protocols for community partners. In these writing projects, students receive course credit or stipends, or both. At the same time, students must recognize their limits of expertise, make realistic demands, and be prepared to accept an increasing degree of autonomy in authorship only as their skills and knowledge of the research project progress. Students begin to develop authorship skills by writing papers and reports for course credit and by preparing pamphlets and presentations for community audiences. As their skills develop, students are invited to work with faculty on academic presentations and on papers for publication in refereed journals.

Both students and research partnerships benefit when faculty are willing to mentor senior students as first authors on academic publications. These generally focus on work done for a masters or doctoral thesis. When students assume the role of first author, they take responsibility for coordinating the work and communicating with publishers or editors. As noted earlier, it is beneficial to students, faculty, and community partners if students dovetail their research with the community–academic collaborations they are part of by developing complementary research. Faculty also invite students, who also may be employees, to assist in publications that are prepared with the assistance of graduate students who are working as employees. This practice broadens the options for writing about project findings and removes some of the burden of dissemination from faculty; it also benefits community partners, particularly when student papers on project data explore questions that are of interest to community partners and the populations they work with.

To facilitate authorship collaborations, students focus on the strengths and benefits of the collaborative process and negotiate with their coauthors, whether those coauthors are other graduate students, faculty, or community partners. It is important to define, early in the process, expectations about authorship and contributions through open dialogue. Those involved may wish to establish a writing timeline and general outline of the contents of the work to be developed. In developing these plans, some flexibility will be required, and student authors should ideally have an opportunity to see the writing process through to the end. If this is not possible, members of a collaboration may wish to withdraw as authors or renegotiate their placing vis-à-vis other group members. It is also beneficial for students to seek faculty support to resolve dilemmas between student members. It is also helpful to have access to third-party faculty members who can mediate any difficulties that arise between students and faculty. As noted earlier in the chapter, these third parties are provided to graduate students in the CAHR as part of their participation in the graduate student colloquiums. Finally, in recognition of the array of considerations in authorship that arise in interdisciplinary, community–academic research partnerships, members of the CAHR project have written policies and procedures for data sharing and authorship. (www.youth.society.uvic.ca/resources/

researchers.html) These protocols apply to students, community members, and faculty, and serve as a guide to graduate students working and studying within the CAHR project.

Conclusion

Today's graduate students will be tomorrow's independent academic researchers. In the CAHR project, the approach taken to training graduate students provides a framework for identifying and managing issues that emerge for researchers-in-training during research collaborations with community partners. By recognizing, exploring, and prioritizing the values that emerge as a result of potentially conflicting loyalties to personal standards, to individual projects, to community partners, and to the university, graduate students are laying the foundation for sound decision-making in their current and future professional endeavours. In this chapter, we have offered examples of how graduate students can negotiate multiple roles with faculty members and community partners. We have also shown how graduate students' responsibilities to both academic research and community partners place them in a unique position to contribute to the resolution of ethics concerns. Finally, we have demonstrated how graduate students can collaborate in negotiating authorship responsibilities.

Our challenge at this stage is to assess the feasibility of adapting the strategies described in this chapter to address other issues that emerge for graduate students as we continue to negotiate our place within community–academic research collaborations. For example, how can graduate students who are still in the training phase of their careers act responsibly when community partners and research participants request informal consultation on matters that extend beyond their professional competence? Through involvement in interdisciplinary, community-based research projects, graduate students can develop valuable research practices, some arising from their own experiences (which may originate in the community), some from graduate seminars, and others from adhering to the institutional guidelines governing academic–community research partnerships. Ethical research practices, and processes for illuminating and resolving conflicts, are the keys to this. Developing such practices may constitute a balancing act for graduate students because of the junior roles they inhabit in academic and community-based partnerships. Further investigations of graduate student roles and positions within community-based research will continue to identify benefits, challenges, and strategies for maximizing the potential of our unique position within community–academic research partnerships.

NOTES

1 Although this chapter refers to graduate students' experiences, undergraduate students have also been involved with the CAHR as research assistants and honours students.
2 Authorship refers to credit given for contribution to the creation of an original work.

REFERENCES

Blevins-Knabe, B. (1992). The ethics of dual relationships in higher education. *Ethics and Behaviour*, 2, 151–63.
Gottlieb, M.C. (1993). Avoiding exploitative dual relationships: A decision-making model. *Psychotherapy*, 30, 41–7.
Hartstock, N.C.M. (1997). Comment on Hekman's 'Truth and method: Feminist standpoint revisited': Truth or justice? *Signs*, 22(2), 367–74.
Marshall, A. (in progress). Development of a graduate course in interdisciplinary research.

14 Stepping into Community-Based Research: Preparing Students to Meet New Ethics and Professional Challenges

MARLENE MORETTI, BONNIE LEADBEATER, AND ANNE MARSHALL

Training in research ethics is too often viewed as inconsequential. In most social science programs, students take course work on ethics separately from courses in the substantive areas of the discipline, and even separately from courses on research design and analysis. In programs offering professional degrees, such as clinical psychology and counselling, students usually complete a course on ethics; however, the content focuses almost entirely on ethical issues related to clinical practice. When research ethics are covered in such courses, students often get the message that research ethics are relatively straightforward and easily resolved through a quick reference to standards and guidelines. Students who are pursuing research careers in the social sciences often have no requirement whatsoever for course work on ethics. Presumably these students learn how to manage the ethical challenges of research through apprenticeships, relying on the tutelage of their research supervisors. Unfortunately, this sometimes resembles training through trial and error, or in worst-case scenarios, trial by fire.

What are we communicating to our students when we teach research ethics in such a cursory way? In this chapter we argue that conventional content and methods of training in research ethics are rooted in a traditional view of science as separate from and impartial to that which it investigates. Such practices, however, are out of step with recent developments in how social scientists approach their work; and as we have seen from the various chapters in this book, such training is insufficient to prepare our students for engaging in community-based research with vulnerable populations. In what follows we discuss the unique issues that arise in teaching ethics related to community-based research; the importance of providing students with an explicit and structured problem-solving strategy; and teaching methods that better equip students to develop competence in responding to the complexities of ethical challenges.

Why Is Traditional Training in Research Ethics Insufficient?

Traditional training in research ethics ensures that students gain a thorough knowledge of relevant ethical codes and guidelines. In social science research, this often includes the ethical codes and guidelines of the Canadian Psychological Association (Canadian Psychological Association, 2000) and the American Psychological Association (American Psychological Association, 2002). Students may also be required to familiarize themselves with specialty guidelines, which are published from time to time and which regulate research and practices with particular populations (such as visible minorities) or for controversial topics and issues (such as recovered memories).

The long-standing procedure for ethical problem-solving in social science research has generally been closed-ended and static: each guideline is considered sequentially as it applies to the proposed study under consideration; concerns, if any, are identified; and methodology is revised to reduce risk in proportion to the potential value of the research. The senior investigator, alone or in consultation with the other investigators, typically completes this process well in advance of beginning the study. She then submits an application – often in the form of an 'ethics checklist' – for approval to the ethics office, review board, or panel at the host institution in which the study will be conducted. Once approved, she begins data collection.

How does community-based research with vulnerable populations compare with standard research procedures for studies conducted in university labs? We focus on two *process-related* issues that we believe set community-based research apart from traditional research endeavours, and that are particularly significant in how we train our students. First, unlike traditional, lab-based studies, community-based research is embedded in multiple social contexts and institutions and typically involves ongoing collaboration across a spectrum of professionals and laypeople. Second, ethical problem-solving in traditional, lab-based studies unfolds sequentially and is completed before a study begins, whereas community-based research involves a dynamic and ongoing interaction with the community; such interaction demands constant monitoring and reassessment of ethical issues. The contextual and dynamic aspects of community-based research raise unique and substantive problems, many of which have been touched on in the other chapters of this book.

Setting the Stage: Developing and Sustaining Relationships among Collaborators

Students may assume that ethical principles apply only in our professional interactions with individuals – typically, clients or research participants. But our interactions with other professional groups, communities, and institutions are guided by the same principles. Each group, community, and institution frequently has its own values, policies, and code of ethics. Thus, ethical principles are not something abstract and external that we consult and apply to solve particular research problems as they arise. Rather, these principles are the very fabric of our social contract with our community partners, and they guide all our interactions.

How does all of this influence the way we teach students ethics in community-based research? We believe it emphasizes the fact that as mentors, we need to teach our students to be sensitive to the ethics of research procedures and methods, and more importantly, to the ethics of their professional interactions with communities, host institutions, and research participants and partners. As teachers, we have traditionally focused on the first issue – the ethics of research methods. It is important that we communicate to students through course content and our teaching practices that ethics is as much about *process* (for example, how a consent form is negotiated between the university and a community service) as it is about *content* (for example, what a consent form states).

When we launch community-based research, at least two systems come into contact – and sometimes collide: the university's system and that of the community under study. We must also consider applicable laws and regulatory acts. Each system comes with its own history and procedures for identifying and resolving problems, as well as its own beliefs, hopes, and fears as they relate to the process and outcome of collaboration. As teachers, we need to help students (a) learn to recognize and respect the explicit and implicit beliefs, standards, and principles within each system, and (b) develop skills to navigate conflicts that inevitably emerge in bringing communities together and keeping them together throughout the project. Both steps are essential to ensuring the success of the study from a purely pragmatic point of view. And both are ethical obligations of researchers. This is captured by the CPA's code of ethics (2000) under the principle of respect for the dignity of persons and responsible caring. Respect for persons extends beyond individuals to the institutions, neighbourhoods, Aboriginal bands, and communities of which they are part.

The instructor's task is to help students develop mindfulness of the diverse standards, values, and procedures embedded in these contexts. It is often useful to use case studies to illustrate common points of conflict. Take, for example, the issue of consent – a central concern discussed in many of the chapters in this book. Many university research offices set a conservative standard for age of consent – often seventeen or older. Medical and mental health settings do not necessarily follow the same guideline, and school boards often utilize yet another standard. Provincial acts also set forth the definition of a minor and the conditions under which minors can provide consent. However, under these acts a specific age of consent is rarely indicated. Rather, whether or not a minor can give consent is defined in terms of his or her competence to fully appreciate the nature and consequences of participation in procedures or services (see, for example, British Columbia, *Infants Act*). Once students grasp the complexities of the standards and definitions that operate across these systems, they will understand that developing a consent form is not as easy as they first thought.

It is not difficult to think of an endless series of similar dilemmas where researchers find themselves on the cusp between educational and research institutions, community agencies, and participants themselves. For example, researchers, community social service agencies, and clients may differ substantially in their estimates of the risks and benefits of research. School boards, teachers, and parents may look at what university researchers consider high- or low-risk methodology quite differently. Students who have the opportunity to interact with community agencies and other sectors will learn to appreciate the diversity of perspectives and standards that come to bear in community-based research, as well as the intricacies of the collaboration process. It is one thing to review in class the ethical codes and guidelines of various agencies, as well as the relevant laws or acts; it is quite another to sit with a panel of teachers and parents and discuss their concerns about children's participation in peer nomination procedures, or to discuss concerns about random assignment and waitlist control paradigms with a panel of mental health service providers. These learning activities go much further in expanding students' appreciation of and respect for the diverse perspectives and positions they will encounter as community-based researchers.

The issues we have identified here should be among the first for students to consider as they embark on community-based research. Students are better equipped to build trusting relationships of the kind that are required to articulate a truly collaborative research program when they recognize all the stakeholders involved in the research and their diverse views and standards. More importantly, we need to emphasize to students that the understandings that are forged during the early stages of collaborative research set the foundations for what comes later. When the foundations are strong and plainly stated, and guided by shared ethical principles, the collaborative process is more likely to be open, successful, and productive.

Key Questions to Pose to Students

1. Who are the relevant stakeholders and gatekeepers involved in the project? Make sure to include public and private agencies to which stakeholders/gatekeepers are accountable.
2. What is the history of the institution or agency, and how does that place them in a particular role relative to the research program and its focus?
3. What ethical guidelines, policies, and procedures exist within each of these institutions, agencies, or communities?
4. How does each institution or agency define the risks and benefits of the research program?
5. Where are the potential domains of conflict in terms of ethical standards, regulations and perceived risks and benefits?
6. Are there relevant laws and acts that pertain to the research?
7. What are your ethical responsibilities to your host institution, the communities collaborating on this project, and the participants?
8. How can you best engender respect, mutual understanding, and commitment to ethical principles and to the research program by all parties?

Dancing in Step with the Dynamic Process of Community-Based Research

Students (and, indeed, traditionally based academic researchers as well) are typically trained to deal with ethical issues at the outset of a study; relatively little attention is paid to monitoring ethical issues over the course of a research program. This is because traditional research para-

digms rarely require active monitoring or reconsideration of procedures for ethical reasons. In contrast, community-based research is
more likely to be dynamic and changing as a function of communications among institutions, communities, and participants. As well,
community-based studies often reach deeper into the personal lives of
participants and may involve some who live in difficult or volatile
situations. Researchers must actively monitor and respond to challenges as they emerge.

There are a host of other factors that can shift during the research
program and that require forethought and planning by the team. For
example, community partners may experience mandate shifts, changes
in staffing, or budget cuts that require a regrouping of roles and partnership obligations. Thus, it is necessary to develop a clear understanding and structure within the team for monitoring and communicating
how research procedures are affecting participants, and whether unanticipated problems or new challenges are emerging. It is impossible to
anticipate everything that might arise, or how issues will affect the
research program and participants, so students must learn to recognize
and prepare for dealing with change and challenges

We must establish the roles and responsibilities of team members and
the procedures that will be followed in responding to arising issues,
and we must do so early instead of leaving them to be sorted out in the
midst or aftermath of their occurrence. We can emphasize to students
the value of striking an advisory committee or 'reflection team' that can
provide a context for monitoring ongoing issues and deciding whether
and how procedures need to change. Decisions need to be made about
the structure and function of such committees. Who best serves the
needs of the various parties involved in the research and represents
the interests of the participants? What issues should be brought to the
committee? Is the feedback from the committee advisory or does it
carry some decision-making authority? If it does not, to whom does the
committee report and what steps come next? How often should the
committee meet? Such questions raise a whole new set of challenges for
students, who likely have little experience constructing such a team if
they have been involved only in lab-based research.

Yet it is important for students to understand that an advisory committee is insufficient in and of itself for dealing with the ethical challenges in community-based research. Indeed, we have sometimes found
that the presence of an advisory committee provides a false sense of
security that everything is under control when what has really hap-

pened is that responsibility has been diffused. It is vital that the roles and responsibilities of team members be explicitly articulated to ensure that problems are actually resolved and that action is taken. In many community-based research programs it is also necessary to identify who is responsible for arising issues and has the authority to respond to them.

If they are to respond to these issues effectively, students must learn to recognize the multiple relationships they enter into once they take on the role of community-based researcher. As professionals, they must remain cognizant of their ethical responsibilities to their community partners and to the participants, and to their scientific field and collaborators as well. Case-based examples can help students identify potential pitfalls and appreciate why it is necessary to build in a system for monitoring and revising procedures at the outset – for example, an advisory committee or a reflection team. It is even better to provide students with opportunities to hear from other researchers who have worked in the field and who have experienced and responded to challenges, both successfully and unsuccessfully. This will better equip them to deal proactively with challenges in their own work.

Not surprisingly, students can sometimes feel overwhelmed when they think about the endless problems that can arise and the crises over which they feel they have little control. It is helpful to reassure them that it is unnecessary – indeed, impossible – to anticipate all problems in community-based research. Rather, the focus should be (a) recognizing that change and challenge are part of community-based research; (b) developing a sound foundation and structure for ongoing problem-solving and collaborative decision-making; and (c) clearly articulating the roles and responsibilities of team members. If the research program is supported by a strong foundation in this sense, it will have both the structure and the flexibility to respond effectively to whatever issues might arise.

Key Questions to Pose to Students

1. Should an advisory committee or reflection team be struck, and if so, what functions will it serve?
2. Who should sit on the committee? How will membership represent the interests of important parties in the research? Will the committee serve a decision-making function, and if not, how will decisions be made?

3. What are the roles and responsibilities of team members vis-à-vis monitoring and responding to ethical issues?
4. Which team members hold the responsibility and authority for responding to ethical concerns or crises that arise?

Covering All the Bases: Special Issues in Community-Based Research

Traditional and contemporary research training touch on common issues, such as minimizing the risk of research procedures, ensuring cultural sensitivity and reliability, gaining informed consent, ensuring and maintaining confidentiality, protecting confidentiality when data are stored and analysed, and ensuring fairness with regard to authorship and the appropriate dissemination of findings. These seem straightforward; however, each is potentially complicated by the contextualized and dynamic quality of community-based research. For example, when we seek informed consent from street kids to participate in interviews about risky sexual behaviour, we face very different challenges than when we seek informed consent from undergraduates completing surveys on sexuality. We need to remember that in the first scenario, questions of competence in understanding the risks and benefits of participation and the limits to confidentiality are much more provocative (see Jansson & Benoit, in this volume). Even simple issues, such as providing financial incentives for participation, take on a special meaning in such scenarios because of the dire conditions in which street kids may be living. How much compensation is appropriate? How much is too little, and what message does it convey? How much introduces undue or coercive influence on the decision to participate in research? Should we be concerned about what kids will do with the money they receive? In what other ways could participants be compensated? Although we might ask similar questions in considering incentives for students participating in university-based lab studies, as researchers we understand that the stakes are higher in research with kids living on the streets. Fortunately, as this book makes clear, the emerging literature on issues related to the research participation of children and youth can provide some guidance to students in making decisions in these domains. Nevertheless, many issues remain murky. Students must be encouraged to practise using ethical principals and consultation to guide their development of new solutions in such situations.

Some issues just never arise in university-based lab studies, or they are emphasized to a greater degree in community-based settings. For example, community-based research is more likely to be conducted with special populations; thus, the validity of measures must to be assessed in relation to issues of social class. Similarly, consent forms, experimental procedures, and confidentiality policies need to be sensitive and respectful (see Riecken & Strong-Wilson, in this volume). The guidelines for conducting research with ethnic minority children and youth recently published by Fisher and colleagues (2002) demonstrate the complexity of these issues.

From the outset of research we must strive to help our students appreciate and be comfortable with openly discussing issues of data ownership and the authorship of publications. This is not easy; students often feel extremely uncomfortable about such discussions. Yet they and their community partners may hold different assumptions about ownership of the data – assumptions that only become clear when the study is completed, at which time they can generate bitter conflict and resentment. Even worse, the use of data can be delayed, restricted, or curtailed. Data ownership and authorship issues need to be clarified early on. If data may be used for other purposes after the study has been completed, guidelines must be established for how this will be negotiated, and the possibility must be noted in consent forms.

As discussed earlier, the individuals and communities involved in community-based research expect and deserve to hear about the outcome of the research, preferably in forms that will benefit them. Students are not typically trained in how to give back to communities, so they require guidance in this regard. A copy of the thesis or a journal manuscript may be appreciated but is unlikely to be sufficient feedback for community partners. Findings need to be reframed and presented in ways that make them more understandable and usable by communities.

Community-based research often involves participants who are vulnerable, and for this reason the dissemination of findings can present unique risks. Students typically underestimate or fail to anticipate the damage that can be done if dissemination is not handled skilfully. They may believe that the results will speak for themselves and be shocked to find that they are represented in ways that they never intended. Thus, students need to become familiar with the risks and benefits of disseminating findings from the participants' perspectives, and with strategies for minimizing risk when it is present. For example, they need to anticipate that findings from research on minority groups, marginalized people, or social service programs are more likely to be picked up by the media and may be sensationalized to the detriment of the participants. It is easy to imagine how findings can be misused to derail social programs and policies, and how the confidentiality of participants can be compromised when they comprise a small and highly visible group. Such risks are substantially greater when the research findings are unanticipated or negative – for example, when they fail to find positive effects from educational enhancement programs or social program initiatives. Students must become practised at anticipating risks, and at presenting findings in ways that do not compromise accuracy but at the same time minimize risk. Teaching students simple strategies can be extremely helpful. For example, they should learn to take sufficient time to discuss and think through the meanings of results in collaboration with community partners instead of responding to pressure to release findings quickly; and they should learn to consider various ways of framing findings to best ensure accurate interpretation. Furthermore, they should recognize the limitations and constraints on generalization.

Finally, because community-based research involves a team, issues of fairness and equity in recognizing contributions when presenting findings at professional and community meetings and in publications need to be worked through. Ideally, such issues are discussed openly at the outset of research; however, contributions often change over time, and avenues for dissemination may arise or vanish unexpectedly. For this reason, an ongoing and frank dialogue about how contributions will be recognized when findings are disseminated needs to be sustained. Ethical guidelines specify the conditions under which authorship is appropriate (American Psychological Association, 2002). However, contributions continue to be framed in traditional academic terms, and definitions may need to be revisited to better recognize the diversity of the intellectual contributions made by community partners. Classroom activities that provide opportunities for students to practise negotiating agreements – such as working through case examples and role playing – can be helpful.

Key Questions to Pose to Students

1. Do procedures minimize risk to participants and maximize the quality of the research?
2. Are procedures and measures respectful and sensitive to cultural, gender, and social class issues?

3. Who needs to provide consent, and how can procedures ensure full comprehension of the risks and benefits of participation?
4. What procedures will be followed to ensure and maintain confidentiality and privacy in storage, analyses, and reporting of data?
5. Who owns the data? Are additional uses of the data anticipated at this time?
6. How can the research team contribute back to the community?
7. Are there risks related to the dissemination of findings? If so, how can they be minimized?
8. How will contributions to the research be recognized in professional and community presentations, and in authorship of publications?

Maintaining Balance: The Importance of Role Clarity and Boundaries

We have emphasized repeatedly that researchers wear many hats throughout the course of community-based research. As researchers, it is imperative that we be clear about our roles and responsibilities and that we preserve boundaries appropriately. This is perhaps the most challenging of all issues in student training. In traditional research, roles and responsibilities are fixed, concrete, and obvious. Research teams are often small and homogeneous in the sense that other members are researchers who share a common understanding of the process. Also, there is typically only one institution – the university or research centre – to deal with, and exchanges between researchers and participants are limited temporally and contextually. In community-based research, students find they must manage professional relationships as part of a diverse team that includes other academic researchers as well as community service providers, administrators, and other community representatives. Research teams are also likely to span diverse disciplines. Students must manage multiple relationships with host institutions and facilities. Moreover, relationships with participants may stretch over a longer period of time, may occur in naturalistic settings, and may involve procedures that are less structured. It can be difficult for students to maintain role clarity and appropriate boundaries, given these unique attributes of community-based research.

We are not advocating that students be trained to adopt a disengaged, overly formal, and rigid role in interactions with collaborators, agencies, and participants; that said, it is important for them to maintain clear roles and boundaries. Take, for example, a researcher who becomes very deeply involved and aligns with collaborators from community agencies or service providers. In doing so, she may be placing herself in a very difficult position if she has to report negative research findings should they emerge or if she has to negotiate authorship credit if conflict emerges. Similarly, consider a researcher who becomes personally involved in the lives of her participants. She may find that having participants open up to her and permit her to enter their lives makes her feel special or influential to their well-being. Despite her good intentions, she may find that these personal relationships make her reluctant to breach confidentiality when necessary. These examples do not mean to suggest that we train our students never to develop personal relationships of any nature with collaborators, and never to feel compassion for their research participants; rather, we are saying that we train them to be aware of the conflicts that such situations may create so that they can anticipate the benefits and costs to both themselves and others.

Students in clinical or counselling training programs receive extensive training on role clarity and on maintaining appropriate boundaries. Even with this training they often falter in managing the complexities of the relationships they develop as professionals. Such training is rarely if ever provided to students in research-focused programs. The lack of this training constitutes a disservice to students and to the profession. Instructors and mentors need to spend sufficient time discussing the subtleties of boundary issues and how they can be managed.

Key Questions to Pose to Students

1. What constitutes appropriate and inappropriate relationships with collaborators or participants?
2. How might compromised roles and boundaries create conflict of interest?
3. How can you remain responsive and engaged while maintaining clear roles and boundaries throughout the research program?

Bringing It All Together: A Model to Guide Ethical Practice in Community-Based Research

We have touched on only a handful of the many ethical issues that arise in community-based research. Novice researchers will find it taxing to keep them all in mind throughout the research process. Decision-making models offer a distinct advantage in that they ensure that relevant issues are routinely considered. Some also offer hierarchies of issues to help researchers identify which ethical principles take precedence over others. Cottone and Claus (2000) provide a comprehensive review of ethical decision-making models as they apply to counselling. But models have not been developed to guide students who undertake community-based research. Drawing on our analysis of the ethical issues involved in community-based research, we offer a model of the steps that can be taken to enhance identification of and effective responsiveness to ethical issues and challenges in community-based research (see Figure 14.1). This model can help students and novice researchers routinely consider key issues in community-based research, from clarifying research interests and developing trusting relationships among team members and stakeholders to managing the dissemination and impact of research findings.

At the heart of this model is a recognition of how important it is for researchers to maintain clarity regarding roles and responsibilities on the team, and regarding the boundaries of the multiple relationships that are inherent in this work. Although the various steps in the model seem sequentially organized, the fact that they intersect emphasizes the dynamic relationship between all steps of the model from the outset to the close of the research program. This model can help students blaze a path through the maze of issues involved in community-based research. It can also be used on conjunction with other ethical decision-making models to resolve specific challenges as they arise.

Ethics by Osmosis or Design?

Some may argue that formal training in research ethics is unnecessary because whatever lessons need to be learned are readily absorbed through active involvement in research and supervision. We believe there are several problems with this position, drawing on Handelsman's (1986) critique of teaching ethics for clinical practice through apprenticeships. First, as we pointed out earlier in this chapter, research practices are changing and community-based research introduces a host of complex factors and situations that must be managed. It is not clear that all supervisors are equipped or available to provide the depth of supervision that students require. Second, each research program presents unique issues, but not all issues are covered in one research program.

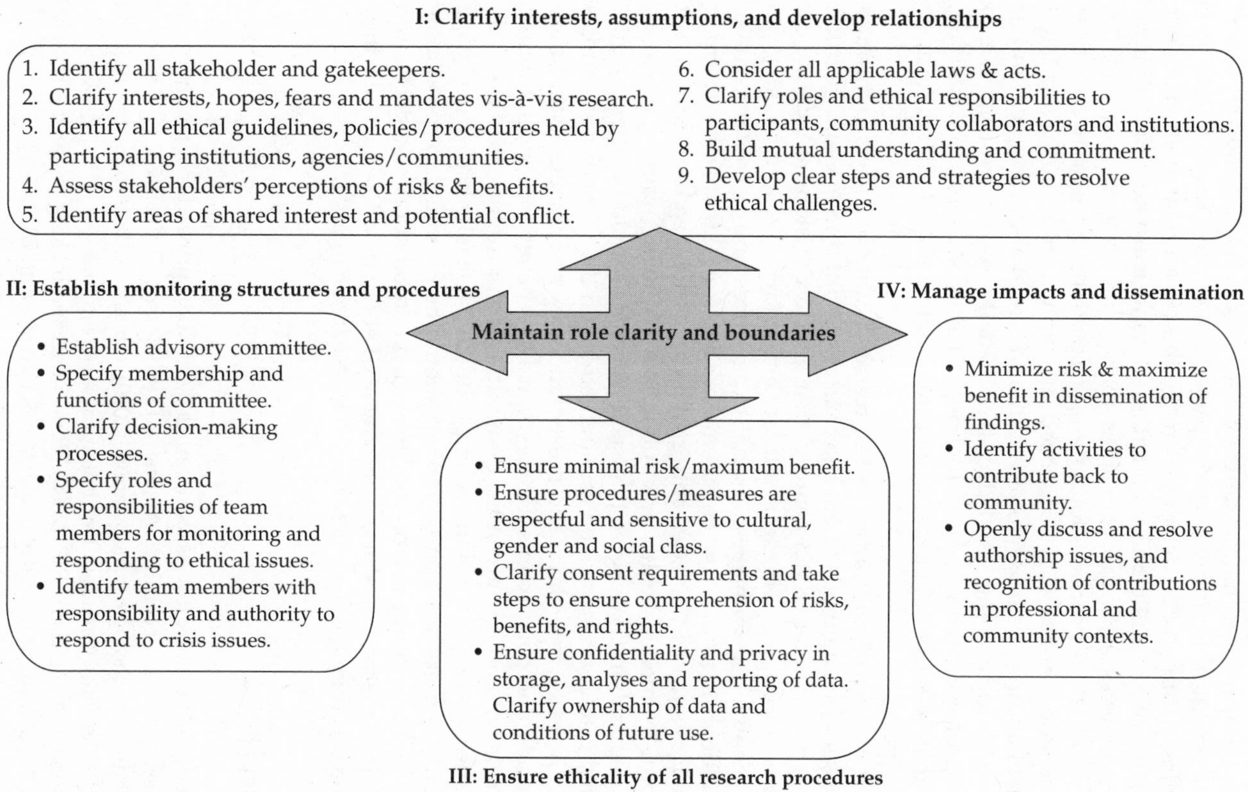

I: Clarify interests, assumptions, and develop relationships

1. Identify all stakeholder and gatekeepers.
2. Clarify interests, hopes, fears and mandates vis-à-vis research.
3. Identify all ethical guidelines, policies/procedures held by participating institutions, agencies/communities.
4. Assess stakeholders' perceptions of risks & benefits.
5. Identify areas of shared interest and potential conflict.
6. Consider all applicable laws & acts.
7. Clarify roles and ethical responsibilities to participants, community collaborators and institutions.
8. Build mutual understanding and commitment.
9. Develop clear steps and strategies to resolve ethical challenges.

II: Establish monitoring structures and procedures

- Establish advisory committee.
- Specify membership and functions of committee.
- Clarify decision-making processes.
- Specify roles and responsibilities of team members for monitoring and responding to ethical issues.
- Identify team members with responsibility and authority to respond to crisis issues.

Maintain role clarity and boundaries

III: Ensure ethicality of all research procedures

- Ensure minimal risk/maximum benefit.
- Ensure procedures/measures are respectful and sensitive to cultural, gender and social class.
- Clarify consent requirements and take steps to ensure comprehension of risks, benefits, and rights.
- Ensure confidentiality and privacy in storage, analyses and reporting of data. Clarify ownership of data and conditions of future use.

IV: Manage impacts and dissemination

- Minimize risk & maximize benefit in dissemination of findings.
- Identify activities to contribute back to community.
- Openly discuss and resolve authorship issues, and recognition of contributions in professional and community contexts.

Figure 14.1. Ethical practice model for community-based research

Do we simply hope that the range of issues is covered through students' involvement in multiple research projects over the course of graduate training? Third, skills developed through active research engagement are often of an implicit nature; that is, students learn how to do things, but not necessarily the principles that guide their actions and the decision-making processes for arriving at solutions. Students need hands-on experience, but they also need an explicit and fully articulated understanding of the issues at hand, of the relevant principles, and of the steps to reaching good decisions. Finally, we believe that it is a breach of our own ethical guidelines to allow students to undertake research without full training because of the potential for harm to participants.

If the ethics of community-based research cannot be learned through osmosis, what methods might better achieve our training goals? Pettifor, Estay, and Paquet (2002) contend that ethical decision-making is best learned through opportunities to acquire knowledge and to integrate that knowledge with the personal experiences and personal involvement flowing from active engagement. They found that active learning exercises such as vignettes and group discussions were rated as most helpful by mental health practitioners in acquiring training in ethical problem-solving. We agree that such activities should be liberally integrated into course work on research ethics, in the form of case studies and vignettes, role plays, and presentations by researchers, community agencies, and participants. However, we also believe that such training alone is not enough, given the demands of community-based research. Because the issues are akin in complexity to those which arise in clinical practice, supervised apprenticeship should be provided to consolidate what is learned in classrooms. Through a combination of didactic and real-life experiences, students are most likely to develop the skills they require as they move forward in their research careers.

REFERENCES

American Psychological Association. (2002). Ethical principles of psychologists and code of conduct. American Psychologist, 57, 1060–73.

Canadian Psychological Association. (2000). Canadian code of ethics for psychologists (3rd ed.). Canadian Psychological Association.

Cottone, R.R., & Claus, R.E. (2000). Ethical decision-making models: A review of the literature. Journal of Counseling & Development, 78, 275–83.

Fisher, C.B., Hoagwood, K., Boyce, C., et al. (2002). Research ethics for mental health science involving minority children and youths. *American Psychologist*, 57, 1024–40.

Handelsman, M.M. (1986). Problems with ethics training by 'osmosis.' *Psychology: Research & Practice*, 17, 371–2.

Pettifor, J.L., Estay, I., & Paquet, S. (2002). Preferred strategies for learning ethics in the practice of a discipline. *Canadian Psychology*, 43, 260–9.

15 Including Vulnerable Populations in Community-Based Research: New Directions for Ethics Guidelines and Ethics Research

BONNIE LEADBEATER AND KATHLEEN GLASS

What have we learned from the case studies of community-based research presented in this book? In this chapter we reflect on the benefits of community-based interdisciplinary research for increasing the inclusion of marginalized populations and for increasing knowledge to help us better address a range of long-standing social problems. We also summarize the ethical dilemmas that warrant continued discussion and research. For some ethical concerns, strategies and guidelines for ethical research practice already exist. For others, we argue that ethical solutions are not merely a matter of adjudicating compliance with an established set of guidelines. Rather, for these a more dynamic, problem-solving approach – one that is fuelled by ongoing dialogue among a wide range of interested parties – is needed in order to identify the varying and sometimes conflicting values related to the risks and benefits of research, not only for individuals but also for families and communities. Ethical dilemmas that arise in these situations are more likely to be resolved through collaborative approaches to ethical decision-making than through present-day approaches in the research community. Funding agencies may also want to consider supporting a longer set-up phase for research, to allow for the processes of establishing ethical practices in community-based research. At the end of this chapter we outline possible directions for empirical research to help guide these discussions.

Why Do Community-Based, Interdisciplinary Research?

In January 2004, advances in communications, science, and technology allowed multidisciplinary teams of engineers, astrologers, geographers, astrogeologists, computer scientists, biologists, and many others to send two small robots, aptly named 'Spirit' and 'Opportunity,' to precise, known locations on the planet Mars. Enormous collaboration was required to coordinate these interdisciplinary and sometimes international teams of professionals and researchers to build, program, land, and monitor these robots, and analyse the data finally transmitted from them – all under the inflexible deadlines set by the opportune positioning of Mars in the solar system in January 2004.

Such accomplishments stand in sharp contrast to our ability to conduct research addressing the earthly social problems experienced by vulnerable populations. These problems include illicit substance use, poverty, lack of education or employment, sexually transmitted infections, and interpersonal violence. Many of these problems are longstanding and involve a complex interplay of biological, physical, socio-economic, and cultural characteristics that differentially affect the health and well-being of vulnerable populations. A recent call for proposals from the Canadian Institutes for Health Research (13 April 2004) cogently summarizes this international concern:

> There is an urgent need to document and analyze disparities across sub-populations in Canada, and to test appropriate interventions to reduce these disparities and promote the health of vulnerable populations. There is also increasing recognition by the international community of the need to develop comprehensive interdisciplinary research programs that investigate ways in which biologic determinants of health link with social, economic and cultural contexts to create and sustain health disparities in society ... reducing socioeconomic, gender-related, ethnic and geographic inequalities in health (through reducing inequalities in access to such fundamental determinants of health as literacy and access to education, food, housing, safe living and working conditions, and health services) is likely to yield health benefits similar in magnitude to those accruing from reductions in conventional 'lifestyle' risk factors for the major chronic diseases.

Despite their complexity and unpredictability, it would be hard to argue that problems related to social systems and human behaviour are more complex or costly to study than the Mars Exploration Rover Mission. Yet as noted in many of the chapters in this book, a collaborative and interdisciplinary approach to research on social problems affecting the health outcomes of specific populations is rarely undertaken. This may stem, in part, from the fact that social science and health scholars are typically trained and rewarded as independent entrepreneurs who work with their own staff and students within a single discipline of study. Moreover, participants in social science research can experience a more inhospitable climate than that of Mars when they agree to subject themselves to the poking and prodding of research tools.

Health and social science researchers also continue to struggle against suspicions generated by a history of unethical research practices with vulnerable groups. Among these are the infamous Tuskegee syphilis experiments. For forty years (between 1932 and 1972), the U.S. Public Health Service involved 399 African-American men diagnosed with syphilis in research experiments without their knowledge. Many of these men were illiterate sharecroppers from one of the poorest counties in Alabama, and thus among the most vulnerable of research participants. They were deceived about the nature of the interventions they were exposed to, and they were denied effective treatments when these became available midway through the research. The Tuskegee project continues to fuel suspicions against researchers today. On the more positive side, Tuskegee and other problematic research has led to dramatic changes in the ways research is conducted. Today, federal and professional agencies regulate the protection of human research participants and set out ethics guidelines that obligate researchers to limit harms, clearly state benefits, obtain informed consent, and protect the confidentiality of participants.

However, efforts to apply ethics guidelines and regulations to vulnerable populations are not always straightforward, and health and social scientists often shy away from the challenges of this research, especially when it also means addressing value-laden social problems related to sexuality, drugs, racism, stigma, and so on. This in turn creates another ethical dilemma when groups are unfairly excluded from the potential benefits of participating in research. This can also create serious gaps in our understanding of the factors that influence disparities in the health status of vulnerable groups.

Hence, while federal regulations and professional and institutional ethics guidelines for research with human subjects have expanded, compliance with these guidelines does not necessarily lead to ethical research practices for community-based research with individuals marginalized by social status, ethnicity or race, culture, stigmas, poverty, unemployment, lack of education, mental status, or sexual orientation. Indeed, even experts who delineate recommendations for ethical guidelines for research that specifically targets vulnerable groups note how difficult it is to resolve cultural differences in values and beliefs with 'one-size-fits-all' guidelines (see for example, Fisher et al. 2002).

There is little consistency across universities or health care institutions as they attempt to apply the existing guidelines to new research approaches. A further problem is created by the general lack of experience of those who draft regulations and guidelines and of those who apply them when dealing with research undertaken outside universities and health institutions. Existing regulations and guidelines may not conform to the norms and practices of the targeted community or population. School boards, for example, often have their own processes for assessing research ethics. Some school boards permit a waiver of written parent consent (that is, parents are informed about a study but not required to give written consent) for minimum-risk research with youth, even though a university's ethics review board (ERB) in the same area may not permit this. Conversely, other school boards require written or verbal consent even though university's ERB does not (see Sippola, in this volume). Careful consideration of value differences and local norms is also central to establishing ethical research practices in Aboriginal communities. In such cases, protocol approval may take place at the community level as well as at the individual consent level. Partnerships in research endeavours, ownership of the data, and dissemination or use of findings can be of significant concern to communities, which resist the perpetration of negative stereotypes in research exclusively focused on risks and problems (see Fisher & Masty; Riecken et al., in this volume). Yet ethics regulations or guidelines generally give little direction for these issues, with the result that many Aboriginal communities have developed their own codes of research ethics, not all of which conform to existing institutional policies (Schnarch, 2004).

The use of age to permit or limit participation in research studies is an example of how current guidelines (or their absence) are fraught with problems of inconsistency and fairness. In a discussion paper, 'Does age matter? Law and the relationships between generations,' the Law Commission of Canada (2004) highlights the need to reconsider the use of age distinctions in law (at both ends of the age spectrum), and their arguments may be important here. The increasing efficiency of eligibility categorizations, using age as a substitute for vulnerability, need, maturity, or ability, or as a tool for distributing resources, can limit individual liberties and fair access and can overemphasize intergenerational stereotypes. The Law Commission argues that distinctions based only on age can compromise equality (full participation with dignity and respect) and justice (protecting human liberties, ensuring only reasonable controls over autonomy and choice, and promoting fair distribution of opportunities), and furthermore, can limit coherence (achieving objectives in ways that are rationally connected rather than arbitrary and inconsistent). The discussion paper appeals for more functional analyses that respect diversity. Noting that developmental transitions such as having the capacity for reason or entering the workforce are not age determined, the authors advocate 'an ethic of discussion' that promotes the 'reevaluation of laws and policies that use age as a marker and that prevent people from participating fully in our society.' They also promote greater acknowledgment of the rights of children (based on the UN Convention on the Rights of the Child) and the elimination of obstacles to full participation based on age distinctions.

Concerns about age-based restrictions have obvious applications for research ethics, particularly with respect to the participation of youth, where the use of age to restrict research participation has become especially arbitrary and inconsistent. For example, youth in British Columbia who are studying complex concepts in high school algebra, and science and who can work, consent to sex or health care, and get a driver's licence, cannot vote and generally require written parental consent for participation in research projects.

As has been shown in the preceding chapters, particularly thorny issues can also arise in community-based research concerning informed consent, reporting requirements, confidentiality, and the dissemination of findings. Moreover, apparent solutions in one research area can create problems in another. For example, statutory reporting requirements that are designed to protect children and youth against risks for abuse or self-harm inherently challenge participants' rights to privacy and confidentiality. The multiple roles of researcher-practitioners are another problem-laden area (see Renold, 2002; Banister & Daly, in this volume). The use of researcher-practitioners can improve trust and help ensure informed consent, but it can also create pressure for clients to agree to be involved in the research in order to please their service providers. Gaining parental consent is another difficult area. Respect for parental authority is intended to protect minors in research studies, but it can also systematically and unfairly exclude children and youth from high-risk or hard-to-reach families, who often do not return the consent forms. This limits the generalizability of research findings and benefits that might come from participation. Some of these dilemmas and the potential solutions for them are summarized below; however, rather than create yet another list of partially adequate guidelines, we suggest changes in the processes of ethical reviews that may facilitate ethical decision-making in community-based research. Shortcomings of current approaches are reviewed first.

How Do Institutional Review Boards Work?

Currently, universities in both Canada and the United States are required to establish institutional review boards (typically called IRBs in the United States and research ethics boards or REBs in Canada) to independently and without bias assess the compliance of proposed research with established regulations and guidelines. Consistent with the widespread practice of using 'peer' reviews to maintain a high quality of university-based research, members of these committees are comprised mainly of scientists, who are appointed from among the pool of experienced researchers at a given university. Individuals who are in any way involved in any particular research protocol under review are excluded from the decision-making process. Typically, these boards are required to have members from the lay community, and they may also include representatives of the university administration. Yet only rarely do they include anyone who represents the values of the local communities where the research is conducted (such as health authorities, school board members, or parent representatives). While the membership of REBs/IRBs is often public, some universities make it a policy to keep confidential the names of actual members; this further minimizes the likelihood of public dialogues on controversial issues.

In fact, only rarely do REBs/IRBs seek to facilitate or inform discussion on the protection of human subjects outside the specific domain of the committee structure. More typically, review boards evaluate funded research proposals (which usually have been reviewed already for scientific merit) prior to the release of funding by the responsible institution. To facilitate the processing of proposals, most review boards have developed specific forms and procedures for submitting research protocols for approval. Moreover, even though they are composed of peers of researchers, and though their membership changes, these boards have a quasi-judicial role in ensuring that protocols comply with ethics standards. Even seasoned researchers are invariably asked to address some areas of concern.

These procedures help ensure independent, unbiased assessments of the ethics of research protocols. However, the growing rigidity of procedures can lead to a kind of adversarial system of adjudication. Indeed, gaining ethical approval for a study is often regarded as one more obstacle to getting the *real* work of the research started. Figuring out how to comply with a committees' specific requirements or how to get the consent forms 'right' in order to gain approval can easily take centre stage in the approval process. A well-known and highly experienced researcher in the area of adolescent development and juvenile justice, Larry Steinberg (2004), has noted that the requirements of review boards are shifting in the direction of becoming more restrictive (for example, by eliminating the use of waivers of parent consent for minimal risk research) as well as more intrusive (for example, by raising research method and design concerns in studies that have already undergone extensive peer merit reviews during the funding process). As we have shown in this book, ethics and the integrity of research interact: particular research methods create challenges for ethical practice, and ethical practice depends on the potential benefits of the study. The benefits, in turn, reflect scientific issues such as the reliability and validity of the measures used and the adequacy of the population that is represented by the research participants. While it is true that a poorly designed study has little chance of benefiting anyone, some guidelines hand REBs/IRBs the task of reviewing the scientific rigour and scholarly merit of the study. Assigning detailed merit reviews to REBs/IRBs can be burdensome, besides detracting from discussions of other important ethical issues.

One common result of all this is that consent forms are growing longer. Most review board protocols include statements of what *must* be contained in consent forms, which typically have to be adapted for individual research projects. These requirements aim to ensure that research participants are aware of their rights (such as the right to understand the nature of the research) and risks (such as those associated with the requirement to report to the appropriate authorities if there is evidence of abuse). However, fulfilling these requirements can result in documents that are several pages long. These can understate benefits, overstate minimal risks, obscure what the research is about, and even intimidate or overwhelm potential research participants. Some researchers resort to a mini-information sheet to explain what participants are going to be asked to do in advance of having them read a lengthy and, sometimes, legalistic consent form. Others have suggested that a minitutorial may be needed, particularly to inform youthful participants of their rights (Bruzzese & Fisher, 2003). While adding to the burden of time required, these tutorials may be increasingly needed to guide participants through the fine print of consent forms.

Efforts to streamline the work of review boards are particularly problematic for community-based research as teams of interdisciplinary researchers step into new territories. This can involve obtaining multiple layers of consent, managing role conflicts, protecting vulnerable individuals and communities, and so on. It is unlikely that REBs/IRBs can adequately solve these complex problems alone, and adding more precise lists of guidelines to their toolboxes will not help (Sieber, 2001). One expert research panel has specifically examined research ethics for mental health services involving ethnic minority children and youth, and listed thirty-two well-considered recommendations for would-be investigators (Fisher et al., 2002). Its recommendations often demonstrate the complexities of ethical problems rather than offering potential guidelines or solutions to them. For example, recommendation 22 advises:

> Criteria for disclosing confidential information about an ethnic minority child's mental health status or risk behaviors need to include careful consideration of mandated reporting laws. Criteria should be culturally valid and should include culturally appropriate means of assessing the following: (a) clinical levels of risk, (b) the truthfulness of reports (c) whether a problem needs immediate attention, (d) whether a child or adolescent is already receiving services for the problem, and (e) sensitivity to the children or adolescent's expectation about the investigator's protective role. (emphasis added, Fisher et al., 2002, 1003)

This recommendation clearly informs the discussion of harms that could result from an unconsidered adherence to mandated reporting laws, but it does little to establish the best ways of applying ethics concerns to specific research projects with children or adolescents.

So who is responsible for ensuring ethical practice in community-based research? Clearly, REBs/IRBs cannot abdicate this responsibility without compromising their valuable independence and adjudicative role. Nevertheless, it is also clear that more innovative, flexible, problem-solving approaches to ethical issues are needed to ensure careful consideration when it comes to developing culturally appropriate, ethical, research practices in this growing area of research. In community-based research, some of these dilemmas can be anticipated and re-solved collaboratively though discussion among representatives of the participants and gatekeepers.

Recommendations for Ethics in Community-Based Research

This book has identified potential concerns that may be encountered in the course of community-based research with vulnerable populations on sensitive social and health issues. The chapters demonstrate efforts to carefully consider potential problems and to generate solutions through ongoing consultations not only with other researchers, but also with research participants and members of the community. The re-searchers have applied creative, innovative solutions both to protect participants from potential harms and to enhance compliance with federal and institutional regulations while reconciling these with com-munity values. The examples of responding to legal requirements to report (Jansson & Benoit, in this volume), and to the requirements to gain informed consent (Vaillancourt & Igneski, in this volume), are briefly reviewed here. They illustrate innovative processes that can support collaborative, problem-solving approaches to resolving ethical concerns in community-based research.

The Dilemma of Mandatory Reporting

As we have seen in this book (Jansson & Benoit, Vaillancourt & Igneski, Walsh & MacMillian), one the most difficult problems for research involving high-risk children and youth concerns mandatory reporting of suspected child abuse or risks for self-harm or harming others. Ironically, there is considerable consensus about the benefits of these regulations. Reporting requirements are consistent across legislative jurisdictions as well as institutional and professional boundaries. How-ever, harms can be created by false, weak, or unsubstantiated evidence, or if the identified individuals or their families go on to be unnecessar-ily entangled in embarrassing or lengthy assessments or legal proceed-ings (Fisher et al., 2002; King & Churchill, 2000). Moreover, these negative outcomes may be more likely for minority or poor families, who stereotypically are thought to be at greater risk for abuse, particularly if the focus of research is on risks, deficits, or dysfunction (Fisher et al., 2002; Leadbeater & Way, 2001). The question of who is to give consent for research participation for victims of child maltreatment also demonstrates the complexities of relying on parental authority (King & Churchill, 2000).

Determining risks for abuse, neglect, or self-harm with any accuracy in the context of a research project can be difficult. Responses to single-item questions about abuse, sexual activity, or suicidal ideation would not be considered valid barometers of abuse, sexual exploitation, or suicidal intentions. However, such responses might suggest risk in the context of high scores on other assessments (such as a depression inventory) or in the context of other evidence of problems (Vaillancourt & Igneski; Jansson et al., in this volume). At the same time, minors living on the street might all be considered at risk by virtue of their living circumstances, or they might report experiences of abuse as a reason for leaving home (Jansson & Benoit, in this volume). Participants enrolled in studies that focus on risk for maltreatment or suicide or on harming or victimizing others, by definition, fall into categories that mandate reporting to appropriate child protection authorities, so how can this be handled?

Researchers have dealt with mandatory reporting in a variety of ways. Consent forms generally require statements that tell participants about the researchers' reporting obligations, but what parents or guardians, children, and youth understand by these statements, or what they anticipate as a consequence of being reported, has not been investigated. Some researchers take elaborate steps to ensure that this information is either anonymously collected or is not revealed (by actively avoiding questions that would elicit this information), and this raises the question of whether help could have been provided and harm prevented in cases where reporting was appropriate. Others recommend follow-up interviews for individual participants when risks are gleaned from questionnaire data so that qualified clinicians can more adequately assess risks (see Yuile et al.; Vaillancourt & Igneski, in this volume). However, such referrals can compromise confidentiality and privacy, particularly in school-based research.

Innovative solutions to reporting concerns are encountered in Jansson and Benoit's longitudinal study of street-involved youth (Jansson & Benoit, in this volume; Benoit et al., in press). Before beginning the study, the researchers set up meetings with representatives of the authority that would be receiving reports of risk for maltreatment to discuss the potential effects of reporting for the youth and to determine a standard protocol for reporting. An individual in the reporting authority was identified who would act as a liaison with the researchers if reportable concerns arose. Discussions led to the awareness that local reporting authorities were unlikely to utilize their limited resources to track down families of youth who were living independently and out of harm's way; however, these authorities would intervene to protect siblings who might still be living at home and who were at risk for abuse.

Solutions to concerns that confidentiality can be compromised by follow-up contacts with youth in school-based studies were resolved partially by Yuile and colleagues (in this volume) through the use of a contact box that any youth could check if he/she wanted to speak to a researcher about anything concerning the research. This provided a way for youth to ask for help, as well as a 'cover' for researchers wishing to contact youth identified as at risk who did not ask for help. All youth were also given referral information to assist them in getting help themselves. Assessments of this method showed that youth who checked the box were at higher risk than those who did not. Jansson and colleagues (in this volume) also dealt with this problem in survey research by ensuring that the survey questions did not accidentally elicit reports of abuse and by training the research assistants who administered the survey to be alert to indicators of reportable concerns and aware of the research protocol for dealing with specific problems.

Informed Consent and Youth Assent in School-Based Studies

A second important question is how to gain informed consent from the parents of youth in school-based studies. Reliance on schools for access to youth participants in research is commonplace and economical. However, this practice often requires that consent be obtained from a hierarchy of gatekeepers, including school principals, school boards, teachers, and parents or guardians. At any point along the way, these gatekeepers can veto efforts to include young people in research projects that could possibly benefit them. This occurs most often when research deals with issues related to sexuality, ethnicity, religion, or illegal activities. Recruiting youth from schools can in itself systematically exclude high-risk youth, who sometimes are alienated from participating in school activities or have already dropped out. Also, cultural values promoting youth autonomy can conflict with demands for youth to get parental or guardian permission for school-based research. When parents are merely informed of a study through forms devised by the researcher, those forms can be lost and never make it home. When written consent procedures are demanded of youth, parents' signatures can easily be forged. Population-based recruitment efforts to identify more representative samples for individual interviews can be costly and time-consuming, but these also have advantages in that they allow direct contact with parents to gain informed consent (Jansson et al., in this volume).

Past research converges in suggesting that youth as young as fourteen understand their rights with respect to participating in research (Bruzzese & Fisher et al., 2001; Underwood et al., in this volume). As we have seen, however, a specific age of consent for participation in research is not delineated by either current legislation or research guidelines. In the absence of other accepted markers of competence, the age of majority in a state or province is used as the point when youth can give their own consent (for example, see Jansson et al., in this volume). Few would debate the need for parental consent for children. That said, the relationship between informed consent and complex issues such as youth competence and autonomy, respect for parental authority, and inclusion in research clearly needs to be discussed more openly by REBs/IRBs, school boards, youth, and parent groups (Law Commission of Canada, 2004).

Petersen and Leffert (1995) argue that even when adolescents are as capable of making decisions as adults, unfamiliar situations can tax their decision-making competence. Adolescent participants in community-based research often have little experience in making decisions about what is safe to reveal in questionnaires or to talk about in a focus group. Decisions about what to reveal can become even more complex when the multiple roles of researcher-practitioners blur the distinction between research and therapy (see Banister & Daly, in this volume). Yet solutions do exist. The lines between research and therapy need to be drawn clearly, and wherever possible, different individuals ought to hold these roles. Moreover, informed consent requires that the risks and benefits of both the research and the intervention be stated clearly. This may necessitate asking for feedback from the adolescents about their understanding of these distinctions, to increase confidence that they have the knowledge they need to make informed choices about participation. Reassessing consent and understanding of the research in the course of a longitudinal research project can provide protection and freedom of choice for vulnerable participants (see Munall, 1988).

Training for community-based researchers needs to reflect the additional care required to respond to the unique demands of close and often ongoing involvement with research participants (see Moretti et al., in this volume). Researchers may need specific skill sets if they are to work ethically with vulnerable groups. For example, focus groups with adolescents require experienced facilitators because such forums raise issues about confidentiality and group process. These issues need to be addressed when training new facilitators. Personal information that is casually shared in groups, and that may or may not be true, can be spread as gossip, reported to parents or teachers, or used for retaliation or victimization. The accelerated pace of adolescents' conversation, in concert with their normal developmental boundary testing tendencies, can also demand strong communication skills, knowledge of group dynamics, and experience with group interviewing in order to maintain a safe environment for the focus group (Banister & Daly, in this volume).

Principles of Ethical Processes in Community-Based Research

Research ethics raises complex issues that are not always easily resolved with reference to legislation or ethics guidelines. Nevertheless, principles for 'careful consideration' do emerge from the chapters in this book. These draw attention to the need to focus on ongoing processes for establishing and maintaining ethical practice in community-based research. Ethical consideration in community-based research should:

1. strive for transparency and openness with participants in the research process;
2. provide ongoing opportunities for community and university dialogue on potential research benefits and harms throughout the research;
3. engage representatives of key stakeholders (youth, parents, schools, service agencies, researchers, and graduate students) in the assessment of research protocols, the development of interventions, and the creation of plans for disseminating findings;
4. provide adequate funding and lead time for discussing ethics in relation to planned research, so as to address both potential harms and benefits and *perceptions* of potential harms and benefits of all involved;
5. involve relevant community members, such as school principals,

parent representatives, and school board officials and authorities responsible for enforcing reporting laws on university REBs/IRBs and research advisory groups; and
6. seek feedback from the participants about their understanding of their rights with respect to the research project or intervention, and continue to assess their consent throughout the research in order to sustain their protection and freedom of choice.

As these principles suggest, increased dialogue with community stakeholders can help researchers articulate more clearly what can be gained from a particular study and also what harms can be anticipated. Furthermore, it can allow researchers to respond to particular community needs. In contrast to research in the physical sciences, where complex issues outside the realm of everyday concerns may be at stake, participants who are asked to engage in research concerning social or health issues may have considerable knowledge about the research questions and may be consulted because of their expertise or experiences (for example, when the research targets children who are victimized, or youth who use illegal substances). With this familiarity and expertise can come a variety of beliefs about and attitudes towards the value and risks of such research, and these can enhance or limit participation. While it is unlikely that all conflicts in views about the benefits or risks of research will disappear, opportunities for more open discussion may serve to clarify common grounds and differences in advance of the project. Some concerns resurface repeatedly – for example, school administrators often raise objections to questions about family socioeconomic status, believing (correctly) that some families in their schools will object to giving this information. However, by being more explicit about why these data are needed (perhaps to substantiate generalizability of findings), and how they will be used (for example, as group data only), they can help overcome concerns. If researchers and stakeholders participate together in public forums to discuss potential harms and benefits of research as well as strategies for minimizing harms and maximizing benefits from participation, more progress can be made in overcoming those limits which preclude the involvement of vulnerable populations in research that addresses entrenched social issues. As an example, dialogues among researchers and school board members, principals, teachers, parents, and youth is overdue in creating up-to-date and ongoing ways not only of monitoring social problems that affect youth – including access to harmful substances, attitudes towards sexuality, and victimization – but also of testing youth engagement models that may help overcome these difficulties.

Raising the Profile of Research on Ethics

While the harms we seek to prevent in research are often clear (such as ongoing child maltreatment or self-harm), too often we know little about the actual or even perceived risks or harms that can result from participation in research on these sensitive issues. We also know little about the effects of current ethics guidelines and research practices on increasing participants' awareness of the potential benefits of the research. Ironically, although many publications reiterate established guidelines for research, ethical concerns have only rarely been viewed as topics for study in themselves. Systematic research and empirical methods have only begun to be used to address ethical questions with vulnerable populations. A handful of studies have looked directly at ethics practices. Variously, they have assessed children's understanding of their research rights (Hurley & Underwood, 2002), children's and youths' capacity to give consent (Bruzzese & Fisher, 2003), and the effects of reporting options (no action, providing referral information, sharing information with parents or counsellors) on the agreement of youth and their parents to participate in research (O'Sullivan & Fisher, 1977).

However, as indicated throughout this book, there are more questions than answers in many areas of community-based research, and generic solutions are not likely to be of help. Many of the chapters point to ethical issues that are specific to certain research methods, and call for increased care to prevent harm. In sociometric studies (see Underwood et al., in this volume), for example, do children who are asked to nominate peers as 'liked' or 'disliked,' or aggressive or non-aggressive, keep these nominations confidential when asked to do so? Do they consider these kinds of rankings of their peers more legitimate, since adult authorities have asked for them, and thus perhaps implicitly sanctioned their validity? Are there, for example, increases in subsequent levels of social exclusion for youth who are nominated as 'unliked' by many students? In studies that use focus groups to elicit youth opinions, do youth reveal confidences gleaned about peers or use these secrets to victimize them (Bell, Dolon & Wessler, 1994; Owen 2001)? We also know little about the effects of different strategies for increasing confidentiality, such as signing confidentiality contracts compared to verbally warning youth about risks (see Banister & Daly; Marshall, in this volume). Longitudinal surveys also challenge researchers to balance participants' needs for confidentiality with researchers' needs for contact information that will permit follow-up (see Jansson et al., in this volume), but what, if anything, are the consequences of collecting these data? Researchers in the United States (but not Canada) have had data collected in a research project subpoenaed by a court order (Lowman & Palys, 2001). Protections for confidentiality of data can be more formalized, as exemplified by the Certificates of Confidentiality that are issued in the United States by the National Institutes of Health to protect identifiable research information from forced disclosure. These allow investigators to refuse disclosure of identifying information on research participants in legal proceedings when it could have 'adverse consequences for subjects or damage participant's financial standing, employability, insurability, or reputation' (see grants1.nih.gov/grants/policy/coc). In Canada, researchers' obligations to protect confidentiality mean that participants are subject to laws, and where these are in conflict, the researcher must decide on the most acceptable course of action (Lowman & Palys, 2001).

Research is especially needed to address ethical considerations related to obtaining informed consent for adolescents (Levine, 1995). How many youth actually object to getting parent permission for participation in research? How does gaining parental consent protect young people? Do parents and youth discuss implications for youth of participating in a study before signing consent forms? Do parents press youth to reveal their answers to confidential research questions as a result of information provided by researchers? Are there age or cultural differences in youths' beliefs about their parents' or principals' authority to permit or prevent them from being recruited into a research study?

Research could also inform best practices for administering consent forms for vulnerable populations. Do different formats (verbal versus written) create different levels of understanding of potential harms, benefits, or participants' right to skip questions or withdraw altogether from a study? What differences might be found if potential stakeholders were to list potential harms from surveys or interventions, compared to those anticipated by researchers? How would these be rated compared to potential benefits of knowledge to be gained? Would these lists differ by levels of education, age of participants, and so on?

Focus groups could be used to elicit community values about the benefits and harms of research. For example, how does obtaining consent for research compare to issues of obtaining parent consent for involvement in sports or school activities? It seems likely that tolerances for risks for injuries in youth who are involved in sports or school activities are much higher than tolerances for minimal risks in research. Also, there is generally no requirement for ethics reviews for data collected and recorded by schools yet for educational purposes (for example, for data on student concerns about their safety or victimization in schools), we do not know how risks for harm differ when these data are collected for research purposes.

We also need to know more about the consequences of mandatory reporting. What is the frequency of reports in community-based research? What happens when youth are referred to authorities after reporting abuse or endorsing suicidal ideation items on research questionnaires? Do they receive help? What criteria would predict greater accuracy in determining risks for abuse, self-harm, or other harm in research protocols?

As chapters in this book illustrate (see Yuile et al., Underwood et al.), some of these issues lend themselves to assessments that can be incorporated into the research process itself. In other cases, key studies need to be proposed and funded. Innovative approaches are also needed to identify and limit real rather than hypothetical harms in order for research to better represent the most vulnerable populations. In any event, it seems imperative that discussion of the values and beliefs about the benefits and harms of research become public and transparent. Opportunities to increase dialogue through community-based research, community forums, and the media are needed. Without this advancement, research will continue to exclude vulnerable populations and to avoid focusing on socially sensitive issues. We will continue to be observers of great advances in space research, while social problems go unaddressed and uninformed by interdisciplinary, collaborative research partnerships.

REFERENCES

Bell-Dolan, D., & Wessler, A.E. (1994). Ethical administration of socio-metric measures: Procedures in use and suggestions for improvement. *Professional Psychology, Research and Practice*, 25, 23–32.

Benoit, C., Jansson, M., Millar, A., & Phillips. R. (in press). 'Community

academic research on hard-to-reach populations: benefits and challenges.'
Qualitative Health Research.

Bruzzese, J.M., & Fisher, C.B. (2003). Assessing and enhancing the research consent capacity of children and youth. *Applied Developmental Science, 7,* 13–26.

Law Commission of Canada (2004). Does age matter? Law and the relationships between generations. Discussion paper, published by Her Majesty the
Queen in Rights of Canada, www.Icc.gc.ca.

Fisher, C., Hoagwood, K., Boyce, C., Duster, T., Frank, D.A., Grisso, T., Levine,
R., Macklin, R., Beale-Spencer, M., Takanishi, R., Trimble, J.E., & Zayas, L.
(2002) Research ethics for mental health science involving ethnic minority
children and youth. *American Psychologist, 57,* 1024–40.

King, N.M., & Churchill, L.R. (2000). Ethical principles guiding research on
child and adolescent subjects. *Journal of Interpersonal Violence, 15*(7), 710–24.

Levine, R. (1995). Adolescents as research subjects without permission of their
parents or guardians: Ethical considerations. *Journal of Adolescent Health, 17,*
287–97.

Munall, P. (1988). Ethical considerations in qualitative research. *Western
Journal of Nursing Research, 10,* 150–62.

O'Sullivan, C., & Fisher, C.B. (1977). The effect of confidentiality and reporting procedures on parent-child agreement to participate in adolescent risk
research. *Applied Developmental Science, 1,* 187–99.

Petersen, A.C., & Leffert, N. (1995). Developmental issues influencing guidelines for adolescent health research. *Journal of Adolescent Health, 17*(5),
286–96.

Owen, S. (2001). The practical, methodological and ethical dilemmas of
conducting focus groups with vulnerable clients. *Methodological Issues in
Nursing Research, 36,* 652–58.

Renold, E. (2002). Privacies and private: Making ethical dilemmas public
when researching sexuality in the primary school. In T. Welland & L. Pugsley (Eds.), *Ethical dilemmas in qualitative research* (pp. 121–34). Burlington,
VT: Ashgate.

Schnarch, B. (2004). Ownership, control, access, and possession (OCAP) or
self-determination applied to research: A critical analysis of contemporary
First Nations research and some options for First Nations communities.
Journal of Aboriginal Health, 1, 80–95.

Sieber, Joan E. (2001). Privacy and confidentiality: As related to human research in social and behavioral science. *Ethical and policy issues in research
involving human participants.* In National Bioethics Advisory Commission:
Ethical and Policy Issues in Research involving Human Participants. NBAC
Report Commissioned Papers and Staff Analysis. Bethesda, MD.

Society for Adolescent Medicine (1995). Guidelines for adolescent health research: Position paper of the Society for Adolescent Medicine. *Journal of Adolescent Health*, 17, 270–6.

Steinberg, L. (2004, March). Ethical Issues in Adolescent Research Roundtable, Presentation at the biannual meeting of the Society for Research in Adolescence, Baltimore, MD.

Weijer, C., Goldsand, G., & Emanual, E. 1999 Protecting communities in research: Current guidelines and limits of extrapolation. *Nature Genetics*, 23, 275–83.